RETHINKING MIGRATION

Challenging Borders, Citizenship and Race

Edited by
Bridget Anderson

BRISTOL
UNIVERSITY
PRESS

First published in Great Britain in 2025 by

Bristol University Press
University of Bristol
1–9 Old Park Hill
Bristol
BS2 8BB
UK
t: +44 (0)117 374 6645
e: bup-info@bristol.ac.uk

Details of international sales and distribution partners are available at bristoluniversitypress.co.uk

British Library Cataloguing in Publication Data
A catalogue record for this book is available from the British Library

ISBN 978-1-5292-3447-3 paperback
ISBN 978-1-5292-3448-0 ePub
ISBN 978-1-5292-3449-7 OA Pdf

Cover design: Andrew Corbett
Front cover image: unsplash/Izuddin Helmi Adnan
Bristol University Press uses environmentally responsible print partners.
Printed and bound in Great Britain by CPI Group (UK) Ltd, Croydon, CR0 4YY

FSC
www.fsc.org
MIX
Paper | Supporting responsible forestry
FSC® C013604

Contents

List of Figures and Tables

Figures

Table

Notes on Authors

Bridget Anderson is Professor of Migration, Mobilities and Citizenship and Director of Migration Mobilities Bristol at the University of Bristol. Her work explores human movement and related experiences, politics, policies and practices, starting from a recognition that the differences between 'migrant' and 'citizen' are socially and legally constructed. She is author of numerous journal articles and books include *Us and Them? The Dangerous Politics of Immigration Control* (Oxford University Press, 2013).

Brid Brennan is an activist researcher and coordinates the Corporate Power Project at the Transnational Institute (TNI) in Amsterdam. She has a long history of organizing with international social movements and is the co-founder of the European Solidarity Centre for the Philippines and RESPECT, a Europe-wide anti-racist network for migrant domestic workers. She has written several articles and edited several books, including *The Great Take Over: Mapping of Multistakeholderism in Global Governance* (TNI, 2021).

Natasha Carver is Senior Lecturer in the School for Policy Studies at the University of Bristol. Her research analyses legal constructions of racialized and gendered identities and how these identities are negotiated by those who are subject(ed) to their force. Her monograph *Marriage, Gender and Refugee Migration* (Rutgers University Press, 2021) won the British Sociological Association 2022 Philip Abrams Prize for the best sole-authored first book in the discipline of sociology.

Manoj Dias-Abey is Senior Lecturer at the University of Bristol Law School. He is a socio-legal scholar interested in the law of work, migration, social movements and political economy, and in particular how Britain thinks about, rationalizes and regulates labour migration.

Lucy Donkin is Senior Lecturer in History and History of Art at the University of Bristol. She specializes in visual and material culture, researching medieval and early modern perceptions of place, with particular reference to Italy and its relationships with the wider Mediterranean region and transalpine Europe. Her recent book *Standing on Holy Ground in the Middle Ages* (Cornell University Press, 2022) focuses on the creation, use and decoration of sacred space.

María Paula Escobar Tello is Senior Lecturer at the Bristol Veterinary School, University of Bristol. As a human geographer, she explores tensions and intersections between livestock farming, conservation and the environment, drawing from studies of regulation as governance, more-than-human geographies, political ecology and the politics of materiality. She is an experienced interdisciplinary scholar and leads research teams in Latin America, particularly her native Colombia. She edited a special issue of *Frontiers in Veterinary Science* (2022) on 'Interdisciplinary approaches to antimicrobial use in livestock farming'.

Angelo Martins Junior is Assistant Professor in Sociology in the Department of Social Policy, Sociology and Criminology at the University of Birmingham. His research focuses on difference, intersectionality, social inequalities and decolonial sociological approaches to contribute to debates on migration and 'modern slavery'. He is author of *Moving Difference: Brazilians in London* (Routledge, 2020), an in-depth ethnographic study of how differences between migrants from the same country travel with them and impact their 'mobile lives'.

Nariman Massoumi is Senior Lecturer in the Department of Film and Television at the University of Bristol. He is a filmmaker and researcher with a background in documentary television production. His research and practice centres on life histories of colonialism and migration with a specific focus on the British/Iranian context through ethnographic and archive-based documentary film practices. His most recent documentary film, *Pouring Water on Troubled Oil* (2023), follows the Welsh poet Dylan Thomas' journey through Iran in 1951 and has screened at various international film festivals.

Laurence Publicover is Associate Professor in Literature and Oceanic Studies at the University of Bristol, where his research focuses on English Renaissance theatre and on the cultural history of the sea. He is author of *Dramatic Geography* (Oxford University Press, 2017) and *Fathoming the Deep in English Renaissance Tragedy* (Oxford University Press, 2024) and co-editor, with Susann Liebich, of *Shipboard Literary Cultures: Reading, Writing, and Performing at Sea* (Palgrave Macmillan, 2021). Alongside Jimmy Packham, he is writing a human and literary history of the seabed, forthcoming from University of Chicago Press.

Holly Rooke is a PhD student in the School of Geography and Planning at the University of Sheffield. She has an MSc in Public Policy from the

University of Bristol. Her thesis focused on the construction of illegality in UK political speeches about asylum seekers. She has worked in the charity sector supporting people experiencing homelessness in Bristol and as a research assistant for Refugee Education UK.

Florian Scheding is Senior Lecturer in Music at the University of Bristol. His research area is music and migration, with a focus on the 20th century. He has published widely on migratory musics in all its forms, ranging across functional, popular and art musics. His first book, *Music and Displacement: Diasporas, Mobilities and Dislocations in Europe and Beyond*, was named Outstanding Publication of the Year by *Choice* magazine. His second book, *Musical Journeys: Performing Migration in 20th-Century Music*, received the Royal Musical Association/Cambridge University Press Monograph Prize in 2020.

Brendan Smith is Professor of Medieval History in the Department of History at the University of Bristol. His work focuses on the character and fortunes of English colonial society in late medieval Ireland. He is editor of *The Cambridge History of Ireland, Vol 1, 660–1550* (Cambridge University Press, 2018) and author of *Crisis and Survival in Late Medieval Ireland: The English of Louth and their Neighbours, 1330–1450* (Oxford University Press, 2013).

Juan Zhang is Senior Lecturer in the Department of Anthropology and Archaeology at the University of Bristol. Her research explores borders and transnational migration in various forms, with a particular focus on Asian borderlands, migrant im/mobilities and transnationalism, and cross-border cultural politics and China.

Acknowledgements

This volume is the collective effort of Migration Mobilities Bristol (MMB), a research institute at the University of Bristol. The editor and authors would like to thank MMB members across the university, who have built and nurtured the research environment that enabled this collection. We particularly thank Emma Newcombe, MMB Manager, for her creativity and organizational and fundraising skills and Emily Walmsley, MMB External Projects Coordinator, for her sharp eye for detail and for encouraging us all to keep to time. We also acknowledge the University of Bristol's Strategic Research Investment Fund 2022 for funding the workshop that brought our thinking together.

Introduction: Rethinking Migration – Challenging Borders, Citizenship and Race

Bridget Anderson

Socioeconomic systems and life itself depend on movement, yet we are poorly equipped to understand mobilities and how they enrich and impoverish our lives. Our habits of thought render some forms of (im)mobilities overly conspicuous and occlude others. The laptop I'm working on has components made from minerals obtained from Australia, Brazil, the Democratic Republic of Congo and Rwanda and was most likely made in China, but its presence on a table in Bristol is unremarkable. The movements required to make it have been naturalized by centuries of forms of rule and technological change; they pass unnoticed, sedimented into everyday life. But other kinds of movement, chief among them 'migration', are exceptionalized. The territorial claims of sovereignty seek to fix people and places, even if trade, data and finance are acknowledged as needing to flow. To understand the apparently contradictory demands of sovereignty and capitalism, of supply chains and immigration controls, we need to look *at* and *from* the national border (Hattam, 2022). And the border is not only at the geographical edges of state territories. From document checks to free ports, via the domains, gateways and passwords of cyberspace, borders hatch the entirety of territory. Bordering processes in their multiple manifestations are part of all our lives, whether or not we are designated 'migrants'.

While there is nothing new about human movement, 'migration' has become a key concern of policy, politics and the media (Manning and Trimmer, 2020; Cole, 2022). Across the world, 'migrants'[1] are positioned at best as a problem that needs managing but more often as a threat to culture, economy and politics, and particularly to the nation. While many of those with a stake in migration debates – including, of course, migrants themselves – challenge the migrant-as-problem framing, they often acknowledge the repertoire they can draw on is limited: migrant as victim of human rights abuse (refugee, modern-day slave, broken body on the shore); or migrant as hard-working contributor (entrepreneurial actor, community builder). Migration academics too are increasingly concerned their scholarship unwittingly reproduces hegemonic representations of migrants as poor, racialized and culturally Other, and they are reflecting on how their research contributes to the widespread perception that migration is a problem (Dahinden, 2016; Schinkel, 2018; Anderson, 2019). A new, more critical scholarly engagement with migration is emerging that asks how we research migration without reinforcing the migrant as a problematic subject. But how do we move beyond critique and intervene to improve policy, practice and organizing rather than simply criticising them from the sidelines?

In scholarly and policy work, and often too in activism, migration (including asylum) is typically treated as a stand-alone issue, overlooking the fact that human movement is inextricably bound up with multiple mobilities (of goods, ideas, data) and socioeconomic processes and that only certain kinds of human movement, and certain kinds of people who move, are legally and socially labelled 'migrations'/'migrants'. Recognizing this and situating analysis of human movement within this broader landscape of processes and relations enables migration scholars to connect their work with other fields. This edited collection has contributions and curated conversations from academics across different disciplines, plus a conversation with a long-term activist, who all share an interest in different aspects of movement but do not necessarily research migration per se. It demonstrates how interdisciplinarity can open new insights into human movement and how the questions we ask across our disciplines are shaped by assumptions about stasis and mobility. Reflecting on ideas and actions centred on migration, with all their assumptions and contradictions, helps us better understand the worlds we are making. This volume offers conceptual, critical and creative approaches with two aims: first, to support academics, activists, policy makers and non-specialist readers in developing new thinking about migration and to make connections between migration and other academic, policy and activist fields; and, second, to demonstrate how academic research can contribute to practice and new thinking without conforming to a policy agenda or reifying policy categories.

This introduction to the book first explores the category of 'migrant'. Who counts as a migrant is highly unclear and variable across policy, practice and academic research. Crucially, if we cannot be clear about who is a migrant, neither can we be clear about who is a citizen, and this has consequences for citizens and non-citizens alike. Having troubled this category, the introduction poses three questions that illuminate three key, interrelated challenges faced by migration studies. These are challenges not only for researchers, but also for policy makers and other non-academic stakeholders. First, *what movements matter?* The separation of human movement/migration from the movement of non-human species and non-living things means our understanding of human movement is often highly partial and distorted, and we misread patterns and miss crucial interconnections. For example, trade and migration, the mobilities of goods and people, are deeply interconnected but typically siloed in research and political debates (though perhaps less in policy practice). Second, *how are we to denaturalize bordering?* The unquestioning assumption of the nation state form means we miss both the work that the nation state does and how it reproduces itself. This is particularly evident in the study of human movement (the nation state form is key to the making of migrants and citizens), but it also raises important issues across the social sciences and indeed beyond – for instance, what does the idea of a 'national dataset' obscure? Third, having problematized and complicated ideas of 'migration', we ask, *what are we to do with 'migration'?* This discusses the power of representation and how social-forensic categories affect what they name – the 'refugee' is subject to restrictions and is expected to act in certain ways, and being labelled or labelling oneself a 'refugee' affects how one feels about oneself. Again, this is not restricted to the label refugee; one could say the same about other social categories, such as a trans person, a COVID-19-immune person or someone who is highly skilled. Names interact with the named, with consequences for research and politics.

Having outlined these challenges, this chapter then sets out the volume's approach and chapters and how they exemplify responses to these challenges and can rethink migration and mobilities, arguing that conceptually based, critical and creative thinking is as important for practice as it is for theory.

The category 'migrant'

If everybody moves, when does movement become migration, who counts as a migrant and why? Even government statisticians, who are rigorous in the search for terminological clarity, do not have a singular definition. The two most common definitions are 'foreign born' and 'foreign national', and the statistics on, for instance, migration and employment, can look quite different depending on which of these definitions is used.

However, in public and political debate the small print of definitions is rarely of interest and the term migrant is loosely deployed. It can be used to describe historically minoritized communities – the Rohingya in Myanmar, rendered stateless under the Citizenship Law 1982, or 'second-generation migrants' in Europe. Furthermore, not everyone who crosses an international border is described as a 'migrant', and the European Commission is adamant that the term should not be applied to 'European mobile citizens', framing debates on the movement of European Union (EU) citizens as completely separate from those on the movement of 'third-country nationals' (Ruhs, 2019). The United Nations takes the purpose of moving as well as the length of time a person stays in a state as relevant to defining migration and distinguishes between short-term and long-term international migrants (for example, United Nations, 1998). In everyday usage too, 'migrant' is distinguished from, for example, tourist or business traveller. But these distinctions are not particularly robust: for instance, the question of whether students should count as migrants is much debated, and northern Europeans and North Americans living abroad tend to think of themselves as expats, not migrants. Foreign-ness does not have to be associated with subjection. Saba Le Renard (2021), for example, has researched Westerners in Dubai not only as privileged migrants but also as local elites who play an important role in reproducing national, racialized, class and gender hierarchies. Putting it crudely, in media coverage – and therefore much public debate – a 'migrant' is a person whose movement, or whose presence, is considered a problem. Meanwhile border controls are typically – in wealthy countries at least – aimed at controlling the mobility of the poor.

The classed nature of migration, rendered visible in everyday understandings of who is a migrant, is evident in policy. Those who are wealthy or educated find it easier to access mobility, whether through global talent schemes or tourist visas, or by purchasing a golden visa or passport. The idea of migrants as working in low-waged jobs is partly a matter of perception, because foreign-born/foreign nationals in high-status work – bankers, professors or neurosurgeons – are not imagined as migrants even if they are subject to immigration controls. Across the world, immigration controls treat the low- and high-waged differently. National immigration regimes are typically twin-track: facilitating entry for the (better-paid) 'brightest and best' while imposing far more restrictions, pre and post entry, for the 'low-skilled'. Visas for the latter are often temporary, with immigration systems designed to make it difficult to achieve legal permanent residence or citizenship.

These distinctions are both managed and obfuscated by the language and ideology of skill. Despite the systemic reliance of employment relations and labour market analyses on its analytical power, what constitutes skill remains remarkably elusive. Skill may be represented in years of education or in qualifications, or subject to special tests, but there is always something extra. One way of capturing this 'extra' is specialization, which can become a proxy for skill, with highly specific skills claimed for certain occupations, winning them improved wages and status. In this skills hierarchy, those who can turn their hand to everything – construction workers who dig and plaster today and lay foundations and build walls tomorrow, domestic workers who clean and cook at the same time as caring for an older person – are 'unskilled' and left to hustle at the bottom of the skills pile. They are typically the most marginalized workers and include, of course, migrant workers who, labelled 'unskilled', are consigned to precarious work and status.

While being a low-skilled worker has specific consequences for migrants because of its associated conditionalities for immigration status, the consequences of the skills regime are deeply felt by citizens too. As Natasha Iskander puts it: 'By denying the unskilled the more abstract, more agentic, and more subjective registers of personhood, these representations reduce the unskilled down to their bodies. Their contribution to the economy and to their jobs becomes recast as corporeal' (2021, p 13). But the framing of migration and migrant labour is such that the low-skilled migrant is positioned as an (unfair) competitor with the low-skilled citizen for access to the labour market, making it difficult to tease out the shared interests in thinking against skills hierarchies.

Migrants can also be citizens. A foreign-born person may be a citizen in law through naturalization or deriving citizenship from a parent, while the possibility of dual and even multiple citizenships in many states means that a foreign national can also be a citizen.[2] If we do not know who counts as a migrant, this has consequences for citizens, as evidenced by the UK's Windrush scandal, which saw Black British citizens wrongly detained and deported, and denied benefits, jobs, medical care and other legal rights. Importantly, neither migrant nor citizen are legal terms alone (nor, indeed, are refugee, skill or asylum seeker). In the academic literature, it is recognized that citizenship is a normative term, and likewise in political debate, being a *citizen* is more than a claim about legal status. This remains unacknowledged when it comes to the term 'migrant', but it is observable that these overlaps are experienced with far greater intensity by poor and negatively racialized citizens. Perhaps the paramount example of this in Europe are Roma people who may be EU citizens yet nevertheless are often removed/deported as criminals, nomads or homeless.

What movements matter?

Our globe is in motion, turning daily on its axis, annually around the star that is our sun. So too is the earth beneath our feet, where tectonic plates birth land. The sea is endlessly shifting, from tides and currents to the deep-sea ocean circulation that can take a thousand years to complete. Reaching for food, driving to work or trekking across glaciers, human beings are part of this movement. Mobilities, human and non-human, are not enacted on a static planet, but are part of patterns that make our worlds. These kinds of relationship have been explored in the work of mobilities scholars. The 'mobility turn' seeks to develop 'a sociology which focuses upon movement, mobility and contingent ordering, rather than upon stasis, structure and social order' (Urry, 2007, p 18). It analyses how social relations are stretched across the world and how they draw on transport, communication and digital infrastructures and on the intersections of mobility infrastructures, such as roads, communications devices and electricity.

That social relations and mobilities are interrelated is not new. Drawing on research in multiple disciplines, including archaeology, linguistics, genetics and anthropology, Patrick Manning (Manning and Trimmer, 2020) argues that 'cross-community migration' was critical to the rapid social evolution and spread of *Homo sapiens*. As humans moved, so too did languages, ideas, technologies and associated ecologies – some argue that plant domestication was not driven by human agency but was an evolutionary response to recruit humans as seed dispersers (Spengler, 2020). These entanglements have become ever more complex as human associated movements have accelerated. Industrialization, colonialism and digital technologies, structured by a global carbon-based capitalism, demand, shape and manage multiple mobilities and set in train processes that are beyond our capacity to anticipate.

Through the multiple effects of climate change, we are experiencing, and for many in the rich world rediscovering, the inextricability of the human and the non-human. Fossil fuel dependence and extractive capitalism are significantly impacting climate and environment and impelling the migration of species, required to adapt, move or die (Shah, 2020). Species move in response to different stimuli and pressures and this movement is often disorderly and difficult to track. But the mobilities of human and non-human species are disrupting the framings of nativity and alienage as the conditions of ecosystem integration. These connections are vividly illustrated in our health. The biologist Rob Wallace has, along with others, researched how multinational agribusiness has undermined local food security across the world and changed the dynamics of land use in complex ways, initiating socioeconomic processes that broaden humans' interface with wildlife (Wallace et al, 2020). Undercut smallholders branch out into wild game or are pushed into areas that are difficult to cultivate. In this context, human movement can expose us to new pathogens and disrupt ecologies that have held them in check. Importantly, the impoverished people who move do so in a local context shaped by global agribusiness, fisheries and livestock production – huge industries owned and controlled by a handful of multinational corporations and invested in by globalized finance capital.

COVID-19 vividly demonstrated the impossibility of disconnecting the socioeconomic and the biological and how both are bound up with movement. Controlling human movement became a critical response to controlling infection and in early 2020 many of us were required to confine ourselves to domestic spaces to contain the virus. Flight bans and quarantines were imposed by multiple states, and across the world there were brutal crackdowns on people on the move. However, human societies and economies cannot function without movement, so at the same time there were multiple exceptions made. Some jobs were declared 'essential', exempting them from the most severe restrictions. How these jobs were defined varied, but food provision, health, logistics and care services were common to lists drawn up by countries across the world (Anderson et al, 2021).

It was notable that most of these essential jobs were designated 'low-skilled' and were poorly paid and low status – for example, crop pickers, food processors, care assistants, shop assistants, delivery workers, cleaners. It is scarcely surprising, then, that in many high-income countries 'migrants' represented a substantial proportion of these essential workers (see, for example, Fernández-Reino et al, 2020; OECD, 2020). Movement was also necessary for the production and distribution of food and essential medical supplies. Take the case of the global demand for rubber gloves, produced largely in Malaysia. Malaysia's rubber glove industry is structurally dependent on migrant labour, and rubber glove supply across the world therefore depends on labour recruitment from Nepal, Indonesia and Bangladesh (Anderson et al, 2023). Trade and human movement are not parallel systems but interconnected, and rubber gloves in a hospital in Washington need immigration bureaucracies in Kathmandu to be functioning effectively. Migration is highly politicized in the country where migrants are physically present, but this politicization does not attach to the goods they make, particularly when they are exported. This means the critical role of migration regimes for global trade can be overlooked even though, in practice, trade policy can often become a form of migration policy and trade policy instruments are increasingly important for international migration governance.

How are we to denaturalize the border?

Our current analysis of human movement is distorted by a focus on migrants, confusion about who is a migrant, and by taking migration as disconnected from other areas of social, economic and biological life. These distortions are informed and compounded by the problem of 'methodological nationalism'. This equates society with the modern nation state, which is seen as a container of social processes. The nation state is assumed and naturalized, thereby invisibilizing how its exigencies shape socioeconomic relations and the multifaceted work – political, legal, social and imaginative – required to reproduce the nation state form.

Methodological nationalism (Wimmer and Glick Schiller, 2002) has, for several decades, been recognized as a challenge across the social sciences, but it has particular and significant consequences for academic and political understandings of migration (Anderson, 2019). Empirically, it treats movements across borders as materially different from movements within borders, particularly in the Global North (in the Global South, 'displacement' commonly refers to both). Normatively, it positions the international migrant as transgressing naturalized territorial boundaries and disrupting the 'national order of things' (Malkki, 1995). Scholars of migration are, then, at the sharp end of the vexing epistemological, empirical and ethical challenges posed by methodological nationalism.

This naturalization of the nation state is not confined to migration scholars, nor to social scientists: 'in a world of nation states nationalism cannot be confined to the peripheries' (Billig, 1995, p 11), and social scientists often fail to reflect on the importance and naturalization of the nation state more generally. Methodological nationalism is in part a manifestation of 'banal nationalism' (Billig, 1995), the quotidian and seemingly mundane reproductions of the nation in routine habits of language and assumptions, in symbols and in reporting on weather, national sports teams, and so on. It allows contradictions to pass unnoticed: consider the claims that the National Health Service (NHS) offers 'universal health coverage', when it patently does not (this was manifest in the then UK Health Secretary Matt Hancock's tweet on 17 November 2019: 'It's the *National* Health Service not the *International* Health Service. … [A]fter Brexit we'll extend the NHS surcharge to all non-UK residents' (Hancock, 2019, emphasis added)). When paired with 'state', the nation describes and renders palatable a form of rule. The 'nation' in nation state humanizes state power: contrast appeals to the 'national interest' with appeals to 'state interest'. It is, moreover, a form of rule that normalizes controls over cross-border mobility. As John Torpey (1999) argues in his history of the passport, modern states' monopoly over the legitimate means of movement is an essential element of the 'state-ness of states'. Nation states can make many different and varied kinds of populations – they may or may not make an autistic population, for example – but they *must* make 'migrants' if they are to be a nation state (Sharma, 2020).

One response to methodological nationalism that has emerged from migration studies is the framework of transnationalism. This recognizes human communities and communications as not restricted to a single nation state and migrants as building social fields that connect across borders (Vertovec, 2007). 'Transnational studies' seeks to decentre the nation state and look across spaces and scales, enabling us to see how the 'global' and the 'local' change when we 'don't assume they are automatically linked to particular types of territory or space' (Levitt, 2011, p 168). In this way, it denaturalizes the borders that make territories and shows how migration and migrant communities adjust to, remake and exceed them. However, transnational approaches engage with methodological nationalism but not 'banal nationalism', keeping the nation inside the nation state portmanteau.

There is much to be learned from paying attention to the work of 'national' when it is not attached to state. 'National' is ambiguous (Mongia, 2018). It can signify a legal relation with, or recognition by, the state – as in 'national territory' or 'national citizenship'. But it can also mean belonging to the nation, with the nation understood as referring to culture/cultures, languages and a people that stretches back in time. It slips between its meanings of formal citizenship status on the one hand and belonging to the nation on the other. Membership of the nation, like citizenship, is claimed through ancestry, but unlike citizenship, national membership is often imagined as independent of and predating the state. It is possible to be considered as belonging to the nation and yet not be a legal citizen, and some states offer fast-tracked naturalization for 'ethnic members' across multiple generations even if they have never set foot on the state's territory. Conversely, some racialized and/or minoritized citizens may have the legal status of citizen but may not be imagined or depicted as belonging to the nation, making them vulnerable to citizenship loss. In India, for example, the implementation of strict requirements for documenting citizenship and the publication of the National Register of Citizens in 2019 removed citizenship from 1.9 million people in the highly diverse region of Assam, rendering linguistic and religious minorities vulnerable to arbitrary and indefinite detention. Who sheds and who retains their migrancy is bound up with nationally specific ways of encoding and remaking race (Lentin, 2014; Mongia, 2018; Sharma, 2020).

David Theo Goldberg argues that the development of the modern state 'depended on the ideological work of manufacturing sameness' and that this sameness became bound up with the ideological work of the construction of race:

> States are racial … because of the structural position they occupy in producing and reproducing, constituting and effecting racially shaped spaces and places, groups and events, life worlds and possibilities, accesses and restrictions, inclusions and exclusions, conceptions and modes of representation. They are racial, in short, in virtue of their modes of population definition, determination and structuration. (Goldberg, 2002, p 104)

The state's projection of political and symbolic power over a territorialized population makes ethnicity and/or 'race' a critical marker of difference. In the nation state form, the emphasis is on belonging to the nation. At the same time, the racializing force of the state form requires navigation around racist ideologies, particularly as ideas of racial group and hierarchies were vocally repudiated by powerful liberal democracies after the Nazi Holocaust. This navigation is facilitated by the ambiguity of the term 'national'. Immigration controls affect to eschew race, but they take nationality as foundational. Indeed, through 'nationality', skills are embodied and acculturated – having small hands, having the right attitude or being naturally more hard-working and obedient can become associated with what country a person was born in. To designate such physical and behavioural characteristics as 'racial' would be unacceptable, and rightly so, but describing them as 'national' can be presented as simple common sense.

The hostility to migration in many states today cannot be understood independently of the migrant as a racialized category, but migration scholarship has demonstrated a certain aversion to discussing 'race' and racism, preferring ideas of ethnicity or culture and, relatedly, integration. But once migration is no longer at the border, it becomes 'race'. While some scholars (such as Paul Gilroy, Claudia Bruns, Goldberg) have taken a transnational approach to racism and resistance, these have largely not been scholars of migration.[3] Yet the imbrication of racism and nationalism shapes who counts as a migrant as well as experiences of migration and relations between different migrant 'communities', which are typically segregated by nationality/country of origin.

What are we to do with 'migration'?

Who counts as a migrant and who counts as a citizen/national is contradictory, contextual and racialized, but this does not mean the category can be abandoned. Being a 'migrant' matters and, for now at least, not only in terms of legal status. Nationalized subjectivities shape how we imagine ourselves and they give rise to many different forms of socialities and politics. Nationalized subjectivities are not confined to citizens. Those legally classified and/or socially imagined as migrants may also feel the importance of language and habits more strongly than they do when they are living 'at home', and much migrant organizing is around country of origin as Brid Brennan discusses in her interview at the end of this volume.

Philosopher Ian Hacking has theorized how human sciences[4] 'make up people' (see Hacking, 2006). His work on 'dynamic nominalism' builds on and critiques the philosophical nominalist tradition that holds, crudely, that taxonomies are created by human beings. When it comes to the classification of people, he argues, names interact with the named, and human action is tightly linked to human description. It is not that bureaucrats and social and human scientists recognize an already existing kind of person, but rather that that kind of person can emerge at the same time as the kind is being invented. Making up categories of people 'changes the space for possibilities of personhood' (Hacking, 1986, p 165); the identification changes how people feel about themselves and their experiences and shapes possibilities for action.

In Hacking's analysis, experts and scientists play an important role in what he calls the 'looping effect', initially in the identification of a potential form of grouping and later in the generation of expert knowledge on the grouping that is both legitimized and disseminated via institutions. Consider the Victim of Trafficking (VoT). Like other recently identified social-forensic categories, from autism to trans identity, once trafficking was identified as a phenomenon, numbers rocketed, and it has become an area of expertise and intervention. Trafficking has seen a huge increase in the numbers of state functionaries, businesses, NGOs and international organizations generating knowledge and policies about trafficking and, more recently, 'modern slavery'.

As categories become socialized, they emerge as groups that are spoken for, on behalf of and negotiated with. Representation is not only about *Darstellung* (portrayal) but also *Vertretung* (speaking for; Spivak, 1988). For minoritized groups, these two are treated as conjoined, but that is not the case for dominant groups. A middle-class White male speaking in a European parliament is rarely regarded as portraying the constituency of middle-class White males or as speaking principally for middle-class White males. In contrast, a Muslim parliamentarian is often, whether or not they want to be, regarded as speaking for all Muslims, as Black people are held to speak for Black people, and migrants for migrants.

What, then, are migration scholars and activists to do with the category of 'migrant'? Here one can turn to critical race theory to look at ways of responding to the epistemological, ethical and conceptual challenges of managing and developing an 'inherited' concept. Mills (2017) helpfully compares 'race' to 'phlogiston' and 'witch'. Both were terms in use in the 17th century. 'Phlogiston' was a gas believed to be emitted by materials on combustion. Phlogiston does not exist, and it has been dropped as a scientific construct. Witches in the sense of evil women with magical powers do not exist either, but the witch is still used in stories and to describe believers of Wiccan religion. 'Race', he suggests:

> is arguably more like 'witch' than 'phlogiston' in that many social and political theorists have contended it can still do useful work for us. [...] Instead of seeing race ... as part of a natural hierarchy, one reconceptualizes it so it refers to one's structural location in a racialised social system, thereby generating a successor concept. People are 'raced' according to particular rules – we shift from a noun to a verb, from a pre-existing 'natural' state to an active social process. (Mills, 2017, p 4)

Migration studies is halfway to a successor concept in the debates about the terminology of illegal/undocumented/unauthorized/clandestine. No one is illegal any more than they are a witch, but they are 'illegalized' through an active social – and state-endorsed – process. Perhaps, then, we can think of 'migrantized people'. In this spirit, there have been calls to 'demigrantize' migration studies; that is, to 'move away from treating the migrant population as the unit of analysis and investigation and instead direct the focus on parts of the whole population, which obviously includes migrants' (Dahinden, 2016, p 2218). This also has the potential to address the increasingly complex relation between migration and race.

Rethinking migration and mobilities

The three questions are discussed separately in this chapter for analytical purposes, but all are related to who counts as a migrant and in (research) practice they cannot be disentangled. They are opportunities as well as challenges. Taken together, they show the richness of thinking both *with* and *against* migration. Thinking with migration shows us how mobility patterns and makes our worlds; thinking against migration exposes how habits of thought and assumptions about migration obscure connections and other ways of living in the world. Both, together, show us how efforts to manage certain kinds of movement are critical to how we are governed.

This volume illustrates how migration can be rethought and how that rethinking can reveal new things about the ways we live in the world. It is *multi*disciplinary in that contributors are writing from their own disciplinary perspective, but it is also genuinely *inter*disciplinary, with introductions to each of the four parts co-authored by academics from a range of different fields. All contributions, in different ways, encourage us to think more broadly about who counts as a migrant, or a citizen, and what we mean by the term 'migration'. Each part foregrounds one of the challenges outlined earlier: 'Multiple Mobilities' shows how human movement is connected to other mobilities and the efforts made to manage some of those mobilities. 'Productive Borders' illustrates the historical contingency of nationhood but also the tremendously productive nature of borders and how this reaches into our ideas of race and nation. 'Transformative Representations' uncovers the dynamic politics of naming and how this can work with and against people on the move. The final part, 'Beyond migrants and migration', examines aspects of the contemporary political landscape and what it tells us about the making and unmaking of difference.

'Multiple Mobilities' comprises three chapters that connect human movement to other mobilities, using these entanglements to explore human/ non-human imbrications and assemblages. Using the case of the Campo Santo Teutonico cemetery in Rome, Lucy Donkin examines how the moving of people and material, particularly soil, made connections between different sites and inspired beliefs and practices. Place became portable and 'the earth functions as a diagnostic device, highlighting connections between different forms of movement' (p 27). What is brought with us as we move, and what does that tell us about our worlds? These relations are often obscured as our imaginations have been so thoroughly schooled in normalizing the contemporary nation state form. With an imagination that starts from the boundedness of place, and a very particular idea of territoriality, it is hard to recover the engagements that render place mobile and allowed pilgrims to visit places as if they were Rome, or that transported soil to make connections between sacred places. Donkin's piece is suggestive of ways of thinking about mobility and place that are not premised on mobility as through place, but rather connect mobility- and place-*making*, meaning that movement does not have to be disruptive of place.

In contrast, Laurence Publicover looks at the early voyages of the East India Company – the first steps in initiating processes of mobility that were to violently disrupt life-worlds across the planet. He describes voyages that suggest in microcosms the unimaginable collisions, partnerships and accelerations that would ensue, attending to the many hidden histories that looking at mobilities in practice (in his case, the sailing ship) exposes. He reveals the role of more-than-human agencies and the materiality and instability of human/non-human assemblages – the shipworms, for example, 'undermined human autonomy within these voyages' (p 60). The fantasy of manly adventurers is exposed in the face of not only the weaknesses but also the multiple dependencies of the Company agents. More particularly, the movement of these Englishmen was only possible because of multiple other movements – of ocean currents, of supplies, animals, goods and other forms of organic and inorganic matter – and these movements did not always further the progress of those who believed they were in charge.

María Paula Escobar Tello's chapter starts from the governing of animal mobilities, more particularly cattle in the UK, charting the historical expansion of the control of the movement of animals to the control of the movement of disease/bacteria to the control of the growth of antimicrobial resistance (AMR) – this latter made ontologically accessible in large part through the policies created to deal with it. She examines how the cow passport 'fastens together the complex assemblage of material objects, documents, regulations, organizations, veterinary inspectors, administrators and others on which policies depend' (p 66). Such an approach reveals how animal and policy mobilities are interconnected, but also how both are embedded in social, economic and historical contexts that stretch beyond efforts to control animal mobilities. She considers the global policies to tackle AMR in the O'Neill report and their potential for application in low- and middle-income countries. In contrast to the unremarked and relatively smooth policy mirroring between the UK and the EU, global AMR policy has proven far more difficult. She explores the impact of differences in context between where policies are devised (in this case, the UK) and where they are implemented (she takes the example of Colombia as emblematic). While policy makers may claim successful policy mobility (diffusion) is a matter of time, she holds that the challenges are far more structural and argues for the relevance of international power relations and colonial histories.

Taken together, these chapters show us how broadening our understanding of 'migration' to make connections with other forms of mobility and with the more-than-human that moves can help us better understand how human movement has and continues to impact on and reflect ecosystems, socioeconomic relations and technological change.

The chapters in 'Productive Borders' take mobility as a lens to denaturalize and historicize borders and expose how they are productive deep within state territory as well as at its edges. People's movements and the huge efforts to govern these movements are, quite literally, world-making and shape how 'migrants' and 'citizens' alike are governed. This part is not only about how movement is controlled but also about how those who move and those who stay are imagined and how they imagine themselves. All three chapters consider all or part of the area of land that today comprises the UK – London (Martins Junior), England (Smith) and the UK (Dias-Abey) – over different periods.

Mobility is a feature of what it is to be human. Brendan Smith parks the question of when mobility became migration by defining 'migrant' as the mobility of those who 'sought to move permanently' (p 95). While borders/frontiers and territory/land were quite differently understood in medieval times, control over *who* lived *where* was, as today, closely associated with rule or sovereignty. Also, as today, there was a variety of reactions towards the stranger, whether challenging or bolstering kingly power. Smith focuses on three groups whose movement was shaped in different ways by 'the royal will' (p 97): exiles, colonists and labourers. His chapter suggests a reading of contemporary immigration controls not only as codifying and bureaucratizing the relationships between ruler and ruled, but also as consequential for the relationships between those who are ruled. It also points to the powerful importance of imaginaries informed by scripture for people's understandings of the meaning and experiences of movement and of exile.

Manoj Dias-Abey's careful analysis of the emergence of the Aliens Order 1920 and its consequences also engages with power and imaginaries but with an eye to their direct contemporary impact. He describes how Britain post World War I, despite still being an imperial power, was confronted by radical shifts in economic conditions and significant changes to the global political economy. The government was also alarmed by increased labour militancy and internationalism (related too to the anti-colonial nationalism organizing in the British Empire). He argues that nationalist divisions between workers that had been sharply drawn during the war were entrenched and normalized by newly introduced restrictions on labour migration. These institutionalized a *national* labour force for a *national* labour market in a context of international radicalism and organizing. Not only did this move enable the government to claim that it was 'protecting' British workers living in the UK, but it also constructed the idea (arguably the ideology) of a distinctively *national* labour market both as an object of knowledge and an object of politics. Seafarers, many of whom were colonial subjects, became a flashpoint in this context. This multinational labour force was then, and continues to be, critical to global trade flows, yet when they put into land their presence, in stark contrast to the goods they bring, is regarded as a threat or danger. The Coloured Seamen Order 1925, which deemed 'coloured' seamen alien unless they could prove their British subject status, evidences the importance of race in both the hostility and the policing of these early immigration control efforts.

Racism is also very much to the fore in the chapter by Angelo Martins Junior. He examines the consequences of illegality as a category signifying both stigma and status. More particularly, he focuses on how it shapes economic and social relationships between Brazilians living in London, and his research participants do not necessarily build nationally solidaristic ties. Race plays an important role here. While in the UK the relation between race and migration is viewed through the prism of nationality, in Brazil there is a close association between race and class. For migrants to London, this means that race maps onto legal status – low-earning people are more likely to find it difficult to enter on appropriate visas given the costs of entry to Europe. Legal status works to undermine national solidarity but also is entangled in complicated ways with race. His chapter demonstrates how social hierarchies are constructed and globalized but also embedded and context dependent, stretching across international borders but also changed by them.

The three chapters in 'Transformative Representations' expose both the complexities and the consequences of the representation of 'migrants'. Juan Zhang explores how Chinese citizens living abroad found their citizenship 'spoiled' or tainted by an Other identity during the COVID-19 pandemic. This became the context of a highly moralizing discourse of deservingness and of blame that circulated in many different forms across the world and was strongly inflected by nationalism. Thus, in China the virus was represented as a foreign import, while in the US and Europe it was often described as 'the Chinese virus'. Chinese people living outside of China were caught by both representations: in their country of residence they often became a target of racism, but those who travelled or returned also found themselves a focus of opprobrium within China, as not only had they left the motherland, but now they were *qianli songdu*, 'spreading the virus for a thousand miles'. In a new take on the association of migrant bodies with disease, the moral citizenship of Chinese living abroad became suspect – some labelled them 'pandemic refugees'. They were represented in both popular and official media as selfish and irresponsible, undeserving subjects who brought risk home. Zhang's chapter illustrates the power of representation in rendering good citizenship precarious and undermining the basic right of citizenship to enter one's state of citizenship. Nevertheless, the underlying values of deservingness and good citizenship were reproduced by many of those living in this dilemma, who responded to stigma by counterclaims that they were good citizens who followed the rules. They located themselves in the deserving camp by living by 'Chinese' pandemic rules and practices even though abroad, thereby proving themselves good citizens with the right to return – in contrast with those who were irresponsible and rightly excluded.

Nariman Massoumi also looks at 'home', but in this case as an intimate space threatened by the chaos of outsiders. In a very different context from that explored by Zhang, he too exposes the hostility that can be directed at co-nationals and how some claim a superior form of cultural belonging over others – for example, that they are more 'civilized' – which shapes and is shaped by racism. In his analysis of the autobiographical film *Persepolis*, he shows that the receptive audience for secular Leftist Iranian representations of their lives and movements is such that the director not only *portrays* but *speaks for* an Iran that is acceptable to Europe and North America. He argues that 'giving voice' to people from marginalized groups – in this case, through diasporic cinema – can reproduce exclusionary nationalisms.

Florian Scheding reminds us that representation is not restricted to the visual but is also about envoicement and silence. Listening to three musical events that were responses to the Russia–Ukraine war, he argues that while they offered support to Ukrainians on the move, they also continued to exceptionalize migration. This is strikingly illustrated by the Concert for Ukraine in Birmingham, in which almost no Ukrainian musicians performed because they were refused UK visas. He examines how borders and nations are made in sound, how these are crossed, and how thinking sonically can help challenge methodological nationalism. All three chapters analyse migration and movement in relation to a crisis (COVID-19, the Iran–Iraq War, the Russia–Ukraine war). This highlights the association of migration with crisis, which often passes unremarked but which, as all three chapters illustrate, profoundly shapes ideas of migration and mobility.

The final two chapters, in 'Beyond Migrants and Migration', return us to migration as a lived experience and as struggle and invite reflection on the relation between academic work and migration in practice. Holly Rooke and Natasha Carver examine the management and reproduction of ideas of race and migration through a textual analysis of British politicians' speeches on migration. This is in a context where draconian immigration legislation was spearheaded by a Home Secretary whose parents were migrants from

Mauritius and Kenya and who described herself as a 'child of Empire'. The highly diverse Cabinet of the British Conservative government pursued extremely harsh immigration policies, demonstrating the dangers of assuming that *Darstellung* is necessarily consonant with *Vertretung*. Rooke and Carver's careful analysis of politicians' language shows how they manage speaking for and in support of the nation. Finally, Brid Brennan from the Transnational Institute, a migrant rights activist for more than four decades, reflects on her experiences of organizing at national and global level. She discusses what can be learned by activists from academic work that is not straightforwardly related to policy.

Conclusion

The ideologically charged migration lexicon is not only a terminological and epistemological challenge, but a conceptual, ethical and theoretical one. Scholars continually risk reifying the figure of the migrant, thereby contributing to the construction of a problem subject. In the past, research on migration tended to reinforce the strongly imagined norm of national and stable communities disrupted by migrants, and its focus on difference contributed to the constructed distinction between the 'migrant' and the 'citizen'. However, this is changing. Migration studies is increasingly reflexive, examining its conceptual tools with an approach that is both critical and creative, striving to think outside policy that is ever more restrictive and to use research to contribute to building radically different worlds. This collection demonstrates the importance of interdisciplinary work to advance our understandings of migration and mobility and to show that intellectual work can help excavate connections and discern surprising patterns. It is an invitation to imagine, think and act across disciplines, institutions and, of course, national borders to undo separations and build connections, not only in the field of migration but across the multiple exclusions and separations that divide our contemporary world.

Notes

[1] As will be discussed, we recognize that what migration means is highly contested. However, for ease of reading, where possible we write migrant and migration rather than 'migrant' and 'migration'.

[2] In many states (for example, Croatia, Myanmar, Spain, UK), citizenship itself is not a singular legal status.

[3] As an exception, see the special issue on 'racism and transnationality' of the *Transnational Social Review*, with an introduction by Caroline Schmitt, Linda Semu and Matthias Witte (2017).

[4] Under the rubric of human sciences, Hacking (2006) includes 'many social sciences, psychology, psychiatry and, speaking loosely, a good deal of clinical medicine … specific sciences should never be defined except for administrative and educational purposes. Living sciences are always crossing borders and borrowing from each other'.

References

Anderson, B. (2019) 'New directions in migration studies: towards methodological de-nationalism', *Comparative Migration Studies*, 7(36). doi: 10.1186/s40878-019-0140-8

Anderson, B., Poeschel, F. and Ruhs, M. (2021) 'Rethinking labour migration: Covid-19, essential work, and systemic resilience', *Comparative Migration Studies*, 9(45): art 45. doi: 10.1186/s40878-021-00252-2

Anderson, B., Khadka, U. and Ruhs, M. (2023) 'Demand for migrant workers: institutional system effects beyond national borders', *Journal of Ethnic and Migration Studies*, 50(5): 1202–25.

Billig, M. (1995) *Banal Nationalism*, London: Sage.

Cole, P. (2022) *Global Displacement in the Twenty-First Century*, Edinburgh: Edinburgh University Press.

Dahinden, J. (2016) 'A plea for the "de-migranticization" of research on migration and integration', *Ethnic and Racial Studies*, 39(13): 2207–25.

Fernández-Reino, M., Sumption, M. and Vargas-Silva, C. (2020) 'From low-skilled to key workers: the implications of emergencies for immigration policy', *Oxford Review of Economic Policy*, 36(Suppl 1): S382–S396.

Goldberg, D.T. (2002) *The Racial State*, Oxford: Blackwell Publishing.

Hacking, I. (1986) 'Making up people', in M. Baigioli (ed) *The Science Studies Reader*, New York: Routledge, pp 161–71.

Hacking, I. (2006) 'Making up people', *London Review of Books*, 28(16). Available from: www.lrb.co.uk/the-paper/v28/n16/ian-hacking/mak ing-up-people (accessed 1 September 2024).

Hancock, M. (2019) 'It's the National…' [Twitter], 17 November. Available from: https://x.com/MattHancock/status/1195997609942560768 (accessed 1 September 2024).

Hattam, V. (2022) 'Border economies/capitalist imaginaries: dispelling capitalism's system effects', *Borderlands*, 21(1): 39–66.

Iskander, N. (2021) *Does Skill Make Us Human? Migrant Workers in 21st-Century Qatar and Beyond*, Princeton, NJ: Princeton University Press.

Lentin, A. (2014) 'Post-race, post politics: the paradoxical rise of culture after multiculturalism', *Ethnic and Racial Studies*, 37(8): 1268–85.

Le Renard, S. (2021) *Western Privilege: Work, Intimacy, and Postcolonial Hierarchies in Dubai*, Stanford, CA: Stanford University Press.

Levitt, P. (2011) 'Constructing gender across borders: a transnational approach', in E. Nang-ling Chow, M. Segal and L. Tan (eds) *Analysing Gender, Intersectionality and Inequalities: Global, Transnational and Local Contexts*, Advances in Gender Research vol 15, Bingley, UK: Emerald Group Publishing Limited, pp 163–83.

Malkki, L. (1995) 'Refugees and exile: from "refugee studies" to the national order of things', *Annual Review of Anthropology*, 24: 495–523.

Manning, P. and Trimmer, T. (2020) *Migration in World History* (3rd edn), Abingdon: Routledge.

Mills, C. (2017) *Black Rights/White Wrongs: The Critique of Racial Liberalism*, Oxford: Oxford University Press.

Mongia, R. (2018) *Indian Migration and Empire: A Colonial Genealogy of the Modern State*, Durham, NC: Duke University Press.

OECD (Organisation for Economic Co-operation and Development) (2020) *COVID-19 and Key Workers: What Role Do Migrants Play in Your Region?*, Paris: OECD Publishing.

Ruhs, M. (2019) '"Migrants", "mobile citizens" and the borders of exclusion in the European Union', in R. Baubock (ed) *Debating European Citizenship*, IMISCOE Research Series, Cham: Springer, pp 163–68.

Schinkel, W. (2018) 'Against "immigrant integration": for an end to neocolonial knowledge production', *Comparative Migration Studies*, 6: art 31. doi: 10.1186/s40878-018-0095-1

Schmitt, C., Semu, L. and Witte, M. (2017) 'Racism and transnationality', *Transnational Social Review*, 7(3): 239–43.

Shah, S. (2020) *The Next Great Migration: The Beauty and Terror of Life on the Move*, London: Bloomsbury.

Sharma, N. (2020) *Home Rule: National Sovereignty and the Separation of Natives from Migrants*, Durham, NC: Duke University Press.

Spengler, R.N. (2020) 'Anthropogenic seed dispersal: rethinking the origins of plant domestication', *Trends in Plant Science*, 25(4): 340–48.

Spivak, G.C. (1988) 'Can the subaltern speak?', in C. Nelson and L. Grossberg (eds) Marxism and the Interpretation of Culture, London: Macmillan, pp 271–313.

Torpey, J. (1999) *The Invention of the Passport*, Cambridge: Cambridge University Press.

United Nations (1998) *Recommendations on Statistics of International Migration: Revision 1*, Statistical Papers Series M, No 58, Rev 1, New York: United Nations. Available from: https://unstats.un.org/unsd/publication/SeriesM/SeriesM_58rev1e.pdf (accessed 1 September 2024).

Urry, J. (2007) *Mobilities*, London: Polity Press.

Vertovec, S. (2007) 'Super-diversity and its implications', *Ethnic and Racial Studies*, 30(6): 1024–54.

Wallace, R., Liebman, A., Chaves, L.F. and Wallace, R. (2020) 'Covid-19 and circuits of capital', *Monthly Review*, 72(1). Available from: https://monthlyreview.org/2020/05/01/ (accessed 1 September 2024).

Wimmer, A. and Glick Schiller, N. (2002) 'Methodological nationalism and beyond: nation–state building, migration and the social sciences', *Global Networks*, 2(4): 301–34.

Multiple Mobilities

Introduction

Lucy Donkin, María Paula Escobar Tello and Laurence Publicover

Our three chapters in Part 1 explore entanglements between human and more-than-human mobilities. In some respects, this is not a groundbreaking topic: we know perfectly well that merchants carry goods (indeed, as Bridget Anderson points out in the introduction to this volume, goods often move across borders far more easily than people), and we know that human movement itself usually depends on the enrolment of non-humans, whether it be aeroplanes, horses or shoes. But we try to demonstrate that there are also more surprising ways in which more-than-human entities co-configure – and sometimes disrupt – forms of human mobility. When we 'follow the thing' (Cook et al, 2004), we may newly illuminate the forces that shape – rather than simply provide the background or context for – human movement, and this may, in turn, encourage us to think in new ways about categories of people in motion and to consider how these categories can overlap or intersect in ways harder to see when we *begin* with the human.

To take one well-known example, the history of the European colonization of the Americas is in some respects a history of the precious metals sought by Europeans because they were relatively easy to melt down, transport across the ocean and exchange for other goods back in Europe. It is also a history of the pathogens those Europeans carried, which killed vast numbers of Indigenous Americans, which in turn contributed to one of the most traumatic and storied episodes in human mobility: the forcible transportation of Africans across the Atlantic to work in the plantations that were left without a ready source of labour. The Columbian Exchange initiated by these wider events in human history, meanwhile, is perhaps the best-known story of more-than-human migration: plants and animals were carried across oceans – sometimes deliberately, sometimes inadvertently – and these reshaped ecosystems globally, a process that continues today as microorganisms are carried in the water providing ballast for container ships. These events, and colonial extraction more generally, have also contributed to the environmental crisis and the broader anthropogenic change that have disrupted the migration patterns of numerous more-than-human species.

In all these ways, human mobility is entangled with that of the more-than-human; and in fact, we would want to insist, appreciation of more-than-human mobility does not always have to be turned back towards a better understanding of human movement – it can have value in and of itself.

Scholarship in human migration and mobility often attends to these issues, either implicitly or explicitly. But there is perhaps scope for further interdisciplinary work that draws on and thinks with scholarship from cognate disciplines. We have already mentioned the 'follow the thing' approach developed in cultural geography,[1] and we would also draw attention to work in the environmental humanities – in particular the field of ecocriticism – which troubles conceptions of the bounded human and stresses the entanglement of humans within more-than-human assemblages; such work has itself drawn on ideas developed within the new materialism, actor network theory, object-oriented ontology, 'thing' theory and posthumanism. Scholarship within migration studies has, of course, long been alert to the limitations of human autonomy in terms of examining which humans are granted the privilege of movement across borders and which are not, due to imbalances of power within the social domain. But there is further work to be done on how human autonomy might also be shaped or compromised by other 'things', some of which are themselves on the move, such as animals, ocean currents, soil and bacteria.

Work in the humanities can also be valuable in addressing these matters because it invites us to think historically. Doing so is necessary because studying the historical movements of people and things can help us understand where we are today (as in the case of the European colonization of the Americas), but more than this, approaching questions of mobility with historical understanding can mean probing the systems of thought that have encouraged the 'human' sciences to divorce human mobility from its more-than-human counterpart. Greg Anderson has written of the 'unapologetic anthropocentrism' of modernity, how it creates in the human and the non-human domains two entirely different orders, assuming the latter to be composed of 'mute lifeforms, inert "resources," [and] subject-less "processes"' (2018, p 93). From the perspectives of other cultures, including that of premodern Europe, examined in Chapter 2 by Lucy Donkin, and the Mughal Empire, referred to by Laurence Publicover in Chapter 3, such assumptions are far from evident. Moreover, many cultures beyond those of European modernity can be far more sensitive to what María Paula Escobar Tello, in Chapter 4, calls animals' 'participation in the (un)making of worlds' (pp 67–8). Such cultures may conceive the world through systems of belief that also shape ideas about movement, whether these encourage or inhibit particular patterns of motion, and attending to these worldviews may involve thinking about mobility in ways framed less by legal, economic and political issues than by emotional and (broadly speaking) 'religious' ones. It may also help us think about the trauma of forced migration; displacement means something different to those whose cosmologies assume human entanglement in a specific life-world than it does to those whose sense of self is shaped through a valuation of unique interiority and personal autonomy (that is, a self that is essentially sealed off from the world). The following chapters can only touch on such vast matters, of course, but they aim to understand how human mobility might be linked to matters such as faith, chivalry and temporality. This is apparent partly in their interest in the life cycle of people and animals that move − the birth of a cow, a death at sea, the slaughter of animals then consumed during a voyage − and the ways in which human bodies are assimilated into specific material places at the end of life.

Time is also important to these essays in another sense. With some notable exceptions, work in migration studies − and indeed in transnational studies − tends to focus on human mobility as a fait accompli rather than a process. Attending to more-than-human agencies can help direct focus onto the journeys themselves − the materials carried and consumed during periods of mobility and the consequences of mobility on both human and more-than-human entities. What this approach also brings into focus is that the thing that arrives is not the same as the thing that left, that both humans and non-humans − sailors, soil − have new meanings and possibilities as they enter new contexts. To some extent, questions like this have long been asked in studies and histories of mobility (not to mention in literary texts). To what extent does the colonial officer posted to the British Raj remain fully 'British'? What happens to the German exile who sets up in 1940s California? But focusing on processes and technologies of mobility itself can help us think in greater detail about the identity (quite literally, the *sameness* or otherwise) of the person who moves. Marcus Rediker, for example, has argued that it was only when they entered the slave ship and experienced the transatlantic passage that Europeans and Africans became 'white' or 'black' (2007, p 10).[2] And beyond this, the more complex picture of the human emerging from scholarship in posthumanism and the new materialism − scholarship which views the human as composed of multiple agencies and stresses that human agency is forever shaped and qualified by the more-than-human world − can help reframe the question of who or what is on the move.

In some more straightforward ways too, including more-than-human elements in studies of mobility brings into greater focus aspects of human experience. Who gets to carry things with them, and who doesn't? What are the materials − tea, spices, clothes − that people carry with them to establish a sense of home during the journey and beyond, and how might we weigh the right to transport a beloved pet with the right to transport a family member? What kinds of more-than-human entities might require passports of some kind, and what material form might these passports take − a chip or an ear tag for an animal, or an imperial document that travels with a box of relics, for example? The legal structures of export controls tend to make a distinction between the border crossing of concepts (that is, technological know-how) and of materials, but a scholarship trained on multiple mobilities might pay greater attention to the material structures through which ideas travel, whether it be scrolls, books, transoceanic cables or physical brains.

In all these ways, we would suggest, a focus on multiple mobilities might lead us to see new patterns and nodes, ones that are connected to – but also exceed or refashion – the usual grid for studies of migration, the boundaries of the state. The chapters that follow focus, for example, on sites that can be considered floating pieces of a state (ships), that serve people from a particular region when they move outside it ('foreign' cemeteries) and that possess their own forms of boundedness (the farm). But more than this, the essays try to show how such sites are comprised of their own ecosystems (sometimes literally, sometimes more imaginatively and metaphorically) and how they are so owing to agencies and movements that are entangled in but also qualify those of the human.

Notes

[1]   For a witty and engaging introduction, see: http://followthethings.com

[2]   Rediker's (2008) work on the sharks that trailed slave ships offers another brilliant example of how human mobility intersects with more-than-human agency.

References

Anderson, G. (2018) *The Realness of Things Past: Ancient Greece and Ontological History*, Oxford: Oxford University Press.

Cook, I. et al (2004) 'Follow the thing: papaya', *Antipode*, 36(4): 642–64.

Rediker, M. (2007) *The Slave Ship: A Human History*, London: Penguin.

Rediker, M. (2008) 'History from below the water line: sharks and the Atlantic slave trade', *Atlantic Studies*, 5(2): 285–97.

2

Mobile People and Places in Premodern Europe

Lucy Donkin[1]

Introduction

In medieval and early modern Europe, connections could be made between sacred places through the movement of stones and soil. The Campo Santo Teutonico, a cemetery close to St Peter's in Rome, belonged to a particularly rich spatial network. It was claimed to contain earth from Jerusalem, and from the late 15th century its own soil was taken to cemeteries and chapels north of the Alps, along with grants of equivalent spiritual benefits. This chapter considers how these beliefs and practices were inspired and enabled by a range of human and non-human mobilities, which were shaped by cultural, social and economic relations. While featuring on pilgrimage itineraries, the Campo Santo was associated with the resident German-speaking community in Rome. It was linked to locations defined as much by trade and industry as by religious custom and sacred space. By tracing the trajectories of the soil and other non-human agents, alongside those of individuals who engaged with the burial sites, I aim to show what these 'portable' places meant to those who moved for faith and work before the establishment of modern states and borders. At the same time, the earth functions as a diagnostic device, highlighting connections between different forms of movement.

A cemetery has particular potential as a site for thinking about mobility. It represents the end of individual trajectories though space and time, which converge on the place of burial. These journeys can be reconstructed through a variety of means: the analysis of human remains, the presence of grave goods or the style and textual content of memorials. In the case of the Campo Santo, these memorials have been carefully recorded. Albrecht

Weiland (1988) identified many of those buried there and traced their presence in other sources. However, the Campo Santo offers further insights into practices and patterns of movement because the site was itself mobile. It was not simply a destination, but also a point of departure. Through the soil from Jerusalem it was claimed to contain and the transalpine movement of its own soil, it was linked materially and conceptually to other cemeteries, each of which was also the final resting place for people from elsewhere. Although these individuals are not as well recorded as in Rome, their origins can be extrapolated from the sites and communities involved. The very fact of these linked places of burial is itself significant, constituting a complex network of dynamic locations.

Moreover, the means through which the cemeteries were connected were entangled with other processes, in ways that challenge neat classifications. The movement of the soil took place alongside a range of human mobilities, including pilgrimage, diplomacy, trade, finance and migration for work. It was part of a spectrum of movement that ranged from the long term to the momentary, and from the long distance and regional to the urban and even smaller scale. The portable earth was connected to the circulation of other material objects, not simply travelling the same routes, or passing through the same hands, but being exchanged for money and discussed in mobile media. In addition to sacred matter such as relics, and the intangible spiritual benefits – indulgences or time off purgatory – with which the soil was associated, two groups of things are particularly resonant: other substances extracted from the ground, including alum, salt, metal ore and the coins into which the latter was minted; and textual and visual sources, from correspondence and legal documents to devotional images and guidebooks.

The first part of the chapter considers the Campo Santo Teutonico in its Roman setting. It relates the site to widely shared practices of pilgrimage and the presence of a resident German community and highlights how phenomena which might today be associated with mobility and migration respectively were closely linked in this context. The second part follows the Campo Santo soil to three destinations in German- and Dutch-speaking northern Europe: Middelburg (Netherlands), Hall (Austria) and Annaberg (Germany). It analyses the relationships, channels of communication and movement of people and things that made this possible and notes other ways in which Rome was made present in those places. While acknowledging common factors and shared identities, it shows how these connections were shaped by the diversity of the individual destinations, in institutional, social, economic and environmental terms, including ways in which they participated in other forms of mobility. Links with Rome were not necessarily the defining feature of the recipient burial sites, and their urban settings acted as centres within circulatory networks in their own right.

Rome

Medieval and early modern Rome was a cosmopolitan city, which prompted forms of mobility that transcended political and physical borders and spoke to multiple identities. Its sacred sites attracted pilgrims from across Europe and beyond, who might be differentiated by the distance and difficulty of their journeys rather than by specific countries of origin. Some pilgrims stayed for a while or even settled, while those travelling for work could also see their presence there in religious terms. Within the city, pilgrimage practices involved a spectrum of micro-mobilities, from a circuit of the major churches to climbing the steps of Old St Peter's. Certain of Rome's churches alluded to a wider sacred topography by including relics and architectural elements believed to have been brought from Jerusalem, notably the Scala Santa, the stairs Christ had trodden on his way to Pontius Pilate. The city's appeal led to movement elsewhere, with some indulgences allowing pilgrims to visit other locations as if these were Rome. Arrangements could involve local churches and sometimes individual altars standing in for particular places in Rome (Kühne, 2017, pp 448–53). There was also a tradition of virtual pilgrimage supported by indulgenced prayers and images, requiring little or no actual movement on the part of the practitioner. In this sense, the whole city was mobile. Rome's status as the headquarters of the papacy also shaped movement to and from the city and the diversity of its population. The papal court lay at the heart of a complex system of faith and finance, which involved the circulation of petitioners, correspondence and coinage throughout Europe (Fonnesberg-Schmidt et al, 2021) and contributed to the development of resident communities of 'foreign' clerics and laypeople in Rome. The perception of these communities reflects the politically fragmented nature of the Italian Peninsula, where belonging and otherness were often defined in terms of a city and its surrounding territory; someone from Florence might be as foreign as someone from France, although *ultramontani* (those from north of the Alps) were thought of as a particular category.

Rome was thus the focus of long-standing practices of devotional movement that concentrated on the tombs of the saints, together with holy images and venerated relics. These sites might be encompassed in a circuit over a few days or visited during an extended stay in the city. Over time, the most important churches became formalized through papal requirements to visit certain locations in Jubilee years, when particularly high numbers of indulgences were available, and the attention devoted to the city's seven main basilicas in indulgence guides. Long-distance and local movement could be explicitly linked. During the first Jubilee in 1300, Pope Boniface VIII required pilgrims or outsiders ('peregrini ... aut forenses') to visit the basilicas of St Peter and St Paul daily for 15 days, while Romans had to do the same for 30 days (Digard et al, 1904, cols 922–3). It was also possible to distinguish between pilgrims in terms of distance travelled and benefits received. One version of the *Indulgentiae ecclesiarum principalium urbis Romae*, printed c 1485–87, differentiates in this way between those coming to St Peter's to see the Veronica, the cloth imprinted with the face of Christ. It promised different levels of remission for Romans, people from the surrounding area ('circa Romam') and those who had travelled over 'over mountains, valleys, hills'.[2]

The Campo Santo played a minor, but distinctive, part in these practices. Guides to the city list indulgences for visiting the site, witnessing a burial, saying prayers for the dead and burial itself. The most influential of these texts was the *Indulgentiae ecclesiarum principalium urbis Romae*. Initially restricted to the seven main basilicas, this was expanded in the later 15th century to include other churches, with the Campo Santo or Gottesacker appearing in this longer list (Miedema, 2001, pp 367–97). In contrast, the *Reliquie rhomane urbis atque indulgentie*, first printed in 1483, refers to the cemetery at the end of its description of St Peter's.[3] However the Campo Santo appears in print, it seems likely that interested pilgrims visited the site in conjunction with St Peter's, although some will have been staying in the surrounding area anyway. In other words, the site fitted into an urban framework and benefited from its proximity to a key basilica and its major relics. The presence of the cemetery on itineraries is confirmed by travel accounts. For example, one pilgrim from Würzburg who visited Rome in 1470 on his way to Jerusalem mentions celebrating Palm Sunday at the cemetery (Röhricht, 1906, p 10).

As this last example implies, the Campo Santo was involved in a second network of long- and short-distance devotional movement. The appeal of the site lay in the legend that it contained soil from Akeldama in Jerusalem, the Potters' Field purchased with the money Judas received for betraying Christ, according to Matthew's Gospel. The *Reliquie rhomane* refers to the Campo Santo as Akeldama, while some versions of the *Indulgentiae* describe the soil as having been brought to Rome by Constantine's mother, Helena. Akeldama itself was visited by pilgrims to the Holy Land and used for their burial. Niccolò da Poggibonsi's *Libro d'Oltramare* of c 1346–50 notes the 'perdonanza grandissima' available and describes how pilgrims recited psalms and prayers for the souls of those buried there (Bacchi della Lega, 1881, vol 1, p 152). In 1431, another Italian pilgrim, Mariano da Siena, took some of the soil for his 'devozione' (Moreni, 1822, pp 57–8). By the late 15th century, Akeldama soil was mentioned in relic lists (Donkin, 2024, p 348). Other cemeteries too were claimed to contain soil from the site, including in Pisa, Cyprus and possibly Acre (Bodner, 2015; Meier, 2022). In Rome, the beliefs regarding the Campo Santo reflect a tendency in the later Middle Ages for the city to be seen to rival Jerusalem, partly through the transfer of matter from sacred places. Soil from Calvary was thought to pave the chapel of St Helena at Sta Croce in Gerusalemme and fill bronze columns in St John Lateran, two of the seven key Roman basilicas (Donkin, 2017). The Campo Santo must thus be seen in the context of pilgrimage to Rome and the Holy Land, a form of mobility which involved the circulation of people and things at differing scales and in a variety of rhythms.

Germany in Rome/Rome in Germany

If these patterns of movement were geographically inclusive, relationships with Rome forged through the Campo Santo also had a specificity that can be seen as 'national', as this concept was understood at the time. Although the name Campo Santo Teutonico postdates the period examined here, the site was already closely connected with the German-speaking lands. The cemetery was run by a confraternity, an association of clergy and laypeople formed for pious purposes. Founded in the mid–15th century, this was officially restricted to Germans, though some members came from elsewhere. The German version of the oldest statutes from c 1490 formulates membership in terms of language ('baydelay man und frauwen von tutscher zungen'), although the Latin version renders things more generally ('utriusque sexus hominum Teuthonicorum'). Both stipulate that the confraternity's priest should speak German well, presumably to aid comprehension by a diverse membership (Schulz, 2002, pp 154, 163). Knut Schulz (2004) has remarked on the wide geographical origins of the founder members and suggested that they experienced a greater sense of affinity in Rome than they would have done north of the Alps. This was probably true for pilgrims too; certainly, Martin Luther's time in the city has been seen to have reinforced his self-identification as 'German' (Roper, 2016, pp 62–3).

Despite a wider remit, the Campo Santo itself also had a national dimension. The cemetery was mainly used to bury pilgrims and foreign residents of the city, reflecting dividing lines between Romans and everyone else found in Boniface's instructions for the first Jubilee of 1300. Indeed, one German-language indulgence guide notes that the cemetery was exclusively for pilgrims and other foreigners ('pilgrin oder sinst fremd leit') and claims that the ground would not hold Romans (Miedema, 2003, p 133). Although memorials at the cemetery and its church, Sta Maria in Campo Santo, do in fact commemorate some individuals from Rome, for the most part they reflect this emphasis on outsiders. The majority of those buried there came from the German-speaking lands, including the Low Countries, with a scattering from elsewhere in Europe, including the rest of the Italian Peninsula, Iberia, France and Poland.

The memorials represent a constellation of individual trajectories, which ended in Rome but encompassed different forms and rationales of mobility. Some people were on pilgrimage, such as Johannes von Rodenstein from the diocese of Mainz, in the city for the Jubilee of 1500, or the Polish nobleman Raphael Chroberski, who died on his way to the Holy Land in 1515 (Weiland, 1988, pp 289–90, 789–91). Later in the 16th century, there were individuals with more varied itineraries, such as Sixtus Lyaukama from Frisia, who died in Rome on his way home from travels in France and Italy (Weiland, 1988, pp 737–9). Yet many of those buried in the cemetery had settled in Rome as part of its German community, which included both laypeople and clerics, and as time went on, some had been born in Rome of German parents. Although the history and composition of this diaspora were shaped by the specifics of the city, flourishing after the return of the papacy to Rome in 1420, it was part of a wider presence of Germans in the peninsula, notably in Trento, Venice and Florence (Maas, 1981; Israel, 2005; Böninger, 2006).

These people did not just come together in death. Not only might visits to Rome fulfil a combination of purposes and more settled residents return temporarily or permanently to northern Europe, but different kinds of mobility were interlinked, with longer-term residents supporting visitors. This was the case for both the Germans at the curia and the lay population. Rome's German community was heavily involved in the running of guest houses, including some close to the Campo Santo, as well as baking and shoemaking, trades utilized by visitors and residents alike (Maas, 1981, ch 1; Schuchard, 1999). Especially in the late 15th century, Germans also dominated the printing trade, which had a particular impact on the circulation of objects, people and ideas. These professions and many others are reflected in the individuals buried at the Campo Santo and enrolled in its confraternity.

The involvement of Germans in printing and the production of pilgrim souvenirs illustrates the intersection of long- and short-term residents as well as the participation of material texts and objects in processes of mobility. A list of inscriptions in Sta Maria in Campo Santo includes the grave of Stephan Plannck from Passau, one of Rome's foremost printers in the later 15th century (Forcella, 1873, p 352). The works he printed included liturgical books for the curia, widely distributed outside the city, and diplomatic speeches delivered by envoys who travelled to Rome to offer obedience to the pope (Duggan, 1991, pp 85–6; Meserve, 2021, pp 269–73). Most significantly, he was active in the production of guides to Rome's antiquities and churches, printing editions of the *Mirabilia Romae* in Latin and the *Historia vel descriptio urbis Romae* and the *Indulgentiae ecclesiarum principalium urbis Romae* in Latin and German, as well as an Italian–German dictionary (Meserve, 2021, pp 180–95). The *Indulgentiae* had a particular agency. It guided the reader through the city's sacred sites, including the Campo Santo. Although several editions were printed north of the Alps, some copies will have been used in Rome and taken home by pilgrims, prompting others to visit the city in their turn or enabling a form of virtual pilgrimage. Alongside such texts travelled devotional images. These served as a sign and souvenir of pilgrimage, but also had a wider appeal, being associated with indulgenced prayers, and circulated independently (Meserve, 2021, pp 162–89). Here too we see the involvement of the German community. Johannes von Lumen, who buried his wife Cornelia in Sta Maria in Campo Santo in 1526, described himself on the tombstone as 'in romana curia veronicarum pictoris' (Weiland, 1988, pp 400–1). The earliest list of members of the Confraternity of the Campo Santo includes individuals with similar occupations, such as 'Martinus van Harlem Vronikemaker', as well as Johann Besicken, another printer (Schulz, 2002, pp 181, 193). Their products are reflected in the expenses of travellers. In the 1450s, Albert van der Molen purchased not only day–to–day necessities and new clothes but also a copy of the *Mirabilia Romae*, a cookbook, and two 'hilgenblade' – devotional prints (von der Ropp, 1887).

The ultimate material mobility was the movement of soil from the Campo Santo as part of a process of establishing cemeteries elsewhere in the likeness of the site. Although this reflected interest in Rome and Jerusalem, and a long tradition of relics of place in Christianity, it also responded to ways in which the burial ground was *not* Roman. The Campo Santo was part of a phenomenon in which parts of Rome were associated with different foreign communities, through 'national' foundations such as churches and hostels, as well as clusters of residences and businesses. For Germans and those from the Low Countries, another important institution was Sta Maria dell'Anima, in the district of Parione, with its own confraternity and burial ground (Maas, 1981, pp 70–114). Across the city, San Gregorio on the Celio was significant too (Israel, 2005, p 81). This is not to imply that such locations possessed an informal extraterritoriality in a period before even the establishment of fixed embassies, but it seems clear that the Campo Santo was perceived as a non-Roman, and more exclusively German, space. Correspondingly, it was mainly to today's Germany, Austria and the Netherlands that its own soil was initially taken, along with two sites in Poland. Perhaps the earliest surviving evidence dates to the 1490s, when the records of the vicar general of the Archbishop of Utrecht include payment for the right to scatter soil from the Campo Santo over the cemetery of the Hospital of St Mary at Middelburg (Heeringa, 1926–32, vol 2, p 54). This was followed by grants of soil and indulgences by Popes Julius II and Leo X to Hall, Kolsass, Innsbruck, Freiburg im Breisgau, Łask, Gniezno and Annaberg (Tietz, 2012, pp 31, 34–8; Szymborski, 2015, pp 414–15; Donkin, 2017).

The majority of these destinations lay within the Holy Roman Empire, a fragmented entity composed of a multitude of independent polities. Relationships forged by these places with the Campo Santo were correspondingly established on an individual basis, with connections between only a few. Nonetheless, it is significant that the region was visualized as a single space in the context of its shared connections with Rome. This is

Figure 2.1: Erhart Etzlaub, *Romweg* map, Nuremberg, 1500. Woodcut, 41.6 × 30.2 cm.

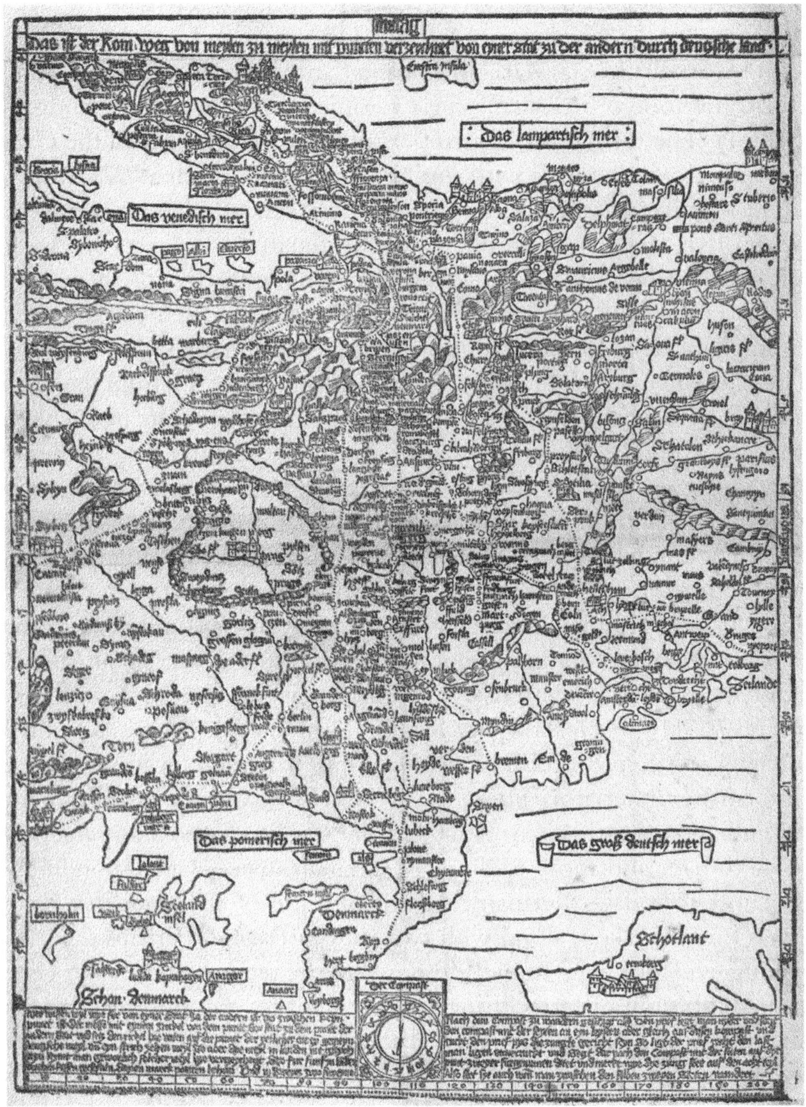

Source: National Gallery of Art, Washington, Rosenwald Collection, 1943.31448 (CC0)

shown in Erhart Etzlaub's *Romweg* map, probably printed in Nuremberg in 1500 for the Roman Jubilee (Figure 2.1; Krüger, 1951). Oriented with south at the top, it stretches from the Baltic Sea and the Noorth Sea ('das groß deutsch mer') to Rome, and extends roughly from Krakow in the east to Bruges in the west. The heading describes the map as showing the way to Rome from one city to another 'durch deutzsche lantt'. It includes no political boundaries within those German lands, and though neighbouring countries and language areas were each designated their own colour by Etzlaub, this has often not been provided in surviving versions. More prominent, therefore, are geographical features such as rivers and mountain ranges, cities and nine itineraries to Rome marked by dotted lines. While this primarily reflects the function of the map, it is in keeping with a tendency in the period, especially within the Holy Roman Empire, to prioritize routes over borders (Scholz, 2020, p 214).

The Campo Santo soil made its way northwards on existing routes as part of a complex motion of people and things. The case studies of Middelburg, Hall and Annaberg illustrate the variety of these dynamics as well as a shared frame of reference. They also demonstrate that the places to which the soil was taken were not blank canvases, to be understood only in terms of their interest in and connections to Rome. Part of their distinctiveness as locations involved the circulation of people and commodities, which in turn framed the reception of the Roman earth.

Middelburg

The soil scattered over the hospital cemetery at Middelburg reflects the presence of individuals from the Netherlands in Rome and journeys made by representatives of that community north of the Alps. In 1493, an agreement was made between a Marian confraternity in Middelburg and that of the Campo Santo, which channelled funds to the latter in return for earth from the cemetery (de Waard, 1907, p 372).[4] The document was drawn up between Wilhelm de Heyck, representative of the German province of the Benedictines in Rome, and Wilhelm Petri, a citizen of Middelburg. The proceedings took place in San Lorenzo in Damaso, a church located – like Sta Maria dell'Anima – in Parione and frequented by merchants from the Low Countries (Vaes, 1919, p 193). The agreement corresponded to wider efforts by the Campo Santo confraternity to engage with the lands from which its members came to raise funds for building a new church. In 1493, the confraternity was concerned about a drop in the number of members resident in Rome and thus paying annual dues, and asked Pope Alexander VI to grant an indulgence to anyone who donated and was inscribed in the list of members. They were allowed to send two men to sell the indulgence, and when the first pair absconded with the proceeds, another was despatched (Baumgarten, 1908, p 54; Maas, 1981, pp 121–2). It is indicative of the importance of regional ties and linguistic divisions that the representatives were sent to their home territory; one man – from Bamberg – went to southern Germany and the other – from Utrecht – to the Netherlands.

The financial relationship between the Middelburg hospital and the Campo Santo was sustained over several years and formed part of a wider set of relations with Rome. The funds were sent via the bank of Willem Pietersz in Mechelen, a firm later responsible for transmitting to the papacy a share of the proceeds from the indulgence granted to the Teutonic Order in aid of its campaign in Livonia, and which acted for Philip of Burgundy in sending funds to his procurator or representative in Rome (Schulte, 1904, p 46; Sterk, 1980, pp 132, 195–7; Kool-Blokland, 1990, p 58). This was not the only direct engagement with Rome in the period. In 1492, Pope Innocent VIII granted members of the hospital confraternities indulgences for work they did with the poor (de Waard, 1907, pp 371–2, 396). Rome was also brought to mind through more concrete means, in communal and private spaces. The hospital accounts for 1513/14 record payment for panel paintings showing the seven churches of Rome, and the same year the room of one resident contained two 'fronika' or Veronica images (Kool-Blokland, 1990, p 26). Paintings of the seven churches, associated with indulgenced prayers, could be hung around a church or religious complex and acted as prompts for virtual pilgrimage (Sugiyama, 2019).

Middelburg, together with its outport of Arnemuiden, was the most important port in Zeeland, involved in trade across the North Sea and into the Baltic Sea and the Atlantic. From the city, located on what was then the island of Walcheren, goods were taken inland, especially to Antwerp. On the *Romweg* map, Middelburg lies close to the route ending in Brussels, Bruges, Ghent and Nieuwpoort (Figure 2.1). The city handled a wide range of goods, including woad and wine from France, iron and fruit from the Iberian Peninsula and alum from the Papal States (Cannelloni, 2017; Goicolea Julián, 2017). Middelburg's identity as a port both meant that elements of its population were highly mobile and led to the presence of foreigners in the city. The Scottish community was particularly well established, with its own conservator or governor, and Middelburg often acted as the staple for Scottish wool and other goods (Catterall, 2005, pp 169, 173; Spufford, 2014). There was also a permanent Spanish community and Portuguese merchants are attested as burghers. The hospital which received the soil catered to the city's transient population as well as to the local poor and sick, and in this sense it replicated the function of the Campo Santo. The complex had dedicated lodgings for passing travellers, such as merchants, craftspeople and pilgrims. In this way, it was a staging-post in the regional and long-distance movement of people and goods. It was customary to enforce a short stay of a few nights, but both long-term residents and short-term guests might come to be buried in the cemetery (Kool-Blokland, 1990, pp 50–1).

Hall

In Hall in the Tyrol, the soil was spread over a family burial chapel in the church of St Nikolaus, forming a site with dynastic and wider significance.

Following a request by Florian and Barbara Waldauf von Waldenstein, soil was granted, along with indulgences equivalent to those available at the Campo Santo, by Julius II in 1508 (Baumgarten, 1908, pp 69–72). Florian Waldauf's eponymous nephew, a cleric, may have acted as an intermediary since 'Doctor Florianus de Waldenstein' was enrolled in the Confraternity of the Campo Santo that year (Schulz, 2002, p 196). The grant benefited the family most immediately, but indulgences were also available to those visiting the chapel. It was part of Waldauf's efforts to amass a large collection of relics, prompted by a vow made during a storm in the Zuiderzee. As a counsellor and envoy of the Holy Roman Emperor Maximilian I, Waldauf was well travelled and well connected, and the rapid growth of his collection was facilitated by these experiences and networks. He drew up an account, intended for publication and accompanied by woodcuts, which details the origins of the relics, drawn from across the German-speaking lands and Hungary (Cárdenas, 2021, pp 254–314). Already prior to the arrival of the Campo Santo soil, the burial chapel was strewn with the ashes of the virgins of Cologne and with holy earth ('heiligen erdrich') from the grave of St Ursula (Garber, 1915, pp lxxv, clxxii). A letter of safe conduct issued by Maximilian requests that Waldauf's chest of relics and another of holy earth should be allowed to pass without incurring duties, showing how the circulation of sacred matter could be part of larger systems of mobility of goods and people (Fabian and Weirather, 2019, p 15). The collection also included relics of Roman saints, such as Peter, Paul and Laurence, and a copy (which still survives) of the image of the Virgin in Sta Maria del Popolo, understood to have been painted by St Luke (Garber, 1915, pp clx–clxiii). Reciting seven Ave Marias in front of this copy of the image earnt 440 days of indulgences. As at Middelburg, then, there was an interest in substituting for Rome, as well as the accumulation of sanctity in a single site.

Hall was a key point on the north–south axis of communications, lying just to the north of the Brenner Pass. On the *Romweg* map, it is shown as the first stop after Innsbruck on the route leading towards Regensburg (Figure 2.1). From Hall, the River Inn was navigable towards the north-east. For example, Andrea de Franceschi's account of Venetian ambassadors' travels in 1492 describes their stay in the city and onward journey by boat to Passau (Simonsfeld, 1903, pp 290–4). Hall drew its prosperity partly from transit trade, especially after c 1500, when a transregional trade fair was established there. A second dimension of its significance lay in the rich mineral resources of the Inn Valley, especially the silver mines at Schwaz. Hall itself was the location of an imperial mint and a centre of operations for the Fugger banking house. It was also an important site of salt production, which de Franceschi describes as providing for the whole of Germany (Simonsfeld, 1903, p 291). If these activities led to the flow of commodities away from the city, they also drew people and things towards it. The mining industry attracted workers, increasing Hall's population to the extent that food had to be brought in by river (Schmitz-Esser, 2015, p 1689). Waldauf himself supervised the saltworks from 1506, and his promotion of his relic collection both tapped into the town's connectivity and generated new momentum. In 1501, the relics were moved from his castle at Rettenberg to St Nikolaus in Hall. The procession was claimed to have attracted thousands of participants and was commemorated in two woodcuts in the Haller Heiltumbuch (Garber, 1915, pp lxxii–lxxiii). The relics were displayed annually until 1524, linked to a market lasting a fortnight, with indulgences available on this and other feast days. Another woodcut pictures this event, with a crowd gathered around the stage, indicating Waldauf's aspirations to encourage pilgrimage (Garber, 1915, p cxxxi).

Annaberg

A different dynamic again led to the transfer of Campo Santo soil to the cemetery of the Hospital of the Holy Trinity in Annaberg (Donkin, 2024). Here it was part of a set of privileges obtained in 1517 by George, Duke of Saxony, for institutions in the town he had founded. The soil and a papal bull granting the cemetery indulgences equivalent to those available in the Campo Santo were brought back by Nikolaus von Hermsdorff, the Duke's procurator in Rome. What he refers to in a letter as 'several pounds of earth from the Campo Santo' was acquired following payment of four ducats to its confraternity (Richter, 1746–1748, vol 1, p 232; Gess, 1891, p 562). Hermsdorff is recorded as joining the confraternity in the year of the negotiations (Schulz, 2002, p 221). Other ducal agents enrolled in that of Sta Maria dell'Anima (Volkmar, 2008, pp 261–8, 295–6). Hermsdorff was aided by allies at the curia who were long-term residents of the city: papal notary Georg Pusch and prominent Dominican Nikolaus von Schönberg. Both came from the Margravate of Meissen, part of the territories ruled by Duke George, reflecting how polities within the Empire dealt with Rome independently. The granting of the soil and indulgences was accompanied not only by documents and correspondence but also the transfer of money. The payment for the earth was very modest compared to the wider costs. Privileges for the main Annenkirche alone cost 500 ducats, while a share of the revenue from the indulgences for that church went towards the construction of the new St Peter's, with monies transferred by the Fugger banking house (Bünz, 2017, pp 195–214). Since Annaberg was a centre of mining and minting, there is a sense in which these funds were literally extracted from the substance of the surrounding territory.

Annaberg was less pivotally located than Hall, but experienced forms of mobility even more dependent on the mining boom. In the early 16th century it was still a very young town, having been founded shortly after silver ore was discovered there in the early 1490s. As such it does not appear on the *Romweg* map, but it lies close to the route that passed through Zwickau (Figure 2.1). One of several new mining towns in the region, Annaberg grew rapidly. Indeed, such was the rush of new arrivals that the 16th-century *Annabergische Annales* compares them to crowds on a pilgrimage ('so großer menge Volcks, wie es sich damals anlies als zu einer Wahlfarth'; Bönhoff, 1910, p 11). All adults in Annaberg at the time of the grant of the Roman soil had therefore grown up elsewhere. The initial group of residents came from the nearby mining town of Geyer, but the bulk of the town's population necessarily came from further afield. More generally, Susan Karant-Nunn (1989) has described the miners of the western Erzgebirge as initially peripatetic and drawn from other social groups, including craftsmen and agricultural workers, as well as miners from the east of the region.

The documents drawn up to request the Roman privileges suggest that it was hoped that these would attract people to the town too (Bünz, 2017, pp 204–14). For the relevant feast days, when a stational liturgy on the model of Rome was anticipated, indulgences were to be available not just to the inhabitants of Annaberg and the diocese of Meissen, but also any other visitors. Similarly, initial plans for the cemetery intended that burial there would be available to anyone, wherever they had lived, although this was dropped in a shortened version of the petition drawn up by Hermsdorff. On the occasion of the consecration of the cemetery in 1519, soil and papal bull were carried in procession from the Annenkirche (Richter, 1746–1748, vol 1, pp 227–48). The feast of the Trinity was subsequently marked by a sermon preached at the cemetery and by wider festivities, which attracted a regional audience. Already prior to the Roman benefits, efforts had been made to gather sources of sanctity, including relics of St Anne brought from Lyon. The town's relics are celebrated in a poem by Hans Schneider, printed in 1510, which mentions a procession on the feast of St Anne and draws comparison with Rome (Richter, 1746–1748, vol 1, pp 27–30). Indeed, Christoph Fasbender (2013, p 115) has suggested that the poem, which details Annaberg's sacred topography, should be related to the Roman guidebook tradition.

Conclusion

The movement of the Campo Santo soil was part of a wider devotional interest in Rome that took material and immaterial form. It did not just accompany indulgences connected to the Campo Santo, but is also found in the company of images of the seven churches of Rome and the Veronica, relics of Roman saints and a copy of the image of the Virgin in Sta Maria del Popolo, as well as other Roman indulgences, all of which were valued more widely. Nonetheless, the soil did not effect a simple translation of

Rome. The Campo Santo clearly had particular meaning for people from the German-speaking lands. Although ultimately neither were exclusively Germanic, both the site and its confraternity brought together people from a wide range of geographical locations within the Holy Roman Empire. As such, they were symptomatic of a phenomenon in which the experience of travelling or living away from one's place of birth fostered a greater sense of affinity between people than they might have experienced back home. In the *Romweg* map, we can see this taking visual form. Mobility in this sense helped to constitute a shared identity. The movement of the soil translated a place that was already in some way transalpine and perhaps even more 'German' than the locations to which it was taken. While it is important to define this against the universal qualities of pilgrimage and the wider use made of earth from sacred places, this 'national' quality should not be overstated. Different constellations of actors were involved in the movement of the soil and the Campo Santo's transalpine relationships, reflecting a range of urban and regional affiliations and linguistic and political divisions.

The mobilities that the Campo Santo and its soil reflected and engendered were not just multiple in terms of number. One important leitmotif has been the integration of movement for faith and work, as well as interconnections between mobilities different in scale or time span. In Rome, the long-term German-speaking population, both clerical and lay, and the transitory population of pilgrims, envoys, bankers and others were mutually dependent. In life, short-term visitors enrolled in the Confraternity of the Campo Santo alongside residents, used their services and bought their products; in death, they could lie alongside each other. Attention to the Campo Santo soil as it was taken and contextualized elsewhere reveals a similarly complex picture. Two of the places discussed here were regional pilgrimage destinations in their own right. All had populations shaped by migration and mobility, whether these involved extractive industries, trade or a combination of the two. Different motivations for movement could be associated both practically and conceptually, in ways that spoke to local particularities. If the annual display of the Hall relic collection coincided with a trade fair that reflected the city's nodal position in a network of land and water communications, the Annaberg 'silver rush' could be conceived in religious terms, being compared in scale and intensity to a collective pilgrimage.

The value of approaching intertwined mobilities through an attention to urban spaces remains relevant in eras where national boundaries and identities dominate. As the headquarters of the papacy, the capital of Italy and the site of international organizations such as the Food and Agriculture Organization of the United Nations, Rome is still home to communities of resident foreigners. Indeed, current patterns of mobility underpin the present study. Not only has the Campo Santo been used as a burial ground into the modern period, but it is home to a German Catholic institute, the

Görres-Gesellschaft, which published some of the scholarship on which this article has drawn. This is just one of many nationally constituted research institutions and religious communities in the city, some of which shaped my own experiences of living in Rome. Scholarship analysing national groups in Rome today also recognizes the importance of ecclesiastical sites and organizations, such as the processions organized by Peruvian confraternities that venerate an image of Christ from Lima (Roldán, 2019). Here urban micro-mobilities and long-distance migration come together in ways that display parallels with premodern phenomena, suggesting the potential of the cityscape as well as institutions when interrogating mobility across time.

A further dimension of the multiple mobilities examined here concerned materiality. The Campo Santo earth was just some of the matter in motion that joined and defined the places discussed. The fact that it was acquired in addition to indulgences suggests a desire for concrete and visible forms of the sacred to accompany intangible spiritual benefits, which we can see in the other artefacts and relics related to Rome. Received in return for payment, it took part in processes of transaction and exchange which encompassed the sacred and the secular. Transportation of the soil was connected to long-distance financial systems, which saw funds collected as coinage sent via paper transfers to the papacy, through banking networks such as those run by Pietersz and the Fuggers. As a site-specific substance taken from the ground, it can be set alongside other extracted commodities: salt and silver from the Tyrol and the Erzgebirge, alum from the Papal States and soil from sacred places in Cologne. Finally, the earth and its movement featured in mobile material texts. These included not only the Roman indulgence guides that were produced north and south of the Alps, inspiring pilgrimage and acting as souvenirs, but also a local equivalent in the Haller Heiltumbuch. Furthermore, the earth generated legal documents and correspondence, which circulated along the same routes.

In this chapter, earth has formed both subject matter and methodology. Attending to the Campo Santo soil, in Rome and as it was taken elsewhere, has shed light on a network of connected, mobile places, people and things. It has also brought into focus and dialogue wider processes of mobility and their interconnections. Pilgrimage, diaspora, diplomacy, banking, trade and extractive industries are all complex phenomena, each of which has a substantial dedicated body of scholarship. Tracing a single substance, it is possible to see some of the ways in which these overlapped and intersected in individual locations. The claims made for the Campo Santo, the particular trajectories of the soil and the wider connections involved are all specific to their time and place. However, both substance and approach are more widely applicable. In the modern era, earth has also been moved in ways that reflect mobility and migration. In the 19th and 20th centuries, emigrants from Greece, Russia, Ukraine and Galicia took with them soil from their places of origin with which to be buried (Harvey and Troper, 1975, p 204; Merridale, 2000, p 47; Papanikolas, 2002, p 53). Taking soil from places with ancestral connections is still carried out by later generations on journeys of return. These burial customs intersected with practices of taking earth from Jerusalem to include in graves (Graham, 1913, p 181), while earth has also been used to create diasporic shrines, such as the Cuban sanctuary in Miami (Tweed, 1997, pp 102–3). At the same time, such customs correspond to a sense in which the place of origin was itself perceived as sacred. Though not all such places of departure were nation states, these practices are often studied as part of national histories. While this is a different dynamic between national and sacred space from that embodied by the Campo Santo and its network, the movement of soil is equally expressive of the movement of people and its significance. Moreover, to trace these practices collectively would engage with patterns and pathways of mobility that transcend the nation and its borders.

Notes

[1] I would like to thank Bridget Anderson for the invitation to participate in this book project and for her helpful comments on this chapter. I am also grateful to Emma Newcombe and Emily Walmsley for their work on the volume and to María Paula Escobar Tello, Laurence Publicover and the other contributors for discussing topics of shared interest across disciplinary divides.

[2] *Historia et descriptio urbis Romae; Indulgentiae ecclesiarum principalium urbis Romae* (Rome: Stephan Plannck, 1485–87), fols 27r–v.

[3] *Reliquie rhomane urbis atque indulgentie* (Basel: Peter Kollicker, 1483), A6r.

[4] Zeeuws Archief Middelburg, Godshuizen Middelburg, Charters, 1343–1574, no 353.

References

Bacchi della Lega, A. (ed) (1881) *Libro d'Oltramare di Fra Niccolò da Poggibonsi*, 2 vols, Bologna: G. Romagnoli.

Baumgarten, P.M. (ed) (1908) *Cartularium Vetus Campi Sancti Teutonicorum de Urbe: Urkunden zur Geschichte des deutschen Gottesackers bei Sankt Peter in Rom*, Römische Quartalschrift, Supplementheft 16, Rome: Forzani.

Bodner, N.B. (2015) 'Earth from Jerusalem in the Pisan Camposanto', in R. Bartal and H. Vorholt (eds) *Between Jerusalem and Europe: Essays in Honour of Bianca Kühnel*, Leiden: Brill, pp 74–93.

Bönhoff, L. (ed) (1910) 'Petrus Albinus. Annabergische Annales de anno 1492 biß 1539', *Mitteilungen des Vereins für Geschichte von Annaberg und Umgegend*, 11: 1–50.

Böninger, L. (2006) *Die deutsche Einwanderung nach Florenz im Spätmittelalter*, Leiden: Brill.

Bünz, E. (2017) 'Johann Tetzel und Annaberg', in H. Kühne, E. Bünz and P. Wiegand (eds) *Johann Tetzel und der Ablass: Begleitband zur Ausstellung 'Tetzel – Ablass – Fegefeuer' in Mönchenkloster und Nikolaikirche Jüterbog vom 8. September bis 26. November 2017*, Berlin: Lukas Verlag, pp 195–214.

Cannelloni, F. (2017) 'Il commercio dell'allume di Tolfa nei Paesi Bassi borgognoni', *Archivio Storico Italiano*, 175(3): 517–46.

Cárdenas, L. (2021) *The Texture of Images: The Relic Book in Late-Medieval Religiosity and Early Modern Aesthetics*, Leiden: Brill.

Catterall, D. (2005) 'Scots along the Maas, c. 1570–1750', in A. Grosjean and S. Murdoch (eds) *Scottish Communities Abroad in the Early Modern Period*, Leiden: Brill, pp 169–89.

de Waard, C. (ed) (1907) *De Archieven, Berustende onder het Bestuur der Godshuizen te Middelburg. Inventaris van de Oude Archieven, 1343–1812*, Middelburg: J.C. & W. Altorffer.

Digard, G., Faucon, M., Thomas, A. and Fawtier, R. (eds) (1904) *Les registres de Boniface* VIII, vol 2, Paris: Boccard.

Donkin, L. (2017) 'Earth from elsewhere: burial in *terra sancta* beyond the Holy Land', in R. Bartal, N. Bodner and B. Kühnel (eds) *Natural Materials of the Holy Land and the Visual Translation of Place, 500–1500*, Abingdon: Routledge, pp 109–26.

Donkin, L. (2024) 'Earth and ore: materialising transalpine relations on the eve of the Reformation', *Journal of Medieval and Early Modern Studies*, 54(2): 333–69.

Duggan, M.K. (1991) *Italian Music Incunabula: Printers and Type*, Berkeley: University of California Press.

Fabian, S. and Weirather, C. (2019) *Florian Waldauf: Eine Karriere unter Maximilian I*, Hall: Ablinger Garber.

Fasbender, C. (2013) 'Die Wiederkehr der Stadt in Hans Schneiders "Ursprung und Herkommen der Stadt Annaberg" (1510)', in G. Mierke and C. Fasbender (eds) *Wissenspaläste: Räume des Wissens in der Vormoderne*, Würzburg: Königshausen & Neumann, pp 101–17.

Fonnesberg-Schmidt, I., Kynan-Wilson, W., Lauge Christensen, E. and Oppitz-Trotman, G. (eds) (2021) *The Papacy and Communication in the Central Middle Ages*, Abingdon: Routledge.

Forcella, V. (ed) (1873) *Iscrizioni delle chiese e d'altri edificii di Roma dal secolo XI fino ai giorni nostri*, vol 3, Rome: Fratelli Bencini.

Garber, J. (1915) 'Das Haller Heiltumbuch mit den Unika-Holzschnitten Hans Burgkmairs des Älteren', *Jahrbuch der kunsthistorischen Sammlungen des Allerhöchsten Kaiserhauses*, 32(6): i–clxxvii.

Gess, F. (1891) 'Ein Gutachten Tetzels nebst anderen Briefen und Instruktionen den Ablass auf St Annaberg betreffend 1516/17', *Zeitschrift für Kirchengeschichte*, 12: 534–62.

Goicolea Julián, F.J. (2017) 'Castilian trade in the Low Countries in the early 16th century: the activities of the merchant Pedro de Arnedo in the town of Middelburg', *Annales Mercaturae: Jahrbuch für internationale Handelsgeschichte/ Yearbook for the History of International Trade and Commerce*, 3: 51–83.

Graham, S. (1913) *With the Russian Pilgrims to Jerusalem*, London: Macmillan and Co.

Harvey, R.F. and Troper, H. (1975) *Immigrants: A Portrait of the Urban Experience, 1890–1930*, Toronto: Van Nostrand Reinhold.

Heeringa, K. (ed) (1926–1932) *Rekeningen van het Bisdom Utrecht 1378 bis 1573*, 3 vols, Utrecht: Kemink.

Israel, U. (2005) *Fremde aus dem Norden: Transalpine Zuwanderer im spätmittelalterlichen Italien*, Tübingen: Max Niemeyer Verlag.

Karant-Nunn, S.C. (1989) 'Between two worlds: the social position of the silver miners of the Erzgebirge, c. 1460–1575', *Social History*, 14(3): 307–22.

Kool-Blokland, J.L. (1990) *De Zorg Gewogen: Zeven Eeuwen Godshuizen in Middelburg*, Middelburg: Koninklijk Zeeuwsch Genootschap der Wetenschappen.

Krüger, H. (1951) 'Erhard Etzlaub's "Romweg" map and its dating in the Holy Year of 1500', *Imago Mundi*, 8: 17–26.

Kühne, H. (2017) 'Ablassvermittlung und Ablassmedien um 1500: Beobachtungen zu Texten, Bildern und Ritualen um 1500 in Mitteldeutschland', in A. Rehberg (ed) *Ablasskampagnen des Spätmittelalters: Luthers Thesen von 1517 im Kontext*, Berlin: De Gruyter, pp 427–57.

Maas, C.W. (1981) *The German Community in Renaissance Rome, 1378–1523*, Römische Quartalschrift, Supplementheft 39, Rome: Herder.

Meier, R. (2022) *'Mio corpo venga sepolto in terra sancta' – Genese und Verbreitung eines Wunderberichts des 13. Jahrhunderts: Der Blutacker in Jerusalem, der heilige Acker in Akkon und der Camposanto zu Pisa*, Wiesbaden: Reichert.

Merridale, C. (2000) *Night of Stone: Death and Memory in Russia*, London: Granta.

Meserve, M. (2021) *Papal Bull: Print, Politics and Propaganda in Renaissance Rome*, Baltimore, MD: Johns Hopkins University Press.

Miedema, N.R. (2001) *Die römischen Kirchen im Spätmittelalter nach den 'Indulgentiae ecclesiarum urbis Romae'*, Tübingen: Niemeyer.

Miedema, N.R. (2003) *Rompilgerführer in Spätmittelalter und Früher Neuzeit. Die 'Indulgentiae ecclesiarum urbis Romae' (deutsch/niederländisch). Edition und Kommentar*, Tübingen: Niemeyer.

Moreni, D. (ed) (1822) *Del viaggio in Terra Santa fatto e descritto da ser Mariano da Siena nel secolo XV: Codice inedito*, Florence: Magheri.

Papanikolas, H. (2002) *An Amulet of Greek Earth: Generations of Immigrant Folk Culture*, Athens: Ohio University Press.

Richter, A. (1746–1748) *Umständliche aus zuverläßigen Nachrichten zusammengetragene Chronica der im Meissnischen Ober-Ertz-Gebürge gelegenen Königl. Churfl. Sächßischen freyen Berg-Stadt St. Annaberg*, 2 vols, St Annaberg: Friese.

Röhricht, R. (1906) 'Die Jerusalemfahrt des Kanonikus Ulrich Brunner vom Haugstift in Würzburg (1470)', *Zeitschrift des deutschen Palästina-Vereins*, 29: 1–50.

Roldán, V. (2019) 'Immigration and multiculturalism in Italy: the religious experience of the Peruvian community in the Eternal City', *Religions*, 10(8): art 478. doi: 10.3390/rel10080478

Roper, L. (2016) *Martin Luther: Renegade and Prophet*, London: Bodley Head.

Schmitz-Esser, R. (2015) 'Travel and exploration in the Middle Ages', in A. Classen (ed) *Handbook of Medieval Culture: Fundamental Aspects and Conditions of the European Middle Ages*, vol 3, Berlin: De Gruyter, pp 1680–1704.

Scholz, L. (2020) *Borders and Freedom of Movement in the Holy Roman Empire*, Oxford: Oxford University Press.

Schuchard, C. (1999) 'Die Anima-Bruderschaft und die deutschen Handwerker in Rom im 15. und frühen 16. Jahrhundert', in K. Schulz with E. Müller-Luckner (eds) *Handwerk in Europa: Vom Spätmittelalter bis zur Frühen Neuzeit*, Munich: R. Oldenbourg, pp 1–25.

Schulte, A. (1904) *Die Fugger in Rom 1495–1523. Mit Studien zur Geschichte des kirchlichen Finanzwesens jener Zeit*, 2 vols in 1, Leipzig: Duncker & Humblot.

Schulz, K. (2002) *Confraternitas Campi Sancti de Urbe: Die ältesten Mitgliederverzeichnisse (1500/01–1536) und Statuten der Bruderschaft*, Rome: Herder.

Schulz, K. (2004) 'Was ist deutsch? Zum Selbstverständnis deutscher Bruderschaften im Rom der Renaissance', in A. Meyer, C. Rendtel and M. Wittmer-Butsch (eds) *Päpste, Pilger, Pönitentiarie: Festschrift für Ludwig Schmugge zum 65. Geburtstag*, Tübingen: Niemeyer, pp 135–79.

Simonsfeld, E. (1903) 'Itinerario di Germania dell'anno 1492', *Miscellanea di Storia Veneta*, ser. 2, 9: 275–345.

Spufford, P. (2014) 'Scottish black money in the Low Countries, c. 1484–1506', *British Numismatic Journal*, 84: 125–39.

Sterk, J. (1980) *Philips van Bourgondië (1465–1525), bisschop van Utrecht, als protagonist van de Renaissance: zijn leven en maecenaat*, Zutphen: Walburg.

Sugiyama, M. (2019) 'Performing virtual pilgrimage to Rome: a rediscovered Christ crucified from a series of three panel paintings (ca. 1500)', *Oud Holland*, 132(4): 159–70.

Szymborski, W. (2015) 'Medieval Rome in Poland: indulgences of the Station Churches of Rome and Jubilee indulgences in medieval Poland', *Biuletyn Polskiej Misji Historycznej/Bulletin der Polnischen Historischen Mission*, 10: 397–424.

Tietz, A.A. (2012) *Der frühneuzeitliche Gottesacker: Entstehung und Entwicklung unter besonderer Berücksichtigung des Architekturtypus Camposanto in Mitteldeutschland*, Halle: Landesamt für Denkmalpflege und Archäologie Sachsen-Anhalt, Landesmuseum für Vorgeschichte.

Tweed, T.A. (1997) *Our Lady of the Exile: Diasporic Religion at a Catholic Cuban Shrine in Miami*, New York: Oxford University Press.

Vaes, M. (1919) 'Les fondations hospitalières flamandes à Rome du XVe au XVIIIe siècle', *Bulletin de l'Institut historique Belge de Rome*, 1: 161–371.

Volkmar, C. (2008) 'Mittelsmänner zwischen Sachsen und Rom: Die Kurienprokuratoren Herzog Georgs von Sachsen am Vorabend der Reformation', *Quellen und Forschungen aus italienischen Archiven und Bibliotheken*, 88: 244–309.

von der Ropp, G.F. (1887) 'Unkosten einer Lüneburger Romfahrt im Jahre 1454', *Hänsische Geschichtsblätter*, 6: 31–60.

Weiland, A. (1988) *Der Campo Santo Teutonico in Rom und seine Grabdenkmäler*, Vol 1 of E. Gatz (ed) *Der Campo Santo Teutonico in Rom,* Römische Quartalschrift, Supplementheft 43, Rome: Herder.

3

The Early Voyages of the East India Company, 1601–17: A Non-Human and Unheroic History

Laurence Publicover[1]

Introduction

As the geographer Tim Cresswell observes, 'human mobilities [are] in an entangled web of "other" mobilities' (2014, p 713): people move along with – and because of – other-than-human 'things', both animate and inanimate. It may seem a crashingly obvious point that such 'things' were important to the early voyages of the English East India Company (EIC); these were, after all, endeavours primarily concerned with trade in goods rather than – like England's contemporary ventures on the other side of the Atlantic – the settlement of peoples or discovery of sea routes.[2] But as I hope to demonstrate across this chapter, a fuller attention to non-human actors can provide fresh perspectives on these voyages. As Bridget Anderson notes in the introduction to this volume, '[t]he separation of human movement/ migration from the movement of non-human species and non-living things means our understanding of human movement is often highly partial and distorted, and we misread patterns and miss crucial interconnections' (p 3). My focus here is on precisely these interconnections – on, that is, the more-than-human factors that shaped these voyages and those who undertook them. I am interested in these impacts both in the more literal sense of how, for example, animals provided sustenance for seafarers and in the more complex sense of how collaboration with and defiance of more-than-human entities shaped seafarers' self-understandings and their sense of their journeys' significance – and here I attend specifically to ideas about travel and heroism particular to early modern England. Finally, this chapter asks how attending to the non-human elements of these voyages can help us interpret them as episodes in *environmental* history. While Richmond Barbour has recently argued that they should be approached in this manner owing to the EIC's providing a prototype for today's resource-hungry – and so often resource-*extracting* – multinational corporations (2021, pp 240, 248–9), I am interested here not so much in how the Company and its agents impacted upon the world, but in how that world acted upon them.

This is an analytic approach that comes with certain dangers. An essay on the EIC in a volume on migration might, quite reasonably, be expected to focus on the large-scale and often traumatic movements of peoples towards which the Company was to contribute. During the EIC's lifetime, its ships transported a substantial number of British men – and later women – to lands within the Indian Ocean, and in particular what would become British India; in total, around 4,600 voyages were undertaken from London (Farrington, 2002, p 23). Relatively few people travelled in the opposite direction during this period, but British involvement in – and exploitation of – South Asia occasioned widespread migration to the UK from that region in the 20th century. Early EIC voyages' contact with the west coast of Africa also helped lay the ground for England's (and later Britain's) involvement in the forced migration of African men, women and children across the Atlantic over the following centuries; and in entering the Indian Ocean world, the EIC was beginning to participate in a geographical region that already had a long history of human movement, including via the trade in enslaved peoples (a business in which the Company would itself become involved, albeit in a relatively small way). Why worry about the non-human when there is so much to say about human experience?

One reason is that attending to the more-than-human world can help refocus attention on the power dynamics that prevailed in early EIC voyages. It can be tempting, from a 21st-century perspective, to see these expeditions as events leading inexorably towards British colonial rule. But as a recent historian of the EIC warns us, 'Teleological thinking elides the radical contingency of historical process [and] overstates the solvency of imperial systems' (Barbour, 2021, p 206). While it later became the most powerful company the world had seen, the EIC was in a fairly weak position in the early 17th century, both in relation to wealthy states with which it sought trade – in particular the Ottoman Empire, which was the great power within the Arabian Peninsula, and the Mughal Empire, which had, during the 16th century, conquered much of what is now India – and in relation to the European powers with which it jostled, Portugal and the Dutch Republic. According to Nandini Das, at the time of the first official English embassy to the Mughal Empire, which took place between 1616 and 1618, the English 'barely had a toehold in the country', and to the Mughals themselves 'they were hardly worth a mention' (2023, p xviii). Early voyages, she notes, were above all marked by 'uncertainty' (Das, 2023, p xix); and this uncertainty, I want to demonstrate, derived in part from non-human factors. Attending to such factors, I would suggest, can help us see the Company's agents less as elements of an implacable force of human history and more as individuals with significant vulnerabilities, and it can therefore provide a more textured sense of the early history of the English in India. It can also steer us away from seeing these figures – as they have so often been seen in British historiography – as heroic adventurers imbued with extraordinary autonomy.

An initial example through which to explore some of these issues can be found in the spaniel belonging to Sir Henry Middleton, the general – that is, the overall commander – of the sixth EIC voyage. In October of 1611, the fleet arrived at Suvali (or Swally) near Surat, beleaguered after what had thus far been a far from satisfactory voyage. They were in a delicate position: to conduct trade, Middleton needed to circumvent a fellow European power – Portugal – which had a more long-standing presence in the region. At Suvali the prospects of successful trade depended on the disposition of Mukarrab Khān, the Mughal governor of Cambay. The EIC fleet waited several weeks for his arrival, which then took place on a grand scale: as recorded by Nicholas Downton, captain of one of the fleet's smaller ships, the governor appeared with 'one hundred horsemen, and many more footmen', as well as 'fiue Elephants, with diuers Camels, Carts and Oxen, for transportation of his prouisions'. In addition, Downton notes, 'he had diuers [that is, several] Carts to carrie his Leopards' (quoted in Purchas, 1625, p 298).

The English could hardly match this multi-species spectacle; in fact, as so frequently in their early voyages to the empires of Asia, they were embarrassed by an absence of impressive gifts to bestow as a means of greasing the wheels of commerce (Das, 2023, p 85). The most noteworthy thing they had brought along, in fact, was their flagship. At 1,300 tons, the *Trades Increase* was enormous by the standard of contemporary vessels; implicitly comparing it with the governor's menagerie, Barbour describes it as 'the marine equivalent of a troupe of castled elephants' (2021, p 140). Mukarrab Khān expressed an interest in visiting the ship, even dining aboard and then spending the night there, and he took the opportunity to eye up items that he felt might be of interest to the emperor or that he fancied himself.[3] Middleton granted the governor whatever he desired, though with some exceptions: he declined the request for 'his perfumed Ierkin' (that is, his jacket) and for 'his Spaniell Dogge' (Purchas, 1625, p 299). Middleton eventually relented, however, after Mukarrab Khān sent messengers the following day once again requesting these items.

The surrender of Middleton's spaniel nicely illustrates the EIC's precarious position in India, both in terms of the animal's basic size – it is dwarfed by the governor's elephants and leopards – and in terms of its significance: Middleton clearly did not wish to give it up, but Mukarrab Khān was not a man he could afford to displease. The spaniel incident interests me most, however, as a way into thinking about non-human agency in these voyages. What was the spaniel doing in Surat, and what was the effect of its presence aboard and then disappearance from the *Trades Increase*? Like other items given as gifts to officials and rulers during early EIC voyages, the spaniel's worth can be regarded both in financial terms – diplomatic gifts were always evaluated in terms of local currency, and they were of course designed to *facilitate* economic exchange – and in more nebulous terms – as an item that was valuable due to its novelty (from the Mughal perspective), in relation to its connection to the giver or their nation, or in terms of the peculiar tastes of the recipient. But was the spaniel always *intended* to be a gift? In later voyages, dogs of this breed, which had a particular connection to English gentlemanly identity, were certainly given as gifts to Mughal officials (Das, 2023, p 163). But Middleton's initial refusal to part with his spaniel may make us wonder whether it was on the voyage to serve a different purpose. It is difficult to imagine that – unlike the horses and attack dogs carried into the Americas and the Caribbean by Spanish conquistadors – it was deemed a *working* animal: spaniels can be used in hunting, but they do not hunt on ships in the manner of cats. Instead, the spaniel may have been taken along as a companion animal: that is, a creature that establishes a dynamic with a human involving two-way dependency (Haraway, 2008). The social historian Keith Thomas points out that the English have always been especially fond of dogs, and that 'it was in early modern times that the foundations [of the nation's] canine obsession [were] laid' (1983, p 108).

Even if the spaniel *had* always been intended as a gift (perhaps to a man of higher rank than Mukarrab Khān), by November of 1611 Middleton would have been travelling with it for around a year and a half. At the very least, it would have served to shore up Middleton's aristocratic identity as he entered lands unfamiliar to him; but there seems no reason not to assume, in addition, that Middleton and the spaniel had developed a mutual affection. What, then, was the impact of its loss? I am keenly aware that even asking this question risks sentimentalizing a man in charge of a venture that contributed – however indirectly and at however great a distance – towards the brutal English (or rather British) colonization of India. But there is surely an equal risk in *refusing* to treat historical actors like Middleton as individuals with vulnerabilities. What we *do* know, mainly from Downton's journal, is that the general's mental health declined considerably as the sixth voyage unfolded: Middleton 'ached with the personal burden of responsibility for [its] failures', the most prominent of which was the loss of the *Trades Increase* at Bantam – in modern-day Indonesia – when the ship was brought onto the beach for repairs (Barbour, 2021, p 227). There, Barbour records, Middleton 'succumbed to disease and despair on 24 May 1613' (2021, p 227). Retaining mental health during long voyages is challenging in any circumstances (Liebich and Publicover, 2021, pp 24–5); doing so in the cramped conditions and perilous circumstances of early EIC voyages must have been almost impossible. In his privileged but isolated position as the voyage's general, facing continual rumbles of discontent from officers, sailors and merchants, whose diverse needs and desires he was compelled to manage and arbitrate between, the loyalty and straightforward affection of a dog – and spaniels are notorious for their affectionate nature – may have been especially meaningful to Middleton.

To put this another way: narrating Middleton's loss of his spaniel gives us a rather different way of thinking about early modern European voyages into the Indian Ocean than might, for example, *Os Lusíadas*, the 16th-century epic poem recounting Vasco da Gama's voyage to India in 1497–99. Though nothing in English matched de Camões' national epic, accounts of English voyages into the global oceans were often, similarly, given heroic trappings; and as Claire Jowitt notes, across the early modern period 'maritime activities and achievements became key cultural markers of, and justifications for, Europeans' beliefs about the superiority of their value systems' (2020, p 533). Heroic narratives of English voyages written and published in the period contemporary with them – most notably Richard Hakluyt's *Principal Navigations* (1589; expanded 1598–1600), a compendium of voyage accounts explicitly aimed at encouraging further English maritime expansion – then 'underpinned the development of the nineteenth-century theory of "Great man" history' (Jowitt, 2020, p 533). Treating men like Middleton not as figures consistently exerting their will on the world, but instead as individuals often at the mercy of – or at least working in collaboration with – non-human agencies, can therefore help us see these voyages less as the early stirrings of an English global expansion fuelled by heroic patriotism and feats of derring-do and more as episodes involving what ecomaterialist scholars might call an 'assemblage of actors'.

Non-human organisms

Organisms of various kinds and in various states shaped long-distance voyages of the early modern period. Pre-slaughtered animals were taken aboard for consumption: one of the more striking examples can be found in the 14,000 dried penguins provisioning an English voyage returning in 1592 from what is now Argentina (Jowitt, 2020, p 543). While early modern English sailors generally survived on a diet of dry salted beef and cod, as well as pickled beef and pork, live animals were also brought aboard to be slaughtered mid voyage, and both live animals and carcasses were sometimes gifted between high-ranking men on different ships as a means of maintaining good relations (Strachan and Penrose, 1971, pp 34–5; Das, 2023, p 66). A stock of live animals could also be taken aboard from island or coastal way stations – frequently, ones that had been stocked deliberately for this purpose. The third EIC voyage of 1607–10 stopped at the Cape Verde islands in the Atlantic, settled by the Portuguese over a century earlier, and the sailors helped themselves to 70 goats (Barbour, 2009, p 158). St Helena was another island stocked with animals for this purpose, and coastal locations around southern tip of Africa became key reprovisioning points for English mariners entering the Indian Ocean.

Organisms encountered overseas could also *disrupt* voyages. Some of these were very small: EIC sailors often lacked immunity from diseases carried by microbes on foreign shores, for example. Bantam, where Middleton died, was known as a particular death-trap for Europeans (Barbour, 2021, pp 205, 227). (In an inversion of this process, diseases carried by European voyages were to cause an almost unthinkable degree of destruction in the Americas.) Larger organisms carried on ships could also prove troublesome. Over the course of the 17th century, many 'exotic' animals were transported on EIC ships, sometimes accompanied by handlers from their point of origin, as in the case of an elephant accompanied by two Bantanese men in 1675 (Farrington, 2002, p 119). These creatures could sometimes pose a physical threat. In one case, a tiger cub unwisely shipped from Surat was killed after it 'severely mauled' a sailor (Farrington, 2002, p 119). Causing far more frequent disruption, however, were rats. As already noted, long-distance voyages in this period typically took cats along so that they could kill rats, which otherwise raided food stocks and destroyed sails. One Tudor text confidently states that there are 'few ships but have cats belonging to them' (Baldwin, 1988, p 14), and the similarity of feline DNA across major global trade routes – for example between Kenya and Sri Lanka – hints at their presence on board ships (Bradshaw, 2014, p 56). Nonetheless, rats continued to present significant problems on EIC voyages. In a journal of 1616–17, one seafarer complained of the damage caused to sailcloth by 'innumerable many Ratts'. It was not, he complained, only stores and sails they attacked. They also attacked sleeping sailors, and they feasted, rather gruesomely, on men who had died in the night: 'some menn … before morning have had their toes eate quite off' (Strachan and Penrose, 1971, p 44; see also Das, 2023, p 64). What is worth noting here is that rats do not simply diminish supplies and harry humans both living and dead; by damaging sails, they also affect the *speed* of the voyage – and the longer the voyage lasts, the more deadly it becomes.

The other organism which consistently affected the speed and safety of early EIC ships was shipworm. As Derek Lee Nelson and Adam Sundberg explain, while these marine parasites – which are 'are actually related to clams' – feed 'mostly on plankton', they have, in an 'evolutionary quirk', also 'learned to eat wood'; some species can 'grow to a meter or more', though most are much smaller, and 'often went undetected by seamen …, who lived in constant fear, never knowing if the ships below their feet were hollowed-out hulks' (2023, pp 38–9). Until the advent of effective copper sheaths (and thereafter iron and steel hulls), shipworms were kept at bay through 'sacrificial' wooden sheaths placed around the hull and through the use of human hair and tar, which, wrote one EIC mariner, 'the worm [...] cannot abide' (quoted in Barbour, 2009, p 220). Another issue presented by long-distance voyages was that ships' carpenters lacked both the materials to repair hulls and dry docks, in which careening (turning a ship on its side for repair) could be safely managed. In fact, the loss of the sixth voyage's flagship occurred because, lacking the proper support when brought ashore for repair in Bantam, its mainmast collapsed, and with no appropriate timber available it was abandoned. In damaging the prospects of the sixth voyage, then, the shipworms and other marine organisms that had ravaged the hull of the *Trades Increase* also helped dispose of its by then spaniel-less general, Henry Middleton.

Vibrant matter

In this section, which sits under a term taken from the new materialist philosopher Jane Bennett (2010), I wish to consider some of the 'things' – that is, the matter beyond living organisms – that shaped these early voyages and the experiences of those who participated in them. Perhaps most important among these were the ships bought or built by the Company; and attending to the agency of shipworms can remind us that these ships were not 'givens', but constantly degrading and emerging entities. Anthony Farrington notes that in the early modern period 'four voyages to Asia over a period of eight to ten years was the expected life of a wooden hull'; and this lifespan assumes a regular regime of repair (2004, p 24). In an Atlantic storm, both the *Trades Increase* and the smaller *Peppercorn* suffered fractured masts – a result, perhaps, of the low-quality timber from which they were built. William Burrell, the man who oversaw the construction of the *Trades Increase* at Deptford, had requested Latvian timber, but it appears this material never arrived (Barbour, 2021, p 34). In any case, new masts – including a mainmast for the *Trades Increase* – were hurriedly fashioned from trees felled on the Cape Verde islands; and as we have seen, it was the flagship's mainmast that eventually fractured during its attempted repair at Bantam. Had the Latvian timber arrived, perhaps Middleton would not have succumbed to despair.

If EIC ships were entangled in the lives of those they transported, then so were the material goods carried in those ships. 'Where wouldn't they go for pepper!' exclaims Marlow, the narrator of Joseph Conrad's novel *Lord Jim* (originally published in 1899). His reflections on the Dutch and English mariners of the early 17th century are worth quoting at length:

For a bag of pepper they would cut each other's throats without hesitation, and would forswear their souls, of which they were so careful otherwise: the bizarre obstinacy of that desire made them defy death in a thousand shapes; the unknown seas, the loathsome and strange diseases; wounds, captivity, hunger, pestilence, and despair. It made them great! By heavens! it made them heroic; and it made them pathetic too in their craving for trade with the inflexible death levying its toll on young and old. […] They left their bones to lie bleaching on distant shores, so that wealth might flow to the living at home. (Conrad, 2007, pp 173–4)

It perhaps takes the vision of a novelist like Conrad – a man who also knew a thing or two about seafaring and about the European footprint in Asia – to bring home the strangeness of all this. Pepper was not unknown in early modern England; during the 16th century, it had been imported from Africa (Dimmock, 2022, pp 39–40). But the Portuguese discovery of sea routes to the Indian Ocean significantly increased its flow into Western Europe from what is now the Indonesian archipelago, and the EIC and Dutch East India Company were able to secure huge profits through its importation. Marlow's ironical apostrophe nicely captures the manner in which EIC agents were in the thrall both of their employers – Company shareholders – and, in some strange way, the pepper itself. Their heroism, in Conrad's vision, is both dependent on and qualified by the relatively mundane matter for which they risked their own lives and took the lives of others.

Another key material carried by early EIC voyages was the paper on which 'remarkable' events were recorded. It is, in fact, what Das calls the EIC's 'obsession with paperwork and record-keeping' that allows us to reconstruct the voyages in relatively fine detail (2023, p xxiv, see also p 63). (English voyages of plunder and discovery have, by contrast, left a piecemeal paper trail.) As well as blank pages waiting to be filled, ships carried journals – or copies of journals – from previous voyages; rather like early modern Rough Guides, these provided information (sometimes unhelpfully outdated) on foreign lands as well as on winds and ocean currents. The reading material carried abroad also included voyage narratives printed for a wider audience, and on the third EIC voyage (1607–10) such material had a particular effect. Unlucky with winds, the *Hector* and *Red Dragon* became stuck in mid-Atlantic, and their decision to seek provisions in Sierra Leone was taken after reading about it in Hakluyt's *Principal Navigations*, the compendium of voyage narratives mentioned earlier (Barbour, 2009, p 14).[4]

Sierra Leone was also the site of the most notorious incident – or possible incident – during these early voyages, which has again to do with texts carried aboard. Two supposed 19th-century transcriptions of the now-lost journal of the voyage's general, William Keeling, record a shipboard performance of Shakespeare's *Hamlet* staged for at least one African man: the Portuguese-speaking Lucas Fernandez, who served as interpreter during the EIC's sojourn. The validity of these transcriptions remains questionable, but a production of *Hamlet* does not seem out of the question. Ambassadors visiting London were often entertained by theatrical performances at Whitehall; in this case, perhaps, the theatre itself was mobile. (In neither instance, it appears, was difficulty in understanding English deemed a significant obstacle.) If this performance *did* occur, it was, we can assume, the first performance of Shakespeare ever to take place outside Europe (*Hamlet* had been written only around seven years earlier), and to make it happen – in whatever form it took – the third voyage would need to have been carrying either the first quarto of *Hamlet*, printed in 1603, or the longer and more familiar second quarto, printed in 1604–05. Transformed into performances, these books contributed towards the voyage's success by facilitating good relations with trading partners.[5]

If the 19th-century transcriptions are to be believed, this was not, in fact, the only performance of Shakespeare during the third voyage of the EIC: there were two subsequent productions staged in mid-ocean, first of *Richard II* and then again of *Hamlet*. The entry recording this final performance also reflects on its purpose: Keeling permitted it 'to keepe [his] people from idleness and unlawful games, or sleep' (Barbour, 2009, p 17).[6] Keeling's remarks – if, of course, they *are* his remarks – can help us reflect on the final form of non-human agency I wish to touch on here: *oceanic* agency. Traversing the oceans before the age of steam was challenging partly because one had to work with an oceanic environment that often refused to cooperate. Journals from these voyages are peppered with anxious entries concerning winds and currents, as well as sandbanks and bars that, in unfamiliar waters, were tantamount to mines, especially for a vessel as large as the *Trades Increase*. As these mariners well knew, though we can sometimes be prone to forget, far from being a blank and smooth surface of connection, the oceanic environment is a site with its own flows and topographies, and it can, in different circumstances, be collaborator or antagonist. Long periods spent in regions without wind – most famously, the doldrums – could have severe consequences on morale; as Cheryl Fury notes in a study of breaches of discipline and their punishment during early EIC voyages, 'for Tudor-Stuart seamen the 2–3 year round trip to the East Indies was one of the most challenging forms of maritime employment' (2020, p 153). Because the Company 'frowned upon cards and backgammon' (Das, 2023, p 65), other forms of entertainment were necessary, and shipboard performances could do for mental health what lemons did for physical health. These did not have to be performances of scripted drama; other 'things' brought on early voyages included musical instruments (Das, 2023, p 42).

People

Shipboard performances were valuable in part because they reminded seafarers of home, in what were unfamiliar lands and waters; and perhaps most unfamiliar, to English mariners, were the monsoon winds, a system they had to learn from pilots and mariners with experience navigating Indian Ocean routes. One individual who directly suffered from the English mariners' lack of knowledge was a man named Nasher. After a brief sojourn in Socotra, an island at the entrance of the Gulf of Aden, the *Hector* and the *Red Dragon* headed east across the Arabian Sea, having spoken with Gujarati merchants about trading prospects on the west coast of India. As they were leaving, Nasher swam out to join them, hoping to escape enslavement on Socotra. Unfortunately for him, however, the ships were attempting the crossing to India too late in the year, and they ran into monsoon winds; when they were forced to retreat to Socotra, the king would only agree to provide provisions if Nasher were returned to him (Barbour, 2008, p 268).

In addition to providing an example of how more-than-human forces might shape individuals' experiences during early EIC voyages, Nasher's aborted journey across the Arabian Sea helps remind us that these voyages involved people other than Englishmen. We have already heard of the Bantanese elephant handlers who sailed to London in 1675. Also in the late 17th century, two ambassadors from the deposed Sultan of Bantam came to London requesting arms; in an echo of the third voyage's visit to Sierra Leone in 1607, they were entertained with an adaption of Shakespeare's play *The Tempest* (Farrington, 2002, p 118). A less voluntary visit to London was made by a man named Corey, abducted in 1613 from Saldanha Bay – around 150 kilometres north-west of what is now Cape Town – by Gabriel Towerson, then captaining the *Hector*, in the hope that he might provide intelligence helpful in future voyages. Staying at the house of the EIC governor Sir Thomas Smythe – who had on his wall an Inuit canoe that served, as Barbour puts it, as 'a reminder of the governor's global interests and the Company's perpetual hope of a northwest passage to Asia' (2021, p 11) – Corey learned enough English to continually express his desire to return home. Granted his wish after six months,[7] he then exacted a degree of revenge on his abductors by disclosing to his countrymen that the brass the English had been using to purchase livestock and other provisions was of little value in London (Stevenson, 2022, p 197). As a result, the price of cattle rose. But Corey also went on to assist English mariners rounding Africa. A journal entry from June 1614 has him providing a 'young steere' to Downton, the colleague of Middleton (Foster, 2016, p 2), and another journal records that inhabitants of a craal in Saldania would greet English mariners by saying 'Sir Thomas Smith's English ships', presumably words learned from Corey (Stevenson, 2022, p 196).

The shorter passage between London and the southern tip of Africa was also undertaken by men involved in the first English experiment with transportation. Nineteen condemned men were taken on the voyage departing in 1615, with ten of them then left at the Cape in the hope that they would establish a way station furnishing provisions for subsequent voyages (that is, that they would become English versions of Corey). This was not a success. The three who had not either died or absconded in Portuguese ships were reconveyed to England in 1616; on arrival home, they deserted and resorted to theft, subsequently being recaptured and then executed (Strachan and Penrose, 1971, p 37). Many more failed to make it home at all. Global voyages in the early modern period were, to say the least, perilous affairs: of the 270 men who departed on Magellan's circumnavigation of 1519–22, only 18 returned (Magellan himself not among them). The rate of attrition in the EIC was not quite so bad, but the figures remain chilling. Of the first 3,000 mariners who departed for the Indian Ocean, only around a third returned, a proportion mirrored in the voyages of the Dutch East India company (Das, 2023, p 48). As one contemporary pamphleteer and critic of the EIC put it: 'though ships come home, yet they leave the men behind' (quoted in Barbour, 2021, p 250).

These men suffered at the hands of various forms of non-human agency. Some died at sea, including in shipwrecks wrought by a combination of heavy seas, marine parasites and deadly shoals. In other cases, placid seas were the problem. During the first EIC voyage (1601–03), a lack of winds in the Atlantic left the ships stuck at the equator for a full month; by the time they arrived at the Cape, a hundred men – a fifth of the voyage's complement – had perished. The mortality rate for the voyage as a whole was around 60 per cent (Fury, 2020, p 153). A direct consequence of losses of this kind was that EIC ships became decidedly multinational spaces, with able seamen picked up in port towns en route. There are records of Indian, Javanese and Japanese mariners on EIC ships, some of whom made it all the way to England. Most of these returned to their native lands on subsequent EIC voyages after staying in England for as long as a year (the fleet leaving England in 1615, for example, carried 11 Japanese men and 14 men from Gujarat; Das, 2023, pp 47–8), but others remained in England for longer, or even indefinitely, gathering especially around the shipyards at Deptford (p 54). Some modern accounts of Corey's sojourn in London suggest that his presence would have been deeply strange to early modern Londoners; but as recent research is demonstrating, London's developing status as a global port in this period was rendering it an increasingly multicultural space – due in no small part to the early voyages of the EIC.

Conclusion

In concluding, I wish to return to issues raised briefly in my introduction: the ways in which these voyages have been ideologically framed and the relevance of non-human agency to this framing. In doing so, I aim also to place this study of mobility within the context of ideas about travel and its effect on the traveller that are more specific to early modern England.

'The restless energy of maritime heroic values dovetails well with colonial ideology', writes Claire Jowitt, 'since continuous expansion and forward movement are the assumptions upon which both are predicated' (2020, p 544). For empire to function, of course, this 'forward movement' needs to be accompanied by return voyages (of ships, if not necessarily of individuals), thus mapping neatly onto the dynamic of movement encountered in chivalric romance, in which the hero moves away from and then returns to the court (Spearing, 1994, pp 138–9). This connection between romance narratives and European voyages of expansion is, in fact, one that has received significant scholarly attention, and for good reason. Famously, conquistadors on their way to the Americas carried romances with them, while Hakluyt's *Principal Navigations* contained (in its first edition, though not its second) the romance-inflected text *Mandeville's Travels*. In short, European voyagers in this period – including English ones – understood their adventures through the lens of the romance narratives with which they were familiar.

Like scholarship within mobility studies, these narratives take an interest in what happens to someone when they travel. The knight-errant's identity depended, as his name would suggest, on mobility ('errant' here conveys wandering or roving), and this mobility allowed the knight to confirm and, in some sense, *update* his – or occasionally her – identity: feats undertaken away from the court established a chivalric heroism whose dependence on movement is apparent in its fundamental relation to horsemanship ('chivalry' is a borrowing from the French *chevalerie*, which itself derives from the French word for 'horse', *cheval*). But *how*, exactly, is the knight-errant understood to move through their environment? It seems fair to suggest that although chivalric heroism is sometimes concerned with stoical endurance, it usually depends on the individual's capacity to *dominate* the space through which they move; the ideal knight-errant, that is, should not be *permeated* by their environment, but instead remain sealed off from it, even while affecting it.

Something like this understanding of heroic mobility feeds into Ben Jonson's epigram addressed to William Roe, cousin of Thomas, the first official English ambassador to the Mughal court. Presumably, William was about to embark on a European tour as a means of completing his education. Published in 1616, the same year Thomas arrived in India, the poem begins thus:

> ROE (and my ioy to name) th'art now, to goe
>   Countries, and climes, manners, and men to know,
> T'extract, and choose the best of all these knowne,
>   And those to turne to bloud, and make thine owne[.]

William should, Jonson advises, *draw on* his experiences in foreign lands as a means of developing his identity. But this does not mean that he should fundamentally *change* through travel:

> So, when we, blest with thy returne, shall see
>   Thy selfe, with thy first thoughts, brought home by thee,
> We each to other may this voyce enspire;
>   This is that good ÆNEAS, past through fire,
> Through seas, stormes, tempests: and imbarqu'd for hell,
>   Came back vntouch'd. This man hath trauail'd well.
>   (Jonson, 1616, p 811)

This is not quite a paradox. Like the knight-errant, Jonson's ideal traveller can *act upon* — can even *choose to incorporate elements of* — their environment, but they will not be *acted upon* by that environment. The 'seas, stormes, tempests' through which they will travel indicate perils that are cultural as much as geographical and meteorological: a fear often encountered in English texts from this period is that travellers might be tainted through contact with foreigners and their customs. And yet, as the enjambment highlights, William will return from these adventures as precisely the same 'selfe', and this is because he will have *worked* at his travel — hence the familiar early modern play on *travel* and *travail* in Jonson's final words — rather than having been worked *upon* by the dangerous world through which he has passed.

What light might this poem — which draws on both classical and medieval notions of travel — throw on the early voyages of the EIC? It is one of the enduring interests of state-sponsored travel that those who journey abroad to 'represent' a state no longer become, in the strictest sense, 'representatives' of that state; instead, they may begin to take on the qualities of, or even sympathize with, the peoples with whom they now associate (which is why, even today, diplomats are moved between postings every three or four years). Would the 'Englishness' of those Englishmen who travelled to the Indian Ocean in the early 17th century have been similarly qualified by the lands into which they travelled? This is certainly the view of Barbour, albeit that he seems to take the more Jonsonian position that these men had a high degree of *control* over their transformations: 'Their opportunistic pursuit of two enormous challenges, survival and profit, freed these mariners from perpetual performance of the Jacobean identities and nationalist Christian agendas ... On unfamiliar shores, they understood the need to adapt and, where possible, collude with local powers of whatever ethical or religious persuasion' (2021, p 136). There is plenty of evidence to back up Barbour's position. The third EIC voyage's William Hawkins spent a long period at the court of the Mughal Emperor Jahangir, becoming known as the 'English

Khan', and while there he married an Armenian Christian named Mariam Khan. (When Hawkins eventually left the court, his wife travelled with him, and they were sailing to England on the same ship as Corey when Hawkins died in mid-Atlantic; Mariam then married Towerson – Corey's abductor – before both returned to India in 1617.)[8] Jonson would, I think we can assume, have disapproved of this degree of acculturation.

It is also worth remembering that, as noted earlier, Englishmen on EIC voyages would have worked and suffered with men from several different parts of the world, again perhaps complicating their sense of national identity. Where we might take this concern with the 'hybridization' of the traveller further, however, is in considering them permeable not only in their capacity to be affected by (or to take on aspects of) different cultural identities, but also in their vulnerability to non-human actors. The knights-errant of medieval and early modern romance narratives frequently fought dragons, or as they were known in Middle English, 'worms'; in doing so, as I have explained, they established their heroism by exerting their will on their environment. The worms which posed challenges to EIC voyagers provide a very different context for considering heroism and vulnerability. Like the ocean currents and monsoon winds affecting the ships' paths through the waters, the microbial organisms invading seafarers' bodies, or the pepper that drew them into the Indian Ocean in the first place, shipworms undermined human autonomy within these voyages. In a sense, this is something that would have been very well understood by the seafarers themselves: as scholarship of the past two decades has demonstrated, early modern men and women perceived their bodies to have a high degree of 'openness' (Paster, 2004). Work focused on travel has demonstrated how this notion of the body's permeability meant that those entering new lands were thought to be affected by climate: what has been called 'geohumoral theory' held that the body's composition was directly shaped by geographical location, adding a more physiological dimension to widespread concerns over how foreign 'cultures' might contaminate the traveller (Feerick, 2006). What work in ecomaterialism can perhaps bring to this understanding of early modern travel, and to studies of mobility more generally, is a fuller sense of how travellers entered into dialogue with 'things' beyond climate and people – how those travellers' agencies, and therefore their identities, were shaped or compromised by other matter(s) both organic and inorganic and both within and beyond the ship, establishing something like the dynamic that Stacy Alaimo (2016) has called 'trans-corporeality'.

To an extent, what this involves is simply focusing greater attention on the voyages *themselves* rather than their consequences and, further, treating the oceans across which these ships moved not as smooth surfaces but instead as textured sites that could in various ways resist as well as collaborate with English expansionism. And if the risk of approaching the voyages in this way is that it may divert attention from the responsibility of those involved for the often-horrific consequences of this expansionism, a benefit is that it can help us see these historical episodes not as faits accompli, but instead in all their perilous contingency. Seawater is, after all, at the very heart of these narratives, for its buoyancy reduces the amount of energy – and therefore cost – required to move goods. Today, '[m]oving a 20-foot container from Shanghai to Frankfurt by ship costs a mere third as much as shifting it by plane' (Armstrong, 2022, p 14); in the early modern period, the choice was between ships powered by wind and arduous journeys across land involving camels and horses. The EIC voyages' negotiation of this watery world can be – and has been – read through a heroic lens, as a tale of dignified suffering and perseverance in the face of adversity.[9] But attending to the non-human agents at play in these endeavours does not need to lead us in this direction. Instead, it can pull into sharp focus the weak position the EIC was in during the early years of its existence; and, more generally, it can help us better understand how, to return to Tim Cresswell's words, 'human mobilities [are] in an entangled web of "other" mobilities' (2014, p 713), from ocean currents to animal carcasses, timber, pepper and spaniels.

Notes

[1]   The author would like to thank Ben Prusiner and Rex Obano, director and author (respectively) of *The Hamlet Voyage* (2022), for stimulating and sharing my interest in the early voyages of the East India Company.

[2]   The work of Philip Stern (2011) has complicated any neat division between 'corporate' and 'state' interests in this historical period by pointing out that corporations like the EIC should themselves be seen as political and social entities. It should also be acknowledged that EIC ships were hardly entering the Indian Ocean with wholly peaceful intention. Previous decades of English predation on the seas had established the principle that commercial practice involved shows of military strength. My point is that it is difficult to draw a straight line between these voyages and the EIC's (and later Britain's) eventual colonization of India. The EIC was not looking to build a Portuguese-style maritime empire; its ambitions were more straightforwardly commercial.

[3]   There is some discrepancy in the records of this episode as to whether the governor offered gifts (or currency) in exchange for these items (Barbour, 2021, pp 141–2).

[4]   This, at least, is the story as it is told in Samuel Purchas' *Purchas his Pilgrimes* (1625), which offers the fullest surviving version of Keeling's journal. Purchas even adds a marginal note: 'This saued the Company, as Sir *Th. Smith* affirmed to me, 20000. pounds, which they had bin endamaged if they had returned home, which necessitie had constrayned, if that Booke had not giuen light' (1625, vol 2, p 188). What brings this claim into some doubt is that William Hawkins, captain of the *Hector* on the third EIC voyage, was quite possibly the same William Hawkins who had been to Sierra Leone in the 1580s. As the entry on Hawkins in the *Oxford Dictionary of National Biography* notes, 'if he was the same man, it is rather surprising that Hawkins's own knowledge of Sierra Leone is not mentioned as influencing Keeling's decision to call there, whereas the favourable reports of Drake and Cavendish [that is, the ones in Hakluyt] are' (www.oxforddnb.com, accessed 21 November 2023). One has to wonder whether Purchas – who was, in effect, writing the sequel to Hakluyt's *Principal Navigations* – exaggerated the influence of his

predecessor's work. It is also possible that Keeling consulted his copy of Hakluyt before conferring with Hawkins; they were, after all, on different ships.

5   For an informative and even-handed discussion of the available evidence regarding these performances, and one that links them thoughtfully to other forms of diplomatic theatre, see Barbour and Klein (2018).

6   There is more direct and conclusive evidence of a play performed on the sixth voyage (Barbour, 2021, p 64).

7   It is unclear whether the intention was always eventually to return Corey to his native land. During John Lok's voyages to West Africa in the 1550s, men were abducted and taken to England to learn English before being returned to their homelands to facilitate English commerce (Dimmock, 2022, pp 37–9).

8   The story does not end well. 'Towerson abandoned Mariam, returned to England in 1619, and then resettled in Amboyna. Mariam made futile appeals to the East India Company for maintenance. The company directed Towerson to address his wife's complaints, but Towerson did not respond. When Towerson was killed, the East India Company bypassed Mariam and awarded Towerson's assets to his brother. There is no record of Mariam Khan's final fate' (Malieckal, 2011, p 98).

9   As Jowitt has demonstrated, ships as well as the men aboard them were celebrated as heroic in early modern England, their images reproduced in jewellery and other forms of material culture. But there are other ways of looking at these ships and of drawing analogies between them and their inhabitants. While early modern ships' heroism was ascribed to their capacity to 'suffer' alongside the men who occupied them (Jowitt, 2020, p 544), there is a difference between considering ships stoically battling the waves – rather as men fend off dragons – and imagining them gradually eaten away by shipworm.

References

Alaimo, S. (2016) *Exposed: Environmental Politics and Pleasures in Posthuman Times*, Minneapolis: University of Minnesota Press.

Armstrong, C. (2022) *A Blue New Deal: Why We Need a New Politics for the Ocean*, New Haven, CT: Yale University Press.

Baldwin, W. (1988) *Beware the Cat*, edited by W. Ringler and M. Flachmann, San Marino: Huntington Library.

Barbour, R. (2008) 'The East India Company journal of Anthony Marlowe, 1607–1608', *Huntington Library Quarterly*, 71(2): 255–301.

Barbour, R. (2009) *The Third Voyage Journals*, London: Palgrave Macmillan.

Barbour, R. (2021) *The Loss of the 'Trades Increase': An Early Modern Maritime Catastrophe*, Philadelphia: University of Pennsylvania Press.

Barbour, R. and Klein, B. (2018) 'Drama at sea: a new look at Shakespeare on the *Dragon*, 1607–08', in C. Jowitt and D. McInnis (eds) *Travel and Drama in Early Modern England: The Journeying Play*, Cambridge: Cambridge University Press, pp 150–68.

Bennett, J. (2010) *Vibrant Matter: A Political Ecology of Things*, Durham, NC: Duke University Press.

Bradshaw, J. (2014) *Cat Sense*, London: Penguin.

Conrad, J. (2007) *Lord Jim: A Tale*, edited by A. Simmons, London: Penguin Classics.

Cresswell, T. (2014) 'Mobilities III: moving on', *Progress in Human Geography*, 38(5): 712–21.

Das, N. (2023) *Courting India: England, Mughal India and the Origins of Empire*, London: Bloomsbury.

Dimmock, M. (2022) *Writing Tudor Exploration: Richard Eden and West Africa*, Cambridge: Cambridge University Press.

Farrington, A. (2002) *Trading Places: The East India Company and Asia, 1600–1834*, London: The British Library.

Feerick, J. (2006) '"Divided in soyle": plantation and degeneracy in *The Tempest* and *The Sea-Voyage*', *Renaissance Drama*, 35: 27–54.

Foster, W. (ed) (2016) *The Voyage of Nicholas Downton to the East Indies, 1614–15: As Recorded in Contemporary Letters and Narratives*, Abingdon: Routledge.

Fury, C. (2020) '"Wicked actions merit fearful judgments": capital trials aboard the Early East India Company voyages', in R. Blakemore and J. Davey (eds) *The Maritime World of Early Modern England*, Amsterdam: University of Amsterdam Press, pp 153–72.

Haraway, D. (2008) *When Species Meet*, Minneapolis: University of Minnesota Press.

Jonson, B. (1616) *The Workes of Beniamin Jonson*, London: Printed by William Stansby.

Jowitt, C. (2020) 'Early modern maritime heroes: idols of the sea', in C. Jowitt, C. Lambert and S. Mentz (eds) *The Routledge Companion to Marine and Maritime Worlds*, London: Routledge, pp 533–58.

Liebich, S. and Publicover, L. (2021) 'Introduction: the stain of the sea', in S. Liebich and L. Publicover (eds) *Shipboard Literary Cultures: Reading, Writing, and Performing at Sea*, New York: Palgrave Macmillan, pp 1–40.

Malieckal, B. (2011) 'Mariam Khan and the legacy of Mughal women in early modern literature of India', in B. Andrea and L. McJannet (eds) *Early Modern England and Islamic Worlds*, New York: Palgrave Macmillan, pp 97–121.

Nelson, D. and Sundberg, A. (2023) 'Shipworms and maritime ecology in the age of sail', in K. Nagai (ed) *Maritime Animals: Ships, Species, Stories*, University Park: Pennsylvania State University Press, pp 38–55.

Paster, G. (2004) *Humoring the Body: Emotions and the Shakespearean Stage*, Chicago: University of Chicago Press.

Purchas, S. (1625) *Purchas his Pilgrimes*, vol 2, London: Printed by William Stansby for Henrie Fetherstone.

Spearing, A. (1994) 'Public and private spaces in *Sir Gawain and the Green Knight*', *Arthuriana*, 4(2): 138–45.

Stern, P. (2011) *The Company-State: Corporate Sovereignty and the Early Modern Foundations of the British Empire in India*, Oxford: Oxford University Press.

Stevenson, E. (2022) 'Corey the Saldanian (d. c.1627)', in N. Das (ed) *Lives in Transit in Early Modern England*, Amsterdam: Amsterdam University Press, pp 193–8.

Strachan, M. and Penrose, B. (eds) (1971) *The East India Company Journals of Captain William Keeling and Master Thomas Bonner, 1615–17*, Minneapolis: University of Minnesota Press.

Thomas, K. (1983) *Man and the Natural World: Changing Attitudes in England 1500–1800*, Oxford: Oxford University Press.

4

Cows on the Move:
The Im(Material) Politics
of Animal Passports and the Risk
# of Antimicrobial Resistance

María Paula Escobar Tello[1]

To the memories of Henry Buller, best companion in farm animal adventures, and Bruno Latour, master tracer of the movements of power.

Introduction

The newborn calf is oblivious to Jack's actions and their significance. All she feels is her mother's tongue assiduously licking her clean, removing fluids, membranes and blood, revealing her unique pattern of black splodges. Two feet away, in the dark of night, Jack, whose presence she will soon grow used to, is writing the date and time of her birth on the farm's whiteboard, the first of her movements to be officially recorded. In the morning, after checking on mum and daughter, Jack transfers the whiteboard's information to the farm book, whose stains of blood and muck and bits of hair and hay attest to the messy business of looking after animals. In the transfer, some pieces of information, like time of birth, are left behind, but others are added, namely the last 6 digits of the 12-digit number on the ear tag that Jack must fit within 36 hours of her birth. The first six digits are the holding's registration number, the seventh is a 'check digit', designed to limit input errors when the farm book data are transferred to the online portal of the British Cattle Movement Service (BCMS). The eighth digit is a place holder, changing whenever the births registered at the farm reach 10,000. The final four are how the newborn will be known to the farm workers: 2356 (Figure 4.1). Within 27 days, Jack must take the book to his office and log into the BCMS to report her birth, quoting the ear tag number. A few days later, 2356 will have her very own cow passport.

Without the passport, ear tags and a movement licence, 2356 cannot move through the circulatory system of UK dairy and cattle farming that connects farms to markets, slaughterhouses and agricultural shows. But the passport and the online tracking system trace far more than 2356's movements, and this chapter shows how animal mobilities, like those of 2356, are woven together with policy mobilities. I look at two policies that seek to control the movement of animals and what their bodies give movement to, such as disease and bacteria, to reveal the materiality and multiplicity of policy mobilities. After a brief overview of the interconnections between animal and policy mobility studies, I discuss the history of the UK/European Union (EU) development of the cow passport. I demonstrate how the passport consolidates and sets in motion a wide range of policies – food safety, public health and market operationality – all of which can be threatened by animal diseases. The cow passport makes these not only 'ontologically accessible' (Atkins and Robinson, 2013, p 1377) but also politically accessible. That is, it makes them governable. It fastens together the complex assemblage of material objects, documents, regulations, organizations, veterinary inspectors, administrators and others on which policies depend and through which they, quite literally, materialize into realities. The chapter then turns to an example of a global policy challenge, the case of antimicrobial resistance (AMR). As a genetic *process*, AMR is more ontologically slippery than disease, and this makes tracing and controlling its movement politically and ontologically challenging: chasing the risk of resistance is not the same as chasing resistant bacteria. Nonetheless, based on the 2016 O'Neill report *Tackling Drug-Resistant Infections Globally*, the UK has developed a policy for its control that is similarly dependent on materiality. As I examine the potential for the UK approach to travel to Colombia, I expose the challenges that context poses to the materialization of policies inspired by the O'Neill report. I also interrogate the report's claims that for these policies to be mobilized successfully in low- and middle-income countries (LMICs), the latter will need time. I end by asking what studies in policy mobilities might learn from taking time seriously (Adam, 2000).

Turns and intersections: animals, policies and mobilities

Building both on Lévi-Strauss' proposition that 'animals are good to think'[2] (1963, p 89) and on Derrida's musing as he stands naked in front of his cat 'before whom I am so numbed with shame' (Derrida and Wills,

Figure 4.1: Calf 2356

Source: Photograph by María Paula Escobar Tello

2002, p 379), the 'animal turn' (Buller, 2013) in social studies has mirrored Derrida's question back onto ourselves. As it trickles through literary criticism, anthropology, sociology, history and, more recently, education, this turn examines what our representations of animals tell us about how we see ourselves as fundamentally different from them. It asks how these othering manoeuvres underlie our treatment of animals and what alternative ethics are made possible by alternative subjectifications of them (Armstrong, 2008; Haraway, 2008; Hinchliffe, 2008; Srinavasan, 2013; Drake, 2015). It has dismantled the binary opposition of humans and animals by suggesting different relational, hybrid and de-essentialized ontologies: more than human, post human (not in a chronological sense but in the sense of beyond; Wolfe, 2011) and humanimal.

Noticing a lingering anthropocentrism in some of this work, a stream within animal studies has sought to 'bring[ing] the animals back in' (Wolch and Emel, 1995, p 636) to show how animal bodies and behaviours have mattered – in the sense of having relevance and in the difference that their specific characteristics and physiologies make to the symbolic and physical places they occupy in our shared histories. This mattering/making a difference demands recognition of animals' animality – rather than semi-humanization – to make them subjects of ethical and legal frameworks. It also demands recognition of their agency and active participation in the (un)making of worlds. This attention to animal places, to our disciplining and ordering of their bodies into specific locations and to the spaces their bodies trace as they move, has been the focus of animal geographies (Wolch and Emel, 1998; Buller, 2013; Hovorka, 2019; Philo and Wilbert, 2000). Attending to the material and organic vitalities of animal bodies and how animals disrupt human orderings of space (becoming feral, pest or invasive) has allowed an embodied understanding of their agency, its limits and the challenges it presents to disciplining efforts. It has offered a lens through which to examine animal politics.

In tracing the networks of relations revealed as animals are followed in and out of material and metaphorical places, scholars have highlighted the role that animal bodies, agencies and behaviours have in human politics. For example, in my analysis of the material refurbishment of Trafalgar Square – to turn it into 'a world-class square for a world-class city' – I show how we enrol animals in policies that are designed to control which humans can access certain public spaces (Escobar, 2014). The removal of the pigeon feed stall, the introduction of a by-law to stop people from feeding the birds and the physical refurbishment of the square, including the inauguration of a cafe, means experiencing Trafalgar Square no longer costs 30 pence for a tin of seeds but £2.45 for a cappuccino. It effectively marginalizes the loners, homeless or working-class visitors associated with the stigmatized figure of the pigeon feeder. However, if animals get passively enrolled in our politics, their presence in our cities also speaks of their agency. Their abundance and persistence despite our attempts to control them, and their adaptation to our urban spaces, including begging behaviour to encourage us to feed them, show that their decision to dwell among us is more on their terms than ours. It is their agency that makes pigeons both feral and pest.

Animal and mobilities studies have met before. Scholars have examined, for example, how animals move through 'globalised networks of production and consumption' (Bull, 2011, p 23), how they move through space (McKiernan and Instone, 2016) and through time (Seaman, 2007) and how they become a new entity as they perform movements with humans (Maurstad et al, 2013). More recently, Hodgetts and Lorimer (2020) offer other potential cross-fertilizations between animal and mobility studies and call for research on how mobilities are experienced by the animals themselves. However, I take a different approach in my effort to connect animal and policy mobilities. Understanding policies as assemblages of objects, documents, discourses and bodies (human and/or not), I explore how policies seek to regulate animal mobilities and how the policies that regulate animals are themselves mobile.

Studies in policy mobilities seek to account for the differences between societies where the policies are designed and those where they are implemented. They compare policy journeys across different socioeconomic, cultural, political and institutional geographies and relate them to different narratives of failure and success (McCann, 2011; Peck and Theodore, 2012; McCann and Ward, 2013; Ward, 2018; Fairbanks, 2019; Lovell, 2019; Malone, 2019). They query the imaginary of fixed, atomized policy components and explore how the assembled elements of policies – technologies, narratives, structures, instruments and institutions – often travel separately and mutate throughout the journey (Fairbanks, 2019). Crucially, they emphasize that policies do not travel in a political vacuum. Above all, policy mobilities studies expose the uneven power relationships along the conveyor belt on which policies move (Ward, 2018).

The field of policy mobilities treats mobility and mutation as imbricated processes: context matters and policies are susceptible to mutation. This emphasis on process requires an engagement with time – Peck and Theodore argue that policy-making processes have accelerated, leading to 'emergent fast-policy regimes' (2015, p 4). Policy mobilities literature has explored the rate at which change happens and the time pressures of policy cycles (Howlett and Goetz, 2014), and more recently it has dissected stages of the policy cycle, from agenda setting and formulation to implementation and evaluation (Lovell et al, 2023). However, to take time seriously is to work with its multiplicity (Griffiths et al, 2013) and think beyond time as clock to consider it as duration and chronology. For Adam (2000), that means thinking about time as context and as multidimensional, to be sensitive to timescapes, or the 'temporal complexity of socio-environmental existence' (Adam, 2000, p 137).

Finally, policy mobilities literature draws heavily on Deleuze and Guattari's (1987) notion of assemblage, as it allows an ontological understanding of policies as a set of heterogeneous elements that work together towards a purpose. In turn, animal studies draw from actor–network theory's relational, heterogenous and flat ontologies, sensitive to the role and agency of material and non-human entities (Law and Singleton, 2014; Drake, 2015; Nimmo, 2019).

It is to assemblage and materiality in policy mobilities that I now turn to show, first, the political role of cows and their passports in the successful deployment of policies to control animal disease in the UK and, second, the mobility challenges that UK policies face as they travel to LMICs in the global effort to control the risk of AMR.

Cattle passports: mobilizing animal, human and market health in the UK

Calf 2356 is a dairy calf. Because she is female and her mum is a good cow (productive, nice temperament, healthy), Jack will rear her as a replacement cow. Other heifers, male calves and cows that are not so 'good' will move across farms, finishing units, markets or the slaughterhouse, depending on the business model and the financial context of farms. All these movements will be made under the general licence of the Animal Health Act 1981, which stipulates the conditions (keeper registrations, standstill rules, prohibited movements, record-keeping requirements) under which movements can take place. Because his farm is not officially free of bovine tuberculosis, Jack needs to apply for a specific movement licence before moving cows off his farm.

The regulation of cattle movements has a long history in UK governance, which I trace later in big leaps to show how the cow passport effectively materializes policies on public health, animal disease and market operationality. Live cattle imports were banned between 1666 and 1842 'for the encouragement of trade' (Spinage, 2003, p 250), but controls within the country were first instigated because of concerns about disease. Cattle plague, or rinderpest, a viral and highly contagious disease that cattle pass to each other through their breath, arrived at dairies near London in July 1714 (Wilkinson, 1992). Aware that farmers hid infection because once it was known that someone's herd had sick animals, 'none would buy their Milk' (Bates, 1718, p 872), the orders were to stop all movement of cows from herds with sick animals, to slaughter and burn (later bury at a minimum depth of eight feet) all sick cows and to stop all contact between keepers of sick cows and those whose herds had no cases. Farmers received 40 shillings for each slaughtered animal, although compensation levels and criteria changed as the disease spread. These controls were largely successful and used again for a rinderpest outbreak in 1745, when movement certificates were first required, setting a precedent for regulating cow movements.

Working with miasmic and environmental theories of disease, the Public Health Act 1848 and the related acts and statutes later compiled by W.G. Lumley in 1859 as 'The New Sanitary Laws', created physical and cultural distances between humans and animals, and included the regulation of animal movements. The routes through which animals could be driven were regulated to alleviate obstruction to pedestrians and establish distance between the filth and nuisance animals created and the increasingly purified lives of humans. Title XXII of the Town Police Clauses Act 1847, for example, stipulated:

> commissioners may make *orders* for regulating the route by which persons shall drive any cart or carriage, or cattle, or the manner in which they shall drive them, in the neighbourhood of such places of worship, during the hours of divine service on Sunday, Christmas Day, Good Friday or any day appointed for a public *fast* or *thanksgiving*. (Lumley, 1859, p 453, original emphasis)

By the end of the 19th century, dairies and slaughterhouses were being pushed outside city centres (Otter, 2006; Maclachlan, 2007).

Cattle plague returned in 1865. With the British imperial government now committed to free trade, the scientific responses to questions about the plague's origins and manner of spread were interpreted under those economic imperatives (Hall, 1962). One of the key actors was veterinarian John Gamgee, who explained its spread through germ theory and traced its origin to Russia (Erickson, 1961).[3] Gamgee was attacked and ridiculed (Hall, 1962; Fisher, 1993; Romano, 1997), but the Royal Commission tasked with investigating the outbreak and coming up with solutions agreed the disease was contagious – though they found the process of contagion unclear (Romano, 1997). Movements to and from markets and fairs, movements via imports and movements through the railway had all contributed to the spread of the cattle plague, but efforts to limit them were resisted by those whose livelihoods depended on these movements. The choice was between draconian slaughtering, which triggered debates about compensation, and a movements-based approach. Some of the 12 commissioners shared Gamgee's view that there should be a ban on all movements alongside compulsory slaughtering with compensation. Others preferred a system of movement licenses (Hall, 1962). Eventually, the magnitude of animal deaths and monetary losses led to the Cattle Diseases Prevention Act 1866, which set precedents for inspections and enforcement powers, transport conditions and disinfection protocols. A Contagious Diseases (Animals) Act was passed in 1869, and through its subsequent amendments and replacements a formerly localized and 'permissive' approach became increasingly centralized and compulsory (Hunting, 1890).

The market approach to the control of animal diseases continued into the 20th century as the internal UK and European markets took shape and developed instruments to trace and control movements and to set the health and welfare conditions under which movements could take place. The UK's Diseases of Animals Act 1950 required licences to move imported cattle from the 'landing place' (the port where they arrived) to the market. These licenses were expected to move with the animal and an initial form of traceability began to take shape in Article 5, which allowed authorities at markets to request from sellers

> the names and addresses, if known, of the persons to whom he has sold animals and of the numbers of each class sold to each person, and may require the person who applies for a licence authorising the movement of animals from the market to state the name and address, if known, of the person from whom he purchased the animals.

In the Tuberculosis Order 1984, licences were required to move animals, manure and slurry if tuberculosis had been identified at the farm, and keepers were ordered to identify every animal moved to be slaughtered except those under 14 days old 'in a visible way'. Hence the additional demands made of Jack to have a movement licence each time he moves cattle off his farm.

European regulations often borrow from precedents established in the UK and vice versa. When the European Community began to consolidate its internal market, Council Directive 34/432/ECC of 1964 'on animal health affecting intra-community trade in bovine animals and swine' established the definitions for animals, herds and areas that were to be considered as brucellosis-free, tuberculosis-free or epizootic-free. This was key to the licensing of movements. It established the obligation to identify bovines with earmarks, consolidated disinfection protocols for modes of transport, established veterinary checks at departure and arrival points and set out the need for animals to travel with either a health certificate or a negative test for either disease. The tests themselves were regulated and standardized for animals and for milk. Templates for individual health certificates were included in the Annexes and were differentiated according to the purpose of the movement: production, breeding or slaughter.

By June 1990, the concern had shifted from dealing with the effects of animal disease on intra-community trade to ensuring the 'harmonious operation of the common market' – which implied free movement of animals and no zootechnical or veterinary barriers. Council Directive 90/425/EEC established the need for national identification and registration systems that made animals identifiable and movements traceable through a computerized system to be developed by each EU member state. It also required holdings to be registered and it reiterated the need for health certificates to accompany animal movements. A few months later, the UK's Bovine Animals (Identification, Marking and Breeding Records) Order 1990 stipulated the requirement for animals to have 'distinguishing marks' and 'approved identification' but with no further detail. It did, however, provide a template (Figure 4.2) for recording movements: a five-column table including date of birth, breed, sex, approved identification and approved identification for the dam (the dam is the birth mother, not necessarily the same as the biological mother). Unidentified animals could not be moved.

Two years later, Council Directive 92/102/EEC refined the understanding of 'approved identification' and introduced ear tags like the one assigned to 2356. These must be tamper-proof and easy to read, and there are currently 17 suppliers approved by the Department for Environment, Food and Rural Affairs (2023). The Directive detailed the information that must be included – an alphanumeric code identifying the holding and the individual animal – as well as their physical characteristics. It also required keepers to have a register of all animals, births, deaths and movements – at least as an aggregate – with details of origin, destination and date.

In the UK's Bovine Animals (Records, Identification and Movement) Order 1995, the ear tag, as the material object designed for identification purposes, was more closely integrated with the paperwork for the control

Figure 4.2: Template to record details of each calf born, following The Bovine Animals (Identification, Marking and Breeding) Order 1990

SCHEDULE (Article 9(1))

FORM OF RECORD

BOVINE ANIMALS (IDENTIFICATION, MARKING
AND BREEDING RECORDS) ORDER 1990

Name and Address of person keeping the record:

[Particulars of each calf]

Date of Birth	Breed	Sex	Approved Identification	Approved Identification of Dam
[1]	[2]	[3]	[4]	[5]

of movements, but the latter was still a record to be kept at the farm. The new template added columns to the 1990 form to record the ear tag number, the date animals arrived on the farm (by birth or by purchase), when they moved off the farm (by death or by sale), the origin of purchased animals and their destination when they left, including the name and address of the person in charge at either point. The final column recorded the total number of animals moved (see Figure 4.3). In the specific case of calves, market operators were required to demand from sellers – and provide to buyers on request – similar details to those recorded for adult cows; that is, place of origin with details of keeper, ear tag number, and dates and places of previous movements. In contrast to 1950, keepers were now required rather than encouraged to record details, so it became their duty to know them, not just an option. As with the 1990 Order, to further facilitate traceability, keepers needed to retain these records for ten years for farm records and three years for any other holdings. Records at markets had to be kept for six months. How to deal with lost and replacement tags was also stipulated. One year later, the UK passed the Cattle Passports Order 1996, which stipulated that no movement could take place without a passport (different passports were created for calves and adult cattle). Issued individually, cow passports became the material instrument where animal movements were recorded. The nuance is significant: whereas what was required before was the recording of movements in a template that included a column for the animal's identification, from 1996 the cattle passport and the animal's uniqueness take precedence in the recording of its movements and always accompany the animal. The cattle passport was introduced at EU level in December 1997 with Council Directive 2629, and veterinary and

Figure 4.3: Template to record animal identification and movement details, following The Bovine Animals (Records, Identification and Movement) Order 1995

SCHEDULE 2

Article 5

Form of Record of Bovine Animals

The Bovine Animals
(Records, Identification and Movement) Order 1995

Record of Animals

Name and address of person keeping the record:

....

To be filled in when applicable		Particulars of each animal filled in for each event			To be filled in when born	To be filled in when tag is lost	To be filled in when animals are moved onto or off holding			
Date of movement onto farm or of birth or of loss of tag	Date of movement off farm or of death	Ear tag number	Breed	Sex	Dam's identification mark	Replacement tag number	Age or date of birth (when known)	Premises from which moved and name and addresses of person from whom delivery taken	Premises to which moved and name and addresses of person taking delivery	Number of animals moved

zootechnical checks required to control animal diseases were integrated into the cattle identification and movement control regulations. The passports were to include the same information required by Council Directive 97/12/EC, dealing with the control of animal diseases – which in fact were the same as those required by the Bovine Animals (Records, Identification and Movement) Order 1995. The same information had to be reported, together with details of each movement, in a computerized database operating as a surveillance system, which each member state was expected to introduce.

In the case of the UK, the system is called the Cattle Tracing System (CTS), and this is managed by the BCMS. The BCMS issues the passport, which has had different designs: from a single-sided A4 sheet to booklets with tear-out pages, and now a double-sided A4 sheet (Figure 4.4a and b). Imported cattle do not need a passport in advance, but they do need one once they arrive. The animal's identity data are visually more prominent than its movements, which are all to be recorded on the back of the page as the animals moves off or onto premises. On each end of a movement, passports are checked and identities are confirmed by the relevant person, whether it be market operators, farmers or official veterinary inspectors.

This regulatory history developed to protect public health, control animal disease and harmonize an integrated market. But it is also a process in which a series of human, animal and material objects that establish human–animal distances – from veterinary inspectors to tests, from health certificates to ear tags – have been positioned to obstruct the path of disease and make markets operational. This placing is inherently spatial: the regulations unfold almost as a surface, punctuated by instances and modes of control, through which cow bodies but no diseases may transit. Disease itself is identified through the tests, and veterinary expertise is distributed along farms, slaughterhouses, markets and borders; the absence of disease is reflected first in the health certificate and then in the movement licence. The ear tag ensures that the tests and licences belong to the correct cow body, and the CTS provides rapid access to information and makes any wrongdoing traceable, whether that be human based – fraud cases, such as the horse meat scandal of 2013 – or animal based – when disease escaped control in the foot-and-mouth outbreak of 2007. While cow bodies and tests make disease ontologically accessible, the ear tags, certificates and licences make the control of the movement of disease politically possible. But it is the cow passport, as a material moving object that grants 'mobile subjecthood' (Cresswell, 2014, p 713) to 2356 and her UK kind, that pulls together the assemblage of objects through which food safety (movement licence), public health (ear tag) and market operationality (BCMS and CTS) policies come into being. The system does not guarantee the containment of disease, but it makes it traceable if it is identified.[4]

But efforts to control disease have produced other material and practical networks that include diagnostic tests, laboratories, pharmaceutical companies

Figure 4.4a and b: Current format and design of a British Cattle Passport

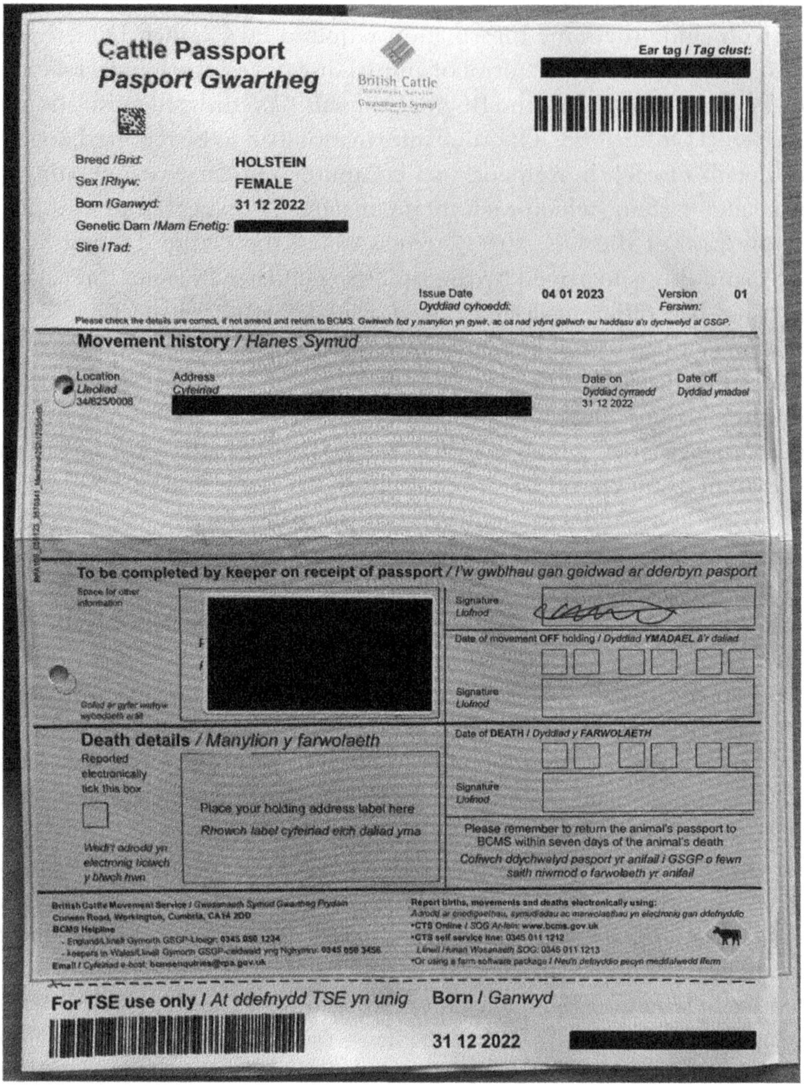

Cattle Passport
Pasport Gwartheg

British Cattle

Ear tag / *Tag clust:* [redacted]

Breed /*Brid:* HOLSTEIN
Sex /*Rhyw:* FEMALE
Born /*Ganwyd:* 31 12 2022
Genetic Dam /*Mam Enetig:* [redacted]
Sire /*Tad:*

Issue Date *Dyddiad cyhoeddi:* 04 01 2023 Version *Fersiwn:* 01

Movement history / *Hanes Symud*

Location *Lleoliad*	Address *Cyfeiriad*	Date on *Dyddiad cyrraedd*	Date off *Dyddiad ymadael*
34/825/0008	[redacted]	31 12 2022	

To be completed by keeper on receipt of passport / *I'w gwblhau gan geidwad ar dderbyn pasport*

[redacted]

Signature *Llofnod*

Date of movement OFF holding / *Dyddiad YMADAEL â'r daliad*

Signature *Llofnod*

Death details / *Manylion y farwolaeth*

Reported electronically tick this box

Place your holding address label here
Rhowch label cyfeiriad eich daliad yma

Date of DEATH / *Dyddiad y FARWOLAETH*

Signature *Llofnod*

Please remember to return the animal's passport to BCMS within seven days of the animal's death
Cofiwch ddychwelyd pasport yr anifail i GSGP o fewn saith niwrnod o farwolaeth yr anifail

For TSE use only / *At ddefnydd TSE yn unig* Born / *Ganwyd*

31 12 2022 [redacted]

Source: Photograph by María Paula Escobar Tello; form available under Crown Copyright: www.gov.uk/guidance/get-a-cattle-passport

and medicines. Medicine residues must not contaminate milk. Jack is required by law to keep a record of every time he doses 2356 with medication so he and his workers can stop her milk from entering the human food chain (Escobar and Demeritt, 2017). However, the circulation of one type of medicine, antibiotics, has resulted in a new challenge to human and animal health: AMR. I now turn to the material policies designed to contain AMR and to the challenges they face as they travel to LMICs such as Colombia.

Figure 4.4a and b: Current format and design of a British Cattle Passport (continued)

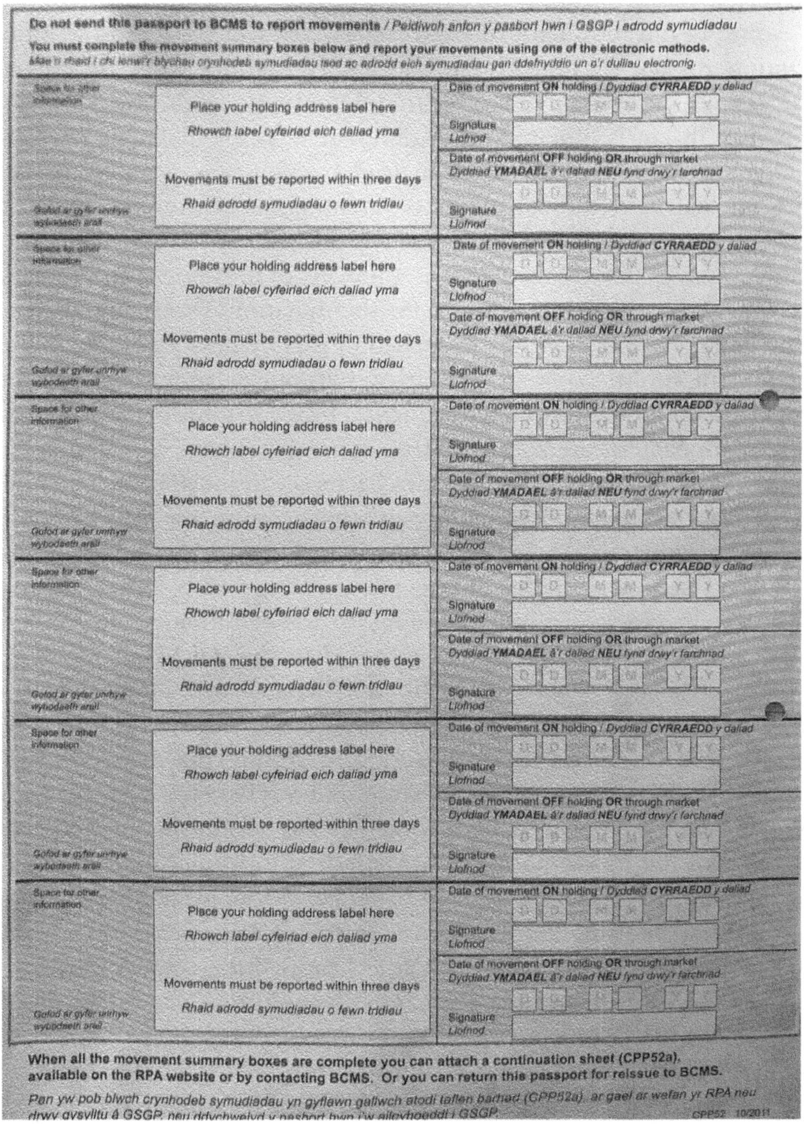

Immaterial and immobile policies: the control of AMR in LMICs

AMR is bacteria's acquired capacity to resist the antibiotics designed to kill them. AMR matters because your attentive body has approximately 3.0×10^3 human cells. Hard as it is to imagine, this number is smaller than the 3.8×10^3 bacteria cells also living inside you. These bacteria are of three main types: commensal bacteria that do no harm to humans and indeed can help keep us healthy; pathogens, which may or may not lead to symptoms and cause disease; and antimicrobial-resistant bacteria, which have lost sensitivity to antimicrobials, particularly antibiotics. Antibiotics work by entering bacteria cells and attacking 'targets' in different parts of the cell. To defend themselves, bacteria mutate in four different ways: by making a change in the target to make it insensitive to the drug; by acquiring an additional target that is not sensitive to the drug; by developing mechanisms to combat the drug's action; or by making it harder for drugs to enter the bacterial cell at all (Avison, 2005). Thus, AMR is a process of movement and mutation with different pathways and drivers for the mutations that materialize it.

The emergence of resistance is shaped in part by how we use antibiotics in a human health context – with or without a laboratory diagnosis, completing or not the course of treatment. However, some of the pathogenic and resistant bacteria are zoonotic; that is, we share them with animals in a complex flow that means that resistant bacteria can move between animals and humans through food, proximity and the environment. The percentage of global antimicrobial sales that is used in livestock is estimated at 73 per cent (Tiseo et al, 2020). Thus, resistance may also be facilitated by practices in livestock farming, including the use of antibiotics to accelerate growth or to deal with the risk – rather than the presence – of disease, although the direct link between AMR from livestock agriculture and human AMR is a contested issue (Woolhouse et al, 2015; Muloi et al, 2018; Coe et al, 2023). The 'misuse' and 'overuse'[5] of antibiotics may be seen to drive the potential for these mutations to occur, but it is less clear how they relate to specific on-farm practices such as medicating healthy animals to prevent contagion or not following dosage or length of treatment indications.

In the first half of the 1990s, national efforts to monitor AMR began to emerge in Finland (the Finnish Study Group for Antimicrobial Resistance was established in 1991), Denmark (the Danish Integrated Antimicrobial Resistance Monitoring and Research Programme was established in 1995) and the US (the National Antimicrobial Resistance Monitoring System for Enteric Bacteria was established in 1996). At EU level, the main on-farm approach has been to reduce the usage of antibiotics by setting benchmarks and targets. In the UK, the Responsible Use of Medicines in Agriculture Alliance (RUMA) put together a target task force that in 2017 set 40 sector-specific targets to reduce the overall use of antibiotics (calculated as milligrams per kilogramme). These include: reducing their sale; increasing sales of alternative treatments (for instance, the use of vaccines or sealant tubes instead of intramammary tubes for the prevention and treatment of mastitis in dairy cows); training farmers and veterinarians; preventing situations and conditions that lead to the use of antibiotics; and reducing antibiotics used in human medicine. This understands AMR as a matter of doses of antibiotics, for whose control a complex assemblage of incentives and regulations has been put in place (More, 2020). These assemblages rely too on the materialities of bottles, tubes, records and vaccines.

The global consumption of antibiotics is estimated to grow by 11.5 per cent by 2030. LMICs drive the trend (Tiseo et al, 2020) as increases in income have led to higher demand for food of animal origin (Henchion et al, 2014), in turn increasing the use of antimicrobials (Van Boeckel et al, 2015). As antimicrobials lose their power, our ability to control the diseases that affect humans is increasingly felt to constitute a 'worldwide health threat' and a 'developing global crisis' (WHO, 2012, p iv). This is particularly urgent in the Global South, where health systems can be more fragile. To contain AMR, the World Health Organization (WHO) developed a global action plan (WHO, 2015a) that includes a global surveillance strategy (WHO, 2015b). In 2014, then UK Prime Minister David Cameron commissioned Jim O'Neill to conduct The Review on Antimicrobial Resistance to analyse 'the global problem of rising drug resistance and propose concrete actions to tackle it internationally' (AMR Review, nd). The O'Neill report pushes ten recommendations into the policy spaces of health, food and agricultural authorities around the globe. In anticipating how the policy approaches it outlines for industrialized economies might travel to the 'poorest countries', the report acknowledges that LMICs will need international 'support to train veterinarians, guide development of regulatory frameworks for antibiotics, build laboratory and surveillance capacity, improve farming practices and other similar methods of capacity building' (O'Neill, 2016, p 24). O'Neill also reiterates a point from his previous report *Antimicrobials in Agriculture and the Environment: Reducing Unnecessary Use and Waste* (O'Neill, 2015), emphasizing that LMICs will need more time.

In the context of journeying AMR policies, thinking of time as chronological implies unpacking time frames, temporalities, timings, tempo, duration, sequence and modalities (Adam, 2000). But time is not only chronological: deciding what steps need to be taken in what time frames and sequences is also contextual. How does kairos – the right time for something to happen (Schwanen and Kwan, 2012) – change for different localities? How long do LMICs have to adjust their context to one where policies based on the control of antibiotics' mobilities à la RUMA become feasible? Answering these questions is not a simple matter; it implies an understanding of the reversibility or not of resistance, and of the impact of periods of resistance on human, animal and environmental health as resistance is reversed. To consider the challenges of AMR policy mobilities and the importance of politics and context, I now turn to Colombia, a regional pioneer in AMR regulations.

Colombia is a representative example of LMICs living a 'livestock revolution' (Delgado, 2003). Efforts to deal with AMR in Colombia predate those of many Global North countries. The Microbiology Group of Colombia's Instituto Nacional de Salud (National Health Institute) was four years ahead of the US and European efforts mentioned earlier; it started monitoring resistance in a series of pathogens in 1987, by which time its legislation to control the presence of antibiotics or other substances in any food or drink product (Law 9, 1979) was already well established. Draconian in character – it punished said presence with product confiscation – Law 9 of 1979 belongs to a wider set of policies designed to protect human and environmental health. Resolution 1326 of 1981 regulates the use of antimicrobial products in domestic animals and Resolution 1966 of 1984 regulates the use of antimicrobial substances as growth promoters or enhancers of food efficiency insofar as they 'pose serious dangers to human and animal health that are related to the transmission of antimicrobial resistance and sensitivity' (Preamble). In fact, no fewer than 27 pieces of legislation scaffold a regulatory architecture that makes strong efforts to control the production, commercialization, prescription, use and even disposal of veterinary medicines, the presence of residues of veterinary medicines in food of animal origin for human consumption, and levels of AMR. Some of these regulations introduce material objects like veterinary prescriptions for the sale of antibiotics or require the presence of a veterinarian at all shops where veterinary medicines are sold and where farmers can receive advice on animal health problems. This speaks to a thoroughly modern country when it comes to the appropriate use and control of veterinary medicines.

Yet the country's efforts to deal with AMR reveal a very different understanding of the problem to that of the UK and Europe. In the livestock farming sector, dealing with AMR is the responsibility of the Instituto Colombiano Agropecuario (ICA; Colombian Agriculture and Livestock Institute), which has a National Plan to monitor the presence of antibiotic residues in milk or meat, and the Instituto Nacional de Vigilancia de Medicamentos y Alimentos (INVIMA; National Medicines and Food Surveillance Institute). The INVIMA is charged with preventing the presence of bacteria in foods of animal origin and their derivates. It conducts inspections and when specific bacteria are found they are tested for sensitivity to a selection of antimicrobials and antibiotics including colistin, a last resort antibiotic considered critically important for human medicine. What is being controlled is the residues, the end of the chain in the use of antibiotics rather than their initial administration. In other words, in contrast to EU and UK regulations concerned with the *emergence* of AMR, the concern in Colombia is focused on its *transferability* to humans.

Between 2016 and 2017, I conducted interviews with officials from the ICA, INVIMA, Ministry of Health and Ministry of Agriculture as part of an Economic and Social Research Council research project looking at animal husbandry practices carrying potential AMR risks, at veterinary medicine prescription practices and at the regulatory system ruling their circulation. My findings suggest the challenges to the mobility of the RUMA approach go beyond the need for additional funding, training and time. The first challenge is the fact that dairy and beef farming operate significantly as part of a traditional peasant economy (DANE, 2020) which is loosely articulated both to processing industries, which in some cases impose product quality and farming practices standards, and to the 'informal' market, through which at least 45 per cent of milk circulates (Minagricultura, 2020). This market operates very locally through *lecheros*, who collect milk on motorbikes, bicycles, horses or donkeys and sell it to local cheese or yogurt makers and bakeries (Chohan et al, 2023). This traditional market was classified as 'informal' as the country made efforts to improve the competitiveness of the national milk sector anticipating the impacts of the free trade agreement signed in 2010 with the EU. Nested in the context of the negotiations, AMR regulations, which included stipulations on the use of veterinary medicines, were strongly associated with the negative consequences of the free trade agreement and therefore were so unpopular that the government withdrew them in the wake of massive agricultural strikes. Second, veterinarians do not hold the monopoly over the sale of antibiotics. Antibiotics are mostly sold at agricultural shops, and the legal requirement of a prescription by a veterinarian is seldom complied with; pharmaceutical laboratories have farm-to-farm salespeople and there is a market in adulterated and smuggled veterinary medicines.

In the language of policy mobilities, in Colombia the material objects that mobilize the RUMA and O'Neill approaches for the control of AMR – intramammary tubes, vaccines, bottles of antibiotics, prescriptions – circulate through systems where the setting of targets cannot be operationalized. First, the key actors in the circulation of veterinary medicines, from laboratory sales representatives to agricultural shops, are very different from those in the UK and Europe. Second, there is a very different understanding of what is being controlled – that is, residues in food products rather than doses of antibiotics in cows. And third, there is a set of costs, to farmers and to governments, beyond the purely financial. The 'formalization' of the 'informal' market transforms complex local economies that shape the social fabric of communities threatening livelihoods and even existence. Efforts to ensure a veterinarian behind the counter at every agricultural shop have also faced political opposition, as veterinarians do not necessarily live near remote milk production localities. Even if they did, farmers often consult over the phone, directly with the shop. According to the O'Neill report, to deal with this difference in context, what Colombia needs, apart from money, is time. But the linear, chronological time assumed in this recommendation obliterates the social, political and economic contexts that policies are generated in and transferred to, and this obliteration is also a manifestation of global inequalities and power relations.

Conclusion

If one pays attention not only to how and where animals move, but also to what they mobilize and to what moves inside their bodies, it becomes evident that animals and their mobilities participate in different ways in our politics. By thinking in a materiality key, I have shown how the control of diseases is made ontologically and politically possible via the complex assemblage of objects and regulations that the cattle passports, material and mobile, bind together. Animal bodies, and the material objects that travel with them, are both the objects and subjects of our politics. By moving together with the animals to whom they give subjecthood, passports mobilize and materialize policies of public health, food safety and market completion and harmonization. The passports accomplish the time trick of offering a window into the past in case it is needed in the future when disease is identified. I have also looked at the mobility of policies to control AMR, a much more ontologically slippery process. The case of Colombia suggests that some temporal tricks are easier to perform than others. It reveals the importance of context and politics that cannot be reduced to an unscrutinized concept of 'time'. Indeed, O'Neill's diagnosis has an implicit politics: What power moves and how does it move in his prescription of the necessity of 'time'? How might the need to grant more time to LMICs be read from a decolonial approach that is awake to its timescapes?

Born 8,000 miles away, Copito receives from his mother Mariposa and his owner Melba the same care as 2356. But he will move through a different world in different ways. How might a more careful politics of time give us a better chance to care for all these lives, human and animal, here and there? How might mobility studies engage with movements that are actually counter-movements, like bacteria becoming resistant or regulations being rejected? And what might studies in policy mobilities learn from processes by which policies are sent back to the place they came from?

Notes

[1]   This research project 'Animal husbandry, prescribing practices and the control of veterinary medicines in Colombia's "Livestock Revolution"' was funded by an Economic and Social Research Council grant (ES/P00475X/1). I am grateful to Ben Hunt and Bex Boenke for information on dealing with cattle passports, to Bridget Anderson for editorial advice and support and to my partner, Trevor Irwin, who listened and challenged and provided writer's retreat conditions as I wrote in Stockholm.

[2]   This statement is very often quoted as 'animals are good to think with' but the original is 'bonnes à penser'. See Garber (2008) and Haddon (2014) for discussions on the addition of 'with'.

³   There were other theories, including that of C.F.W. Schrader, who believed it originated in Dutch and German ports (Erickson, 1961).

⁴   I want to signal two points I cannot go into here. First, passports also materialize the power and borders of the state (see Torpey, 1997); second, the system is not infallible – it has blind spots that reveal the limits of such power and borders.

⁵   These labels carry political consequences that are beyond the scope of this analysis. I want to at least acknowledge them by referring to them within inverted commas.

References

Adam, B. (2000) 'The temporal gaze: the challenge for social theory in the context of GM food', *British Journal of Sociology*, 51(1): 125–42.

AMR Review (nd) 'Review on antimicrobial resistance'. Available from: https://amr-review.org/ (accessed 12 June 2024).

Armstrong, P. (2008) *What Animals Mean in the Fiction of Modernity*, London: Routledge.

Atkins, P.J. and Robinson, P.A. (2013) 'Coalition culls and zoonotic ontologies', *Environment and Planning A: Economy and Space*, 45(6): 1372–86.

Avison, M. (2005) 'New approaches to combating antimicrobial resistance', *Genome Biology*, 206(13): art 243. doi: 10.1186/gb-2005-6-13-243

Bates, T. (1718) 'A brief account of the contagious disease which raged among the milch cowes near London, in the year 1714. And of the methods that were taken for suppressing it', *Philosophical Transactions of the Royal Society of London*, 30(358): 872–85.

Bull, J. (2011) 'Introducing movement and animals', in J. Bull (ed) *Animal Movements. Moving Animals. Essays in Direction, Velocity and Agency in Humanimal Encounters*, Uppsala: Uppsala University, pp 23–40.

Buller, H. (2013) 'Animal geographies I', *Progress in Human Geography*, 38(2): 308–18.

Chohan, J.K., González Téllez, J.L., Eisler, M.C. and Escobar, M.P. (2023) 'Agropastoralism and re-peasantisation: the importance of mobility and social networks in the páramos of Boyacá, Colombia', *Agriculture and Human Values*, 41: 715–29.

Coe, S., Balogun, B. and Sutherland N. (2023) *The Use of Antibiotics on Healthy Farm Animals and Antimicrobial Resistance*, House of Commons Debate Pack CDP 2023/12. Available from: https://researchbriefings.files.parliament.uk/documents/CDP-2023-0012/CDP-2023-0012.pdf (accessed 8 December 2023).

Cresswell, T. (2014) 'Mobilities III: moving on', *Progress in Human Geography*, 38(5): 712–21.

DANE (Departamento Administrativo Nacional de Estadística) (2020) *Comunicado de prensa, Encuesta de Cultura Política, Identificación subjetiva de la población campesina*. Available from: www.dane.gov.co/files/investigaciones/ecpolitica/cp_ecp_poblacioncampesina_19.pdf (accessed 8 December 2023).

Department for Environment, Food and Rural Affairs (2023) 'Approved cattle ear tag suppliers', *GOV.UK*. Available from: www.gov.uk/governm ent/publications/approved-cattle-ear-tag-suppliers/approved-cattle-ear-tag-suppliers (accessed 3 December 2023).

Deleuze, G. and Guattari, F. (1987) *A Thousand Plateaus*, trans Brian Massumi, Minneapolis: University of Minnesota Press.

Delgado, C.L. (2003) 'Rising consumption of meat and milk in developing countries has created a new food revolution', *Journal of Nutrition*, 133(11): 3907S–3910S.

Derrida, J. and Wills, D. (trans) (2002) 'The animal that therefore I am (more to follow)', *Critical Inquiry*, 28(2): 369–418.

Drake, P. (2015) 'Marxism and the nonhuman turn: animating nonhumans, exploitation, and politics with ANT and animal studies', *Rethinking Marxism*, 27(1): 107–22.

Erickson, A.B. (1961) 'The cattle plague in England, 1865–1867', *Agricultural History Society*, 35(2): 94–103.

Escobar, M.P. (2014) 'The power of (dis)placement: pigeons and urban regeneration in Trafalgar Square', *cultural geographies*, 21(3): 363–87.

Escobar, M.P. and Demeritt, D. (2017) 'Paperwork and the decoupling of audit and animal welfare: the challenges of materiality for better regulation', *Environment and Planning C: Politics and Space*, 35(1): 169–90.

Fairbanks, L. (2019) 'Policy mobilities and the sociomateriality of U.S. offshore aquaculture governance', *Environment and Planning C: Politics and Space*, 37(5): 849–67.

Fisher, J.R. (1993) 'British physicians, medical science, and the cattle plague, 1865–66', *Bulletin of the History of Medicine*, 67(4): 651–69.

Garber, M. (2008) 'Good to think with', *Profession*: 11–20.

Griffiths, M., Rogers, A. and Anderson, B. (2013) *Migration, Time and Temporalities: Review And Prospect*, COMPAS Research Resources Paper. Available from: www.compas.ox.ac.uk/wp-content/uploads/RR-2013-Migration_Time_Temporalities.pdf (accessed 6 December 2023).

Haddon, M. (2014) 'Dirk, Dolly and Dolores', *AEON*. Available from: https://aeon.co/essays/animals-have-things-to-say-they-re-just-not-say ing-them-to-us (accessed 8 December 2023).

Hall, S.H. (1962) 'The cattle plague of 1865', *Medical History*, 6(1): 45–58.

Haraway, D. (2008) *When Species Meet*, Minneapolis: University of Minnesota Press.

Henchion, M., McCarthy, M., Resconi, V.V. and Troy, D. (2014) 'Meat consumption: trends and quality matters', *Meat Science*, 98(3): 561–8.

Hinchliffe, S. (2008) 'Reconstituting nature conservation: towards a careful political ecology', *Geoforum*, 39(1): 88–97.

Hodgetts, T. and Lorimer, J. (2020) 'Animals' mobilities', *Progress in Human Geography*, 44(1): 4–26.

Hovorka, A. (2019) 'Animal geographies III: species relations of power', *Progress in Human Geography*, 43(4): 749–57.

Howlett, M. and Goetz, K.H. (2014) 'Introduction: time, temporality and timescapes in administration and policy', *International Review of Administrative Sciences*, 80(3): 477–92.

Hunting, W. (1890) 'Suggested amendments of the Contagious Diseases (Animals) Act', *Journal of Comparative Pathology and Therapeutics*, 3: 16–26.

Law, J. and Singleton, V. (2014) 'ANT, multiplicity and policy', *Critical Policy Studies*, 8(4): 379–96.

Lévi-Strauss, C. (1963) *Totemism*, trans R. Needham, Boston: Beacon.

Lovell, H. (2019) 'Policy failure mobilities', *Progress in Human Geography*, 43(1): 46–63.

Lovell, H., Nixon, C. and Betzold, A. (2023) 'Policy mobilities and the policy cycle: an analysis using two smart grid case studies', *Geoforum*, 144: art 103818. doi: 10.1016/j.geoforum.2023.103818

Lumley, W.G. (1859) *The New Sanitary Laws*, London: Shaw and Sons.

Maclachlan, I. (2007) 'A bloody offal nuisance: the persistence of private slaughter-houses in nineteenth century London', *Urban History*, 34(2): 227–54.

Malone, A. (2019) '(Im)mobile and (un)successful? A policy mobilities approach to New Orleans's residential security taxing districts', *Environment and Planning C: Politics and Space*, 37(1): 102–18.

Maurstad, A., Davis, D. and Cowles, S. (2013) 'Co-being and intra-action in horse-human relationships: a multi-species ethnography of be(com)ing human and be(com)ing horse', *Social Anthropology*, 21(3): 322–35.

McCann, E. and Ward, K. (2013) 'A multidisciplinary approach to policy transfer research: geographies, assemblages, mobilities and mutations', *Policy Studies*, 34(1): 2–18.

McKiernan, S. and Instone, L. (2016) 'From pest to partner: rethinking the Australian White Ibis in the more-than-human city', *cultural geographies*, 23(3): 475–94.

Minagricultura (2020) *Cadena láctea colombiana. Análisis situacional Cadena láctea*, UPRA Colombia. Available from: www.andi.com.co/Uploads/ 20200430_DT_AnalSitLecheLarga_AndreaGonzalez.pdf (accessed 8 December 2023).

More, S.J. (2020) 'European perspectives on efforts to reduce antimicrobial usage in food animal production', *Irish Veterinary Journal*, 73: art 2. doi: 10.1186/s13620-019-0154-4

Muloi, D., Ward, M.J., Pedersen, A.B., Fèvre, E.M., Woolhouse, M.E.J. and van Bunnik, B.A.D. (2018) 'Are food animals responsible for the transfer of antimicrobial-resistant Escherichia coli or their resistance determinants to human populations? A systematic review', *Foodborne Pathogens and Disease*, 15(8): 467–74.

Nimmo, R. (2019) 'Biopolitics and becoming in animal-technology assemblages', *HoST – Journal of History of Science and Technology*, 13(2): 118–36.

O'Neill, J. (2015) *Antimicrobials in Agriculture and the Environment: Reducing Unnecessary Use and Waste*, The Review on Antimicrobial Resistance, London: HM Government and Wellcome Trust. Available from: https://amr-review.org/sites/default/files/Antimicrobials%20in%20agriculture%20and%20the%20environment%20-%20Reducing%20unnecessary%20use%20and%20waste.pdf (accessed 6 December 2023).

O'Neill, J. (2016) *Tackling Drug-Resistant Infections Globally: Final Report and Recommendations*, The Review on Antimicrobial Resistance, London: HM Government and Wellcome Trust. Available from: https://amr-review.org/sites/default/files/160525_Final%20paper_with%20cover.pdf (accessed 6 December 2023).

Otter, C. (2006) 'The vital city: public analysis, dairies and slaughterhouses in nineteenth-century Britain', *cultural geographies*, 13(4): 517–37.

Peck, J. and Theodore, N. (2012) 'Follow the policy: a distended case approach', *Environment and Planning A: Economy and Space*, 44(1): 21–30.

Peck, J. and Theodore, N. (2015) *Fast Policy: Experimental Statecraft at the Thresholds of Neoliberalism*, Minneapolis: University of Minnesota Press.

Philo, C. and Wilbert, C. (eds) (2000) *Animal Spaces, Beastly Places: New Geographies of Human-Animal Relations*, London: Routledge.

Romano, T.M. (1997) 'The cattle plague of 1865 and the reception of "the germ theory" in mid-Victorian Britain', *Journal of the History of Medicine*, 52(1): 51–80.

Schwanen, T. and Kwan, M.P. (2012) 'Critical space-time geographies', *Environment and Planning A*, 44(9): 2043–8.

Seaman, M.J. (2007) 'Becoming more (than) human: affective posthumanisms, past and future', *Journal of Narrative Theory*, 37(2): 246–75.

Spinage, C.A. (2003) *Cattle Plague: A History*, New York: Kluwer Academic/Plenum.

Srinivasan, K. (2013) 'The biopolitics of animal being and welfare: dog control and care in the UK and India', *Transactions of the Institute of British Geographers*, 38(1): 106–19.

Tiseo, K., Huber, L., Gilbert, M., Robinson, T.P. and Van Boeckel, T.P. (2020) 'Global trends in antimicrobial use in food animals from 2017 to 2030', *Antibiotics*, 9(12): art 918. doi: 10.3390/antibiotics9120918

Torpey, J. (1997) *Coming and Going: On the State Monopolization of the Legitimate Means of Movement*, Center for the Study of Democracy CSD Working Papers, UC Irvine. Available from: https://escholarship.org/uc/item/2n49r2s3 (accessed 8 June 2024).

Van Boeckel, T.P., Brower, C., Gilbert, M. and Laxminarayan, R. (2015) 'Global trends in antimicrobial use in food animals', *Proceedings of the National Academy of Sciences*, 112(18): 5649–54.

Ward, K. (2018) 'Policy mobilities, politics and place: the making of financial urban futures', *European Urban and Regional Studies*, 25(3): 266–83.

WHO (World Health Organization) (2012) *The Evolving Threat of Antimicrobial Resistance: Options for Action*, Geneva: WHO. Available from: www.afro.who.int/publications/evolving-threat-antimicrobial-resistance-options-action (accessed 8 December 2023).

WHO (World Health Organization) (2015a) *Global Action Plan on Antimicrobial Resistance*, Geneva: WHO. Available from: www.who.int/publications/i/item/9789241509763 (accessed 8 December 2023).

WHO (World Health Organization) (2015b) *Global Antimicrobial Resistance Surveillance System: Manual for Early Implementation*, Geneva: WHO. Available from: www.paho.org/en/documents/global-antimicrobial-resistance-surveillance-system-manual-early-implementation-2015-2017 (accessed 8 December 2023).

Wilkinson, L. (1992) *Animals and Disease: An Introduction to the History of Comparative Medicine*, Cambridge: Cambridge University Press.

Wolch, J. and Emel, J. (1995) 'Bringing the animals back in', *Environment and Planning D: Society and Space*, 13(6): 632–6.

Wolch, J. and Emel, J. (eds) (1998) *Animal Geographies: Place, Politics and Identity in the Nature-Culture Borderlands*, London: Verso.

Wolfe, C. (2011) 'Moving forward, kicking back: the animal turn', *Postmedieval: A Journal of Medieval Cultural Studies*, 2(1): 1–12.

Woolhouse, M., Ward, M., van Bunnik, B. and Farrar, J. (2015) 'Antimicrobial resistance in humans, livestock and the wider environment', *Philosophical Transactions of the Royal Society B Biological Sciences*, 370(1670): art 20140083. doi: 10.1098/rstb.2014.0083

PART 2

Productive Borders

Introduction

Manoj Dias-Abey, Angelo Martins Junior and Brendan Smith

Borders demarcate the territory over which a state exercises its sovereignty. In addition, the policing and maintenance of borders perform several vital state-making functions, including the legitimation of political authority (Barker, 2017), the fashioning of particular social relations (Anderson, 2010) and even the formation of certain kinds of subject (Auchter, 2012, p 294).

Our three chapters in Part 2 look at this from quite different disciplinary and temporal perspectives, enabling us to discern interesting patterns, similarities and differences. The sovereign has always regulated movement and used a variety of tools to do so. The methods relied on change with prevailing conditions and ideas, but there are common themes that echo over time. For example, easing labour supply at a time of labour shortage, tightening it when it is hard to find work and, in both contexts, dampening labour unrest are important factors in understanding government responses to and efforts to control mobility. In Chapter 5, Brendan Smith, a historian of the Middle Ages, describes how Edward III's government rushed through the emergency legislation in 1349 in response to the massive changes in the labour market being wrought by the Black Death, and then revised and extended its approach in the Statute of Labourers of 1351. In Chapter 6, Manoj Dias-Abey, a lawyer, describes the emergence of the Aliens Order 1920 and the demarcating of the 'national' labour market in the context of unemployment and growing labour internationalism. While both chapters might be deemed historical, they use quite different methods. Dias-Abey uses a particular regulatory instrument to uncover how the state has thought about and regulated migration over the course of the 20th century. Smith is less interested in the instruments per se and more on their sociopolitical consequences.

In Chapter 7, Angelo Martins Junior, a sociologist, explores the varied experiences of Brazilians who have made it through the UK border. He finds that they carry with them to London a range of differences relating to social class, gender, 'race' and regional background, which originate in Brazil's colonial past and are reconstituted in an environment that is suspicious of, and unsympathetic towards, 'migrant communities'. Legal status is critical to this reconstitution and to the creation and magnification of differences among Brazilian migrants in London. Legal categories are imagined as imposing order on the world, but both Martins Junior and Dias-Abey demonstrate that they both interact with social differences and call those social differences into being. The controversies that arose in the late 14th century about whether subjects of the English king who had been born outside of the kingdom were entitled to be regarded as English before the law when they moved to England speak to this same blurring and confusion. That is, questions of legal status reveal that the law and social relationships are entangled in complex ways. Martins Junior powerfully shows us how officially generated categorizations both reproduce and overlook significant social divisions, and Dias-Abey shows us that these categorizations can be mobilized to the advantage of capital.

Smith's chapter considers mobility and marches (migration and borders) in England and its neighbours from the 11th to the 15th century, taking as his starting point that the fact throughout this period English kings ruled, and claimed to rule, territories beyond England itself. Subjecthood in its medieval sense, in other words, was less directly associated with territoriality than was to be the case in later centuries. Suspicion of the outsider/stranger, however, was always strong in medieval communities, and the word 'foreigner' was synonymous with these terms until the late Middle Ages, when the concept of 'alien' (that is, foreign born) grew in prominence. Both Dias-Abey and Martins Junior's chapters also problematize a simple mapping of subjecthood onto territory. The former examines the introduction of the regulatory instrument of the 'work permit' in the Aliens Order 1920, which required any alien seeking to work in the British Isles to produce to their employer a work permit issued by the Ministry of Labour. Colonial subjects were not aliens and therefore not covered by this Order, and anyway they were not present in significant numbers on the British Isles themselves. However, seafarers were a notable exception, and the Coloured Seamen Order 1925 made it difficult for racialized subjects to find a home or even temporary residence in the heart of Empire.

While immigration policy is, as Anderson argues in the introduction to this volume, bound up with ideas of nation, it is ostensibly race neutral. Dias-Abey and Martins Junior suggest this is otherwise in practice. The latter notes how 'good' and 'bad' become 'legal' and 'illegal' and that legal status is both racialized and classed. While these chapters focus on England and London, respectively, Martins Junior's contribution helps us see that processes of racialization are not confined to the former British imperial power. Brazilians who come to London bring with them their own colonially inflected ideas of race and hierarchies that adapt to the British sociolegal context. What borders produce in this context is newer forms of disunity, and fear of deportation deepens old divisions and generates new ones among Brazilian migrants, some of whom internalize the rhetoric of 'good citizens' on the one hand and 'non-citizens' or 'dodgy citizens' on the other in order to distance themselves from the stigmatized figure of 'the migrant'.

Taken together, the chapters demand that we take a critical view of not only traditional narratives and officially sponsored terminologies and rhetoric, but also accepted chronological and geographical frameworks. Centuries before the appearance of modern states, powerful political entities like the medieval English kingdom were deeply concerned with issues of mobility and sought to direct their course. This is not to claim that 'there is nothing new under the sun'. Good history takes nothing for granted and eschews teleology. It is also sensitive to changing vocabularies and to the changing meaning of words that appear in both the past and the present. Rather, it claims that understanding contemporary mobility is enriched by an appreciation of how important it has been in the past and how histories of movement and efforts to control it, not only in England but elsewhere, shape our contemporary landscape. Dias-Abey shows that attending to histories of mobility control helps us understand how the 'national labour market' was made, Martins Junior reminds us that ideas of race and class stretch across and are changed by borders. We consider in different settings how the choices made by those who hold power over borders affect the lives of those who cross those borders. The crossing may be a moment in time, but the consequences of those choices may stretch over generations. Taking the configuration of the social world as a continuum, made of connections, ambivalences and paradoxes, these three chapters illuminate how the global mobile present is connected to the legacies of the colonial past, both national and global. 'Here' and 'there', 'present' and 'past' are always entwined – creating and recreating racialized inequalities and difference, including unequal access to the privilege of mobility.

References

Anderson, B. (2010) 'Migration, immigration controls and the fashioning of precarious workers', *Work, Employment and Society*, 24(2): 300–17.

Auchter, J. (2012) 'Border monuments: memory, counter-memory, and (b) ordering practices along the US-Mexico border', *Review of International Studies*, 39(2): 291–311.

Barker, V. (2017) 'Penal power at the border: realigning state and nation', *Theoretical Criminology*, 21(4): 441–57.

5

Migrants and Borders in the Medieval English World

Brendan Smith

Introduction

'Migrations', we are told, 'are as much part of the human condition as birth, reproduction, sickness and death' (Bade, 2003, p ix). To acknowledge migration – by which I mean an expression of mobility usually involving permanent relocation – as a historical constant is not to dispute that it had distinctive features in different ages and in different parts of the world. Nor is it to suggest that anxiety about it is characteristic only of some societies in recent times. Debates about present-day migration stand to benefit from greater engagement with the historical dimensions of the issue, not because the past provides answers to the questions we ask about our current concerns, but because 'the long view' encourages us to move beyond judgement to understanding. Migration in its various forms – immigration, internal migration, emigration – in the context of the UK in the 21st century is different in a host of obvious and important ways from migration in medieval England, yet some appreciation of the latter has the potential to enrich consideration of the former.

If this is to be achieved, the issue of terminology must first be addressed. There were no equivalents in the languages of medieval England – Latin, English and French – for the words 'migration', 'borders', 'citizenship' and 'race' as we use them today. Historians, in negotiating the challenges presented by linguistic change over time, seek to avoid anachronism while escaping the constraints that strict adherence to the vocabularies of an earlier age imposes (Davies, 2003; Armstrong et al, 2022). They recognize that the permanent relocation of newcomers, the presence of territorial boundaries, the notion of subjecthood and the recognition of the existence of different peoples were all medieval commonplaces. At the same time, however, they see the 12th- and 21st-century manifestations of these phenomena as distinct. Bernard Gueneé has observed that '[h]istorians find the awarding of prizes for modernity irresistible', but an acceptance of the reality that mobility, including migration, is as old as our species surely lessens the temptation to burden consideration of the past of this topic with the particular concerns of the present (1985, p 18).

Consideration of migration in today's UK, for instance, to a considerable extent concentrates on the crossing of the borders that give the nation state its meaning (Ellenblum, 2002; Anderson, 2024). Medieval England was not a nation state (Watts, 2002). Furthermore, the borders of the English kingdom were not the borders of the king of England's territories: at various times in the Middle Ages the monarch claimed, and often exercised, authority over the other countries of the British Isles as well as adjacent and more distant parts of France (Gillingham, 2014). The borders of the kingdom of England and of what some historians call 'the first English empire' were not static and were not imagined to exercise a function related to migration control (Davies, 2000). Yet kings of England showed interest in regulating who moved into and out of their kingdom – sometimes promoting such movement, at other times limiting it – and recognized that their ability to display their power in this context helped shape the nature of their rule as well as the fortunes of their lands.

Recent scholarship on the 'global Middle Ages' has demonstrated that human mobility in the medieval period was more widespread than has often been imagined (Holmes and Standen, 2018). The traditional and still prevalent idea that 'in pre-modern times the default assumption was that nobody was allowed to travel anywhere – often not even to the next town – without official permission' (Harford, 2021, p 16) is being superseded by one urging that 'we assume mobility in the medieval past unless or until the evidence invalidates this null hypothesis and demonstrates stasis' (Horden, 2007, p xxxiv). Helpful as this 'mobility turn' (Urry, 2007; Anderson, 2024) is in reframing our perception of the scale of human movement in the past, it must be fine-tuned in relation to migration. It may be true, as Horden suggested, that in the Middle Ages 'almost everyone was mobile' (Horden, 2007, p xxx), but not everyone who was mobile sought to move permanently. This explains why this chapter is not concerned with English pilgrims who visited Santiago de Compostela or Rome, English schoolmen trained at Paris and other continental universities, English traders who resided for periods in merchant colonies at Cologne and elsewhere, or English royal administrators and soldiers whose employment involved service outside of England. In all these cases, the presumption was that the individuals concerned would return home; their sojourns abroad spoke to their mobility, not to any commitment on their part to permanent relocation beyond the kingdom. In contrast, this chapter focuses on those whose mobility constituted what one historian has called 'a one-way ticket' (Khazanov, 2015, p 359).

Medieval migration often involved traversing frontiers, and the study of frontiers has long been a preoccupation of medieval historians (Bartlett and Mackay, 1989; Power and Standen, 1999; Abulafia and Berend, 2002). Medieval charters recording the transfer of land reveal the deep interest of the parties involved in identifying with precision the boundaries between neighbouring parcels of real estate (Berend, 2001). But designating the borders of larger territorial/political units – duchies, kingdoms and empires, for instance – was not to be achieved by simply upscaling thinking that prevailed at the level of the village or the manor. Linear frontiers delimited by natural features such as rivers were to be found in various parts of the medieval West, such as Normandy–France and England–Scotland, but much more common were zonal frontiers. Since Carolingian times, these had been designated by the term 'mark' or 'march', from which we have 'Denmark' and, closer to home, 'the Welsh Marches' (Power, 1999; Barrow, 2003; Lieberman, 2010). Indeed, even a linear (as opposed to zonal) frontier such as that established between England and Scotland in 1237 came to be enclosed within a larger frontier zone that operated its own 'march laws' (Neville, 1998; Armstrong, 2022). Whether 'frontier societies' developed in some of these zones – whether, in other words, we should see 'the frontier not simply as a place but as a set of attitudes, conditions and relationships' – has intrigued historians and is often discussed in relation to the militarized nature of these places (Abulafia and Berend, 2002 p 34; see also Frame, 1989). Undoubtedly, the persistence of sporadic armed conflict in many marches had consequences for patterns of settlement and migration (Barrow, 1989; Frame, 2012). Intermittent warfare on the Anglo-Scottish border and in parts of northern France contested between the French and English in the 14th and 15th centuries, for instance, led to the depopulation of parts of these frontier zones (Allmand, 1983; Ellis, 1999).

There was, therefore, a link between frontiers and mobility in England and its empire in the Middle Ages. To appreciate how different that link was from what prevails today, one need only consult the website of the UK Border Force, where one reads that '[w]e secure the UK border by carrying out immigration and customs controls for people and goods entering the UK' (Border Force, nd). Medieval frontiers were not 'secure'; they were open, and they operated no 'controls' on the temporary or permanent movement of people across them (Ormrod et al, 2019). We must look elsewhere than its borders if we wish to understand England's medieval migration history. We must look instead at the centre, since in a king-centred polity it was with the monarch and his government that the power lay to influence the permanent relocation of people. This chapter therefore focuses on three groups whose experiences of migration were shaped by the royal will: exiles, colonists and labourers who moved in search of work.

Exiles

Medieval Christians, familiar with the story of the expulsion of their first parents from the Garden of Eden, recognized migration in the form of exile as the original punishment for human sinfulness. However, the exile that began when '[t]he Lord said to Abram, "Go from your country and your kindred and your father's house to the land that I will show you"' (Genesis 12:1), was clearly not motivated by divine displeasure. The idea that exile might have a positive dimension was also to be found in the classical heritage that the medieval West cherished. In detailing the struggles and achievements of Aeneas, Virgil offered a powerful story of defeat and exile that concluded in triumph. It was no wonder that when the barbarian peoples of the West began to write of their origins from the seventh century onwards, they portrayed themselves as descendants of migrants who had suffered and struggled before securing the lands which they subsequently called home (Geary, 2003).

The ability of kings to send their enemies into exile attested to their power in a particularly visible manner (Gibney, 2020). Reflecting on King Edward I's (1272–1307) expulsion of England's Jewish population in 1290, one chronicler remarked: 'You have achieved in one day what the Pharaohs of ancient Egypt failed to do' (Scales, 2007, p 299). For the elite of medieval England, exile, either as punishment or as a means to avoid it, was a familiar feature of political life. The upheavals of the 11th century, both before and after 1066, led to members of Earl Godwin's family and supporters and descendants of King Edward the Confessor (1043–1066) relocating to parts of Europe as far flung as Ireland, Scandinavia, Hungary and the shores of the Sea of Azov (Barlow, 2002; Parsons, 2019). In like manner, exiling supporters of the king against his will represented a very public challenge to royal power. Magna Carta, issued by a reluctant King John (1199–1216) in 1215, contained a clause ordering the removal from the kingdom of named individuals described as *alienigena* – that is, outsiders, aliens, of foreign origin – who were deemed to be a bad influence on the monarch. This marked the first appearance of this significant term in an official English record (Davies, 1984). The expulsion from the kingdom of foreign royal favourites by opponents of the king was a feature of the troubled reigns of Henry III (1216–1272) and Edward II (1307–1327), but as events in the reign of Richard II (1377–1399) demonstrated, exile was not a political weapon reserved solely for use against foreigners. In the late 1380s, Richard's enemies secured the exile of his leading favourites, Michael de la Pole, earl of Suffolk, and Robert de Vere, earl of Oxford, and when

Richard returned to the ascendant in the second half of the 1390s, he in turn exiled his aristocratic opponents (Saul, 1997; Prestwich, 2005).

In medieval England, as a result of the development of the legal procedure known as abjuration of the realm, exile was not an experience confined to the nobility. Reaching its mature form in the reign of Henry II (1154–1189), abjuration of the realm – 'this picturesque episode of medieval justice', as Maitland called it (quoted in Pollock and Maitland, 1968, p 590) – saw those accused of felony (usually robbery or murder) and those who had sought sanctuary in church property swear before the local coroner that they would leave England immediately, never to return on pain of death. This form of outlawry was a punishment, but it was also an act of royal mercy in that it spared the life of the guilty party and forbade attacks on him or her. It thus resembled God's judgement of Cain following the murder of Abel: 'You shall be a fugitive and a wanderer over the earth ... And the Lord put a mark on Cain, lest any who came upon him should kill him' (Genesis 4:12, 15; Jordan, 2015). Most felons who abjured were poor, and the lands and chattels they forfeited to the Crown once they had sworn the oath were usually of little value. Perhaps 10 per cent of abjurers were women, and in some instances, husbands and wives abjured together. The procedure offered to individuals and families with little to lose the opportunity to start a new life abroad, but was usually ruinous to those who already enjoyed local status (Shoemaker, 2011; McSheffrey, 2017).

Maitland believed that as a result of abjuration, 'large numbers of our felons were induced to relieve England of their presence and were shipped off at Dover to France or Flanders' (quoted in Pollock and Maitland, 1968, p 591), while Hunnisett argued that

> it would be surprising to discover that more than a minute proportion of all abjurors ever left the kingdom or even reached their ports. What must have happened in the vast majority of cases is that the abjurors sooner or later left the highway and took up residence unmolested elsewhere. (Hunnisett, 1961, pp 48–9)

Most recently, Jordan has argued persuasively that evasion of exile was the exception rather than the rule and has suggested that in the period from 1170 to 1330, at a conservative estimate, 'approximately 75,000 men and women were sent into perpetual exile through abjuration' (2015, p 26).

An aspect of abjuration and of other forms of exile pertinent to the issue of migration and borders concerned the destination of those who were expelled. From the time of King John, the principle prevailed that one and the same law (*una et eadem lex*) operated in the kingdom of England and the lordship of Ireland. Yet the great legal commentary on English common law, *Bracton*, which was probably composed in the 1230s, made clear that in relation to abjuration, each component of the king's domains remained legally distinct (Hand, 1967). Abjured felons from England could, and did, relocate to Ireland, free from fear of further punishment for their felonies, while England became home to felons who had abjured in Ireland (Jordan, 2015). Abjured English felons were also to be found in the king's French lands. During his sojourns in Gascony in 1242–43 and 1253–54, Henry III granted scores of pardons to felons who had abjured there having committed murder in England (Hurnard, 1969). When the disgraced chief justice of the common bench, Thomas Weyland (c 1230–98), was permitted to abjure the realm in 1290, he promised on oath never to return to England or any other of the king's territories, and made his way to Paris (Brand, 1992; Freeman, 2007).

The destination of exiles from England during the political conflicts of Richard II's reign mattered to those who forced them from the kingdom. The king's noble favourites, the earls of Suffolk and Oxford, were expelled beyond the king's territories – the former died in Paris in September 1389, the latter expired in or near Louvain in the duchy of Brabant in August 1392. The six judges who were exiled at the same time for having supported the king's legal rights against his enemies, on the other hand, were ordered instead to remove themselves permanently to Ireland, and were referred to subsequently as 'justices qe demourent bannyz en Ireland' (the justices who remain exiled in Ireland; Given-Wilson, 2005, p 263). Anthony Goodman's (2011) droll remark with reference to one of the judges, Sir John Cary, that 'parliament eventually decided that life exile in Ireland was an appropriate substitute for death', perhaps misses the larger point that the 'internal exile' of the judges meant something different than expulsion beyond the king's lands. Richard II seems to have understood this: at the Revenge Parliament of 1397, which saw him seek to destroy those who had opposed him a decade earlier, he ensured that the earl of Warwick was banished to the Isle of Man and that John, Lord Cobham, was sent to Jersey, with both islands being described as 'hors du roialme' (beyond the realm; Given-Wilson, 2005, pp 416, 420). Henry Bolingbroke, too well connected to be allowed to remain in the king's lands, was instead expelled beyond them and moved to Paris, from where he launched the coup of 1399, which saw him crowned as King Henry IV (1399–1413) (Given-Wilson, 2017). It appears that for both the humble and the exalted, the complicated nature of the borders of the English king's lands involved opportunities and dangers.

Colonists

For the inhabitants of medieval England, colonization was a form of mobility with a pedigree similar to that of exile, featuring as it did in both the Bible and in classical texts. 'Colony' and the words derived from it have the root meaning of working the land, and medieval Christians remembered that '[t]he Lord God took the man and settled him in the Garden of Eden to till it and keep it' (Genesis 2:15; Crooks, 2022). They also knew that God had later reminded the Israelites: 'I gave you a land on which you had not laboured, and cities which you had not built, and you dwell therein; you eat the fruit of vineyards and oliveyards which you did not plant' (Joshua 24:13). Colonization in the medieval West, unlike the introduction of the first parents to Eden, involved taking land from those who already held it. When, in the 1590s, Edmund Spenser justified English policies in Ireland with the remark 'for it is usually in the Conquest of anye Countrye that manie of the Conquerers doe plant them selves in the lande of the Conquered', he encapsulated succinctly an approach to colonization that had an ancient pedigree (Hadfield, 1993, p 398; Veracini, 2010; Wilson, 2018). In the century and more before Duke William conquered England in 1066, rulers of Normandy had settled their vassals on the lands they conquered from their neighbours in Brittany and Maine, and they adopted a similar approach to securing their position in the British Isles after the Conquest (Searle, 1988; Hagger, 2017). Under its Norman kings, England became a colonized land into which, at the behest of William I (1066–1087) and his sons and successors, communities of Jews from Rouen, as well as large numbers of Flemings and inhabitants of various parts of northern France, moved and put down roots (Golding, 1994; Holt, 1997).

These kings also used colonization as a means of securing territories taken from neighbouring rulers in the archipelago. At the time of the Conquest, Cumbria was in the hands of the King of Scots, but in 1092 King William II (1087–1100) of England captured Carlisle and expelled its Scottish ruler. The *Anglo-Saxon Chronicle* reports that he then 'sent many peasants there with their wives and livestock to live there and cultivate the land' (quoted in Bartlett, 2000, p 82). The approach was articulated in a royal charter for the first time in 1171–72. Granting his newly acquired city of Dublin to 'my men of Bristol', King Henry II (1154–1189) declared that the Bristolians were to have it 'ad inhabitandam' (for the purpose of living in; Duffy, 2005). Edward I's (1272–1307) conquest of Wales, which was complete by 1284, was followed by the settlement of large numbers of English peasants and townsfolk, some from as far away as Kent, around Denbigh and Ruthin in the north of the country (Korngiebel, 2007). As part of this campaign, displaced Welsh peasants were resettled in the vicinity on land of inferior quality, in a process which Rees Davies has described as 'more like internal exile than fair exchange' (1974, p 11).

Edward I's attempts to conquer Scotland after 1296 were rooted in the same way of thinking. Following his capture of Berwick and the massacre of its inhabitants in March 1296, he summoned representatives of 24 English towns to meet him at Bury St Edmunds in November of that year to advise him on how to make his ongoing resettlement of Berwick with English colonists a success (Tout, 1919; Watson, 1998). Efforts were also made to plant English settlers in Berwickshire and Lothian by King Edward III (1327–1377) after he renewed his grandfather's efforts to conquer the northern kingdom after 1333 (Brown, 2007; MacInnes, 2012). Edward III also saw colonization as crucial to the success of his policies in France. 'I wish to repopulate Calais with pure-blooded English', a later chronicler reported the king declaring after the capture of the town in August 1347 (Rose, 2008, p 1).[1] Edward issued a proclamation in the northern and eastern counties of England appealing for colonists to move to the town, promising them liberties and commercial privileges if they did so and, in imitation of his grandfather's actions after the capture of Berwick, summoned representatives of English towns to meet him at Calais to advise him on its future. Almost 200 grants of tenure were issued in a short space of time to English settlers, and an English presence was established that endured for two centuries (Greaves, 1918; Le Patourel, 1984). Finally, after his victory at Agincourt in 1415, Henry V (1413–1422) sought to colonize with English subjects those parts of Normandy and adjacent territories – the *pays de conquête* – that he took from the French. It was his stated wish following his capture of Harfleur in 1417, a chronicler reported, to 'stuffe the toun with English peple' (Allmand, 1968; see also Massey, 1984).

Not all English migrants who settled in new lands did so as part of efforts by the English Crown to extend its territories. It would be inaccurate, for instance, to describe the large numbers of English peasants, town dwellers, knights and clergy who in the century after c 1150 were enticed by successive kings of Scots to settle north of the border as 'settler colonists' (Sharma and Wright, 2008; Veracini, 2010; Oram, 2011). Nor were all the lands claimed by English kings acquired by conquest – Aquitaine/Gascony and Ponthieu, for example, came to the Crown through marriage and witnessed little settlement by English folk. But in those places that were acquired by conquest, the exercise of royal authority and the presence of English colonial subjects were viewed as inseparable. For this reason, the migration to England in the 14th and 15th centuries from Wales, Scotland and Ireland, and from the 1440s Normandy also, of large numbers of peasants and townsfolk of English settler stock, was viewed by the Crown and by Parliament as a serious problem. Noting the campaigns to repatriate Irish-born residents living in England in the 1390s, the St Albans chronicler Thomas Walsingham wrote that 'such a multitude had come to England in the hope of gain that [Ireland] was almost emptied of cultivators and defenders', with the result that parts of the island no longer obeyed the king (quoted in Frame, 2006, p 452). A petition from the Irish parliament to the king in 1421 argued that because so many 'tenants of the land, artificers and labourers' had moved from Ireland to England, 'the husbandry of your said land is greatly injured and disused, and your said lieges greatly weakened in their power of resisting the malice of your said enemies' (Berry, 1907, p 569). Laws passed by the parliament in Ireland to prevent people moving to England, and the king's commands that people from Ireland residing in England should return across the Irish Sea had little impact on the situation. England's medieval borders remained open and as its empire shrank the kingdom became home to many migrants whose ancestors had set out from England to other parts of the British Isles and to parts of France as colonists in earlier times (Ormrod and Mackman, 2017).

Labourers

Late medieval England became home not only to migrants from other parts of the English empire, but also to individuals and families who moved there from adjacent and in some instances more distant parts of Europe. Anxiety about the political allegiance of such people at a time when England's war with France was going badly was one motivating factor behind the introduction in 1440 of an alien subsidy (the first of its kind in Europe), the purpose of which was to identify and raise revenue from those residing in the kingdom of England who had been born beyond its borders. Initially, even English subjects who had been born in other parts of the Plantagenet lands were included in its remit, but the howls of protest of those concerned quickly reached the ear of the king and they were speedily removed from its provisions (Ormrod et al, 2019). England's medieval immigrants entered the kingdom in search of a better life. This was a motivation they shared with those individuals born in England who chose to relocate within the kingdom. Exiles, colonists, various pied noir groupings and immigrants from beyond the empire were part of medieval England's migration story. Most of those who migrated in medieval England, however, were born there and died there. In an age of open borders, and one in which the 'methodological nationalism' of which Bridget Anderson writes in the introduction to this volume was absent, no very sharp distinction was drawn between 'internal' and other forms of migration in medieval England (Dyer, 2020). It may be fruitful to see the alien subsidy initiative of 1440 in part, at least, as the latest in a series of attempts by the Crown, beginning in the middle of the 14th century, to influence patterns of labour mobility.

'The Black Death', it has recently been argued, 'provides a prominent and early example of a government taking decisive action at a moment of national crisis to protect what it regarded as the welfare of its peoples and to promote its notion of a good society' (Bailey, 2021, p 334). A crucial expression of this policy was the Statute of Labourers, enacted in 1351. In response to the removal by death from plague in the previous three years of some 40 per cent of the workforce, the Statute sought to increase the supply of labour and limit its cost by, among other provisions, requiring labourers to remain in their villages and enter only into long-term work contracts with their employers (Steinfeld, 1991). In other words, the Crown used parliamentary legislation to try to limit the scale of mobility within the kingdom (Palmer, 1993; Hatcher, 1994). Attempts later in the century to force Irish-born residents in England to return to Ireland, and from 1440 to identify and tax workers who had been born abroad, stemmed from the same desire on the part of the Crown to direct and control the movement of labour.

This mobility had been a feature of English society for centuries before the advent of plague in 1348 (Postles, 2000). So prevalent was it that one historian has remarked that '[l]abour seems sometimes to have flowed almost at random, as if movement occurred for its own sake' (Dyer, 2005, p 226). Unfree tenants, that is serfs or villeins, who accounted for some 40 per cent of the peasantry by the late 13th century, had always been among those who relocated within England, either to towns or to other parts of the countryside, despite theoretical restrictions on their freedom of movement. In the 13th century, when the population was rising and pressure on land was increasing in some areas, it suited some lords to turn a blind eye to the departure of a number of their serfs, though this may in turn have increased the proportion of town dwellers in places such as London and Norwich who were living in destitution (Bailey, 2014; Campbell, 2016). It seems probable that the scale of peasant migration increased after the Black Death, and this has plausibly been identified as the most important factor in the rapid decline of serfdom in the kingdom in the late 14th century (Razi, 1993). In the wake of plague, lords sought to curtail the mobility of their unfree peasants, and the Statute of Labourers 1351 and the Statute of Cambridge 1388, which required labourers who left their manors to carry with them letters stating why they were travelling and when they would return, were designed to help them in this regard (Clark, 1994).

Campaigns to discover and forcibly return flown villeins to their native manors were undertaken by some lords following the enactment of these statutes, but no momentum in this regard could be sustained by these individuals, and the policy was clearly a failure (Schofield, 2003). Those lords and town officials who welcomed migrant serfs were under no obligation to return them to their 'true' lords, and – despite parliamentary statutes – the legal system did not offer much help in the retrieval of those who relocated. A lord had only four days in which to find and bring back an unfree tenant who had fled before being required to purchase a common law writ of recovery to help achieve this end. This involved unwelcome expense and was no guarantee that, once returned to his native manor, the serf would not simply flee again at the next opportunity. The frustration encountered by the aggrieved lord as he sought to curtail the mobility of his unfree peasants, only to find that the authority of his own manorial court had been undermined by Parliament, is captured nicely in Mark Bailey's observation that '[t]o make matters worse, an English lord who retrieved a serf already bound in a contract of employment with a third party was vulnerable to legal challenge for breaching the contract clause of the Statute of Labourers' (Bailey, 2021, p 105; see also Given-Wilson, 2000).

Migration was not confined to villeins; free peasants, artisans and traders were also on the move in late medieval England. The young were so noticeably mobile that it has been suggested that 'mobility may be perceived as a facet of youth'. This included young women, and the incidence of female migration, especially to towns, was extensive (Goldberg, 1992; Goldberg, 2004, p 91). Population densities in different parts of the kingdom were altered as a result of the permanent relocation of so many individuals and families in the century and a half after 1348. The thriving cloth industry of the south-west of England enticed migrants to the region, while the transition from arable to pastoral farming in the east midlands reduced employment opportunities and promoted movement elsewhere (Dyer, 2005). Towns had been unable to sustain their population levels even before 1348 and always needed to attract newcomers if they were to survive. In the era of plague, registers of freemen and toponymic surnames suggest that in most English towns first- or second-generation immigrants constituted at least a third of the population (Dobson, 2000). Smaller towns in most cases attracted migrants from within a 12-mile radius, but 'regional capitals', such as Exeter, York, Winchester and Norwich drew up to half of their immigrants from a distance greater than 20 miles (Postles, 2000; Childs, 2006). Bristol's migration hinterland was even larger, and Peter Fleming (2007) has suggested that in the early 15th century between 5 and 8 per cent of its inhabitants were Irish born.

Conclusion

Fleming has drawn attention to the hostility displayed towards its Irish community by the authorities in Bristol in the late Middle Ages, while attacks on foreigners, of which the massacre of London's Flemish community in the course of the Peasants' Revolt of the summer of 1381 is the most notorious, were, it has been argued, 'a more frequent occurrence than the fragmentary and scattered scholarly literature on the subject might lead readers initially to suppose' (Scales, 2007, p 286). On the other hand, recent and intense scrutiny of the experience of 'aliens' in England in the late Middle Ages – which in this context means subsequent to the expulsion of the Jews in 1290 – suggests that animosity towards foreigners was rare and arose from local economic problems rather than a more general xenophobia. In a minority of cases, migrants were known to their neighbours by the surnames 'Scot' or 'Irish' and might be targeted for harsh treatment at moments of political tension, but what has more often caught the eye of historians is the 'apparently high levels of assimilation and toleration of immigrants found in England during the later Middle Ages' (Ormrod and Mackman, 2017, p 10; see also Bolton, 2000).

It was certainly the case that it was not only around migrants from beyond the kingdom's borders that disputes within urban communities might revolve. Samuel K. Cohn Jr has drawn attention to the 'struggles between newcomers, who had immigrated to Shrewsbury from its hinterland since the Black Death, and the town's old order on the eve of England's second wave of pestilence in 1361' (2013, p 124). Initially at least, all newcomers were strangers and the suspicion of the mobile stranger, which was widespread in medieval society, did not distinguish in a consistent manner between those who were English born and those of foreign origin. In *Piers Plowman*, successive versions of which were written between the 1360s and 1380s, William Langland wrote: 'Truth's command to Piers was to stay at home and plough his fallow lands' (Schmidt, 1992, p 75). The most popular tales circulating in late medieval England concerned Robin Hood, a put-upon yeoman who never strayed far from his own neighbourhood and wished only to leave his refuge in the forest, go home and be left to mind his own business (Keen, 2000; Crook, 2020).

If those who did not wander were seen in a positive light, the stranger was viewed with intense distrust. Christ had told his listeners: 'Then the king will say to those at his right hand, "Come, O blessed of my Father, inherit the kingdom prepared for you from the foundation of the world. For … I was a stranger and you welcomed me"' (Matthew 25:34–5). But the Christians of medieval England did not find welcoming strangers easy, whether they originated within or beyond the borders of the kingdom. One of the earliest English law codes, that of Wihtred, king of Kent (c 695–96), decreed: 'If a man who has come from afar or a stranger goes off the road, and if he neither shouts nor blows a horn, he is to be considered a thief, either to be slain or redeemed [by a fine]' (Neville, 2007, p 207). Some five hundred years later, the Assizes of the Watch, enacted between 1233 and 1253, laid down that in the summer months each vill was to employ at least four watchmen, whose job it was to take any passing stranger into custody and pursue them if they fled. Offering hospitality to a stranger without providing a pledge was also frowned upon, being restricted to a single day. Court records, which survive in abundance from the late 13th century onwards, suggest that a link between the presence of strangers and criminal activity was firmly in place in the communal imagination. At the Bedford eyre (circuit court session) held in 1287, for instance, 'almost every criminal was said to be either a vagrant or a stranger' (Summerson, 1979, p 326).

Before the 14th century, the various words for 'stranger' in use in England – which included terms best translated as 'foreigner' – implied no distinction between people born in the kingdom and those born elsewhere. By then, however, it was commonly held that Englishness was defined by place of birth and parentage, and over time the word 'alien' came to be used more frequently to identify strangers who were not from England (Ruddick, 2013; Ormrod et al, 2019). But England's borders remained open and throughout the Middle Ages people from England migrated to other countries just as migrants arrived in the kingdom from the rest of the British Isles and from mainland Europe. The nature of borders and migration in medieval England was different from their nature today. But the migrant's tale from any era is fascinating, instructive and, Scripture promises, potentially revelatory: 'Let brotherly love continue. Do not neglect to show hospitality to strangers, for thereby some have entertained angels unawares' (Hebrews 13:1–2).

Note

[1] 'Blood' in this context relates to ancestry, customs and place of birth, rather than to ideas of race based on biological 'purity' (see Ruddick, 2013).

References

Abulafia, D. and Berend, N. (eds) (2002) *Medieval Frontiers: Concepts and Practices*, Aldershot: Ashgate.

Allmand, C.T. (1968) 'The Lancastrian land settlement in Normandy, 1417–50', *Economic History Review*, 21(3): 461–79.

Allmand, C.T. (1983) *Lancastrian Normandy, 1415–50: The History of a Medieval Occupation*, Oxford: Oxford University Press.

Armstrong, J.W. (2022) 'Frontier', in J.W. Armstrong, P. Crooks and A. Ruddick (eds) *Using Concepts in Medieval History: Perspectives on Britain and Ireland, 1100–1500*, Cham: Springer, pp 89–106.

Armstrong, J.W., Crooks, P. and Ruddick, A. (2022) '"Tyrannous constructs" or tools of the trade? The use and abuse of concepts in medieval history', in J.W. Armstrong, P. Crooks and A. Ruddick (eds) *Using Concepts in Medieval History: Perspectives on Britain and Ireland, 1100–1500*, Cham: Springer, pp 1–14.

Bade, K. (2003) *Migration in European History*, Oxford: Basil Blackwell.

Bailey, M. (2014) *The Decline of Serfdom in Late Medieval England: From Bondage to Freedom*, Woodbridge: Boydell Press.

Bailey, M. (2021) *After the Black Death: Economy, Society and the Law in Fourteenth-Century England*, Oxford: Oxford University Press.

Barlow, F. (2002) *The Godwins*, Harlow: Pearson.

Barrow, G. (1989) 'Frontier and settlement: which influenced which?', in R. Bartlett and A. Mackay (eds) *Medieval Frontier Societies*, Oxford: Clarendon Press, pp 3–21.

Barrow, G. (2003) *The Kingdom of the Scots* (2nd edn), Edinburgh: Edinburgh University Press.

Bartlett, R. (2000) *England under the Norman and Angevin Kings, 1075–1225*, Oxford: Oxford University Press.

Bartlett, R. and Mackay, A. (eds) (1989) *Medieval Frontier Societies*, Oxford: Clarendon Press.

Berend, N. (2001) *At the Gate of Christendom: Jews, Muslims and 'Pagans' in Medieval Hungary, c. 1000-c. 1300*, Cambridge: Cambridge University Press.

Berry H.F. (ed) (1907) *Statutes and Ordinances and Acts of the Parliament of Ireland: King John to Henry V*, Dublin: His Majesty's Stationery Office.

Bolton, J. (2000) 'Irish migration to England in the late Middle Ages: the evidence of 1394 and 1440', *Irish Historical Studies*, 32(125): 1–21.

Border Force (nd) 'About us', *GOV.UK*. Available from: www.gov.uk/gov ernment/organisations/border-force/about (accessed 21 November 2023).

Brand, P. (1992) 'Chief Justice and felon: the career of Thomas Weyland', in P. Brand (ed) *The Making of the Common Law*, London: Hambledon Press, pp 113–33.

Brown, M.H. (2007) '*Scoti Anglicati*: Scots in Plantagenet allegiance during the fourteenth century', in A. King and M. Penman (eds) *England and Scotland in the Fourteenth Century: New Perspectives*, Woodbridge: Boydell Press, pp 94–115.

Campbell, B.M.S. (2016) *The Great Transition: Climate, Disease, and Society in the Late-Medieval World*, Cambridge: Cambridge University Press.

Childs, W. (2006) 'Moving around', in R. Horrox and W.M. Ormrod (eds) *A Social History England 1200–1500*, Cambridge: Cambridge University Press, pp 260–75.

Clark, E. (1994) 'Social welfare and mutual aid in the medieval countryside', *Journal of British Studies*, 33(4): 381–406.

Cohn, S.K., Jr (2013) *Popular Protest in Late Medieval English Towns*, Cambridge: Cambridge University Press.

Crook, D. (2020) *Robin Hood: Legend and Reality*, Woodbridge: Boydell Press.

Crooks, P. (2022) 'Colony', in J.W. Armstrong, P. Crooks and A. Ruddick (eds) *Using Concepts in Medieval History: Perspectives on Britain and Ireland, 1100–1500*, Cham: Springer, pp 51–71.

Davies, R.R. (1974) 'Colonial Wales', *Past and Present*, 65(1): 3–23.

Davies, R.R. (1984) 'Lordship or colony', in J. Lydon (ed) *The English in Medieval Ireland*, Dublin: Royal Irish Academy, pp 142–60.

Davies, R.R. (2000) *The First English Empire: Power and Identities in the British Isles, 1093–1343*, Cambridge: Cambridge University Press.

Davies, R.R. (2003) 'The medieval state: the tyranny of a concept?', *Journal of Historical Sociology*, 16(2): 280–300.

Dobson, B. (2000) 'General survey, 1300–1540', in D.M. Palliser (ed) *The Cambridge Urban History of Britain I: 600–1540*, Cambridge: Cambridge University Press, pp 273–90.

Duffy, S. (2005) 'Town and crown: the kings of England and their city of Dublin', in M. Prestwich, R. Britnell and R. Frame (eds) *Thirteenth Century England X*, Woodbridge: Boydell Press, pp 95–117.

Dyer, C. (2005) *An Age of Transition? Economy and Society in England in the Later Middle Ages*, Oxford: Oxford University Press.

Dyer, C. (2020) 'Migration in rural England in the later Middle Ages', in W.M. Ormrod, J. Story and E.M. Tyler (eds) *Migrants in Medieval England c.500- c.1500*, Oxford: Oxford University Press for the British Academy, pp 238–64.

Ellenblum, R. (2002) 'Were there borders and borderlines in the Middle Ages? The example of the Latin Kingdom of Jerusalem', in D. Abulafia and N. Berend (eds) *Medieval Frontiers: Concepts and Practices*, Aldershot: Ashgate, pp 105–20.

Ellis, S. (1999) 'The English state and its frontiers in the British Isles, 1300– 1600', in D. Power and N. Standen (eds) *Frontiers in Question: Eurasian Borderlands, 700–1700*, Basingstoke: MacMillan, pp 153–81.

Fleming, P. (2007) 'Identity and belonging: Irish and Welsh in fifteenth century Bristol', in L. Clark (ed) *The Fifteenth Century VII: Conflicts, Consequences and the Crown in the Late Middle Ages*, Woodbridge: Boydell Press, pp 175–93.

Frame, R. (1989) 'Military service in the Lordship of Ireland 1290– 1360: institutions and society on the Anglo-Gaelic Frontier', in R. Bartlett and A. Mackay (eds) *Medieval Frontier Societies*, Oxford: Clarendon Press, pp 101–26.

Frame, R. (2006) 'The wider world', in R. Horrox and W.M. Ormrod (eds) *A Social History England 1200–1500*, Cambridge: Cambridge University Press, pp 435–53.

Frame, R. (2012) *Colonial Ireland, 1169–1369* (2nd edn), Dublin: Four Courts Press.

Freeman, J. (2007) 'And he abjured the realm of England, never to return', in P. Horden (ed) *Freedom of Movement in the Middle Ages: Proceedings of the 2003 Harlaxton Symposium*, Donington: Shaun Tyas, pp 287–304.

Geary, P. (2003) *The Myth of Nations: The Medieval Origins of Europe*, Princeton, NJ: Princeton University Press.

Gibney, M.J. (2020) 'Banishment and the pre-history of legitimate expulsion power', *Citizenship Studies*, 24(3): 277–300.

Gillingham, J. (2014) *Conquests, Catastrophe and Recovery: Britain and Ireland, 1066–1485*, London: Penguin.

Given-Wilson, C. (2000) 'Service, freedom and English labour legislation, 1350–1500', in A. Curry and E. Matthew (eds) *Concepts and Patterns of Service in the Later Middle Ages*, Woodbridge: Boydell Press, pp 21–37.

Given-Wilson, C. (ed) (2005) *The Parliament Rolls of Medieval England, 1275–1504, Volume 7, Richard II, 1385–1397*, Woodbridge: Boydell Press and The National Archives.

Given-Wilson, C. (2017) *Henry IV*, New Haven, CT: Yale University Press.

Goldberg, P.J.P. (1992) *Women, Work and Life Cycle in a Medieval Economy: Women in York and Yorkshire, c.1300–1520*, Oxford: Oxford University Press.

Goldberg, P.J.P. (2004) 'Migration, youth and gender in later medieval England', in P.J.P. Goldberg and F. Riddy (eds) *Youth in the Middle Ages*, York: York Medieval Press, pp 85–99.

Golding, B. (1994) *Conquest and Colonisation: The Normans in Britain, 1066–1100*, Basingstoke: Palgrave MacMillan.

Goodman, A. (2011) 'Cary, Sir John (d. 1395), justice', *Oxford Dictionary of National Biography*. Available from: www.oxforddnb.com/view/10.1093/ref:odnb/9780198614128.001.0001/odnb-9780198614128-e-4839 (accessed 10 March 2023).

Greaves, D. (1918) 'Calais under Edward III', in G. Unwin (ed) *Finance and Trade under Edward III*, Manchester: Manchester University Press, pp 313–50.

Guenée, B. (1985) *States and Rulers in Later Medieval Europe* (2nd edn), trans J. Vale, Oxford: Basil Blackwell.

Hadfield, A. (1993) 'Briton and Scythian: Tudor representations of Irish origins', *Irish Historical Studies*, 28(112): 390–408.

Hagger, M.S. (2017) *Norman Rule in Normandy, 911–1144*, Woodbridge: Boydell Press.

Hand, G.J. (1967) *English Law in Ireland 1290–1324*, Cambridge: Cambridge University Press.

Harford, T. (2021) 'The undercover economist', *FT Weekend Magazine*, 21–22 August.

Hatcher, J. (1994) 'The aftermath of the Black Death', *Past and Present*, 144: 3–35.

Holmes, K. and Standen, N. (eds) (2018) 'The global Middle Ages', *Past and Present*, Supplement 13, Oxford: Oxford University Press.

Holt, J.C. (1997) *Colonial England, 1066–1215*, London: Hambledon Press.

Horden, P. (2007) 'Introduction: towards a history of medieval mobility', in P. Horden (ed) *Freedom of Movement in the Middle Ages: Proceedings of the 2003 Harlaxton Symposium*, Donington: Shaun Tyas, pp xvii–xxxiv.

Hunnisett, R.F. (1961) *The Medieval Coroner*, Cambridge: Cambridge University Press.

Hurnard, N.D. (1969) *The King's Pardon for Homicide before A.D. 1307*, Oxford: Clarendon Press.

Jordan, W.C. (2015) *From England to France: Felony and Exile in the High Middle Ages*, Princeton, NC: Princeton University Press.

Keen, M. (2000) *The Outlaws of Medieval Legend (rev edn)*, New York: Routledge.

Khazanov, A.M. (2015) 'Pastoral nomadic migrations and conquests', in B.Z. Kedar and M.E. Wiesner-Hanks (eds) *The Cambridge World History: Expanding Webs of Exchange and Conflict, 500 CE–1500 CE*, Cambridge: Cambridge University Press, pp 359–82.

Korngiebel, D.M. (2007) 'English colonial ethnic discrimination in the Lordship of Dyffryn Clwyd: segregation and integration, 1282-c.1340', *Welsh History Review*, 23(2): 1–24.

Le Patourel, J. (1984) 'L'occupation anglaise de Calais au XIVe siècle', in M. Jones (ed) *Feudal Empires: Norman and Plantagenet*, London: The Hambledon Press, pp 228–41.

Lieberman, M. (2010) *The Medieval March of Wales: The Creation and Perception of a Frontier, 1066–1283*, Cambridge: Cambridge University Press.

MacInnes, A.I. (2012) '"To be annexed forever to the English Crown": the English occupation of southern Scotland, c.1334–1337', in A. King and D. Simpkin (eds) *England and Scotland at War, c.1296-c1513*, Leiden: Brill, pp 183–201.

Massey, R. (1984) 'The land settlement in Lancastrian Normandy', in A.J. Pollard (ed) *Property and Politics: Essays in Later Medieval English History*, Gloucester: Alan Sutton, pp 76–91.

McSheffrey, S. (2017) *Seeking Sanctuary: Crime, Mercy and Politics in English Courts, 1400–1550*, Oxford: Oxford University Press.

Neville, C. (1998) *Violence, Custom and Law: The Anglo-Scottish Border Lands in the Later Middle Ages*, Edinburgh: Edinburgh University Press.

Neville, J. (2007) '"None shall pass": mental barriers to travel in Old English poetry', in P. Horden (ed) *Freedom of Movement in the Middle Ages: Proceedings of the 2003 Harlaxton Symposium*, Donington: Shaun Tyas, pp 203–14.

Oram, R. (2011) *Domination and Lordship: Scotland 1070–1230*, Edinburgh: Edinburgh University Press.

Ormrod, W.M. and Mackman, J. (2017) 'Resident aliens in later medieval England: sources, contexts and debates', in W.M. Ormrod, N. McDonald and C. Taylor (eds) *Resident Aliens in Later Medieval England*, Turnhout: Brepols, pp 3–32.

Ormrod, W.M., Lambert, B. and Mackman, J. (2019) *Immigrant England, 1300–1550*, Manchester: Manchester University Press.

Palmer, R.C. (1993) *English Law in the Age of the Black Death, 1348–1381: A Transformation of Governance and Law*, Chapel Hill: University of North Carolina Press.

Parsons, S.T. (2019) 'The inhabitants of the British Isles on the first crusade: medieval perceptions and the invention of a pan-Angevin crusading heritage', *English Historical Review*, 134(567): 273–301.

Pollock, F. and Maitland, F.W. (1968) *The History of English Law Before the Time of Edward I*, (2nd edn, reissued with a new introduction and select bibliography by S.F.C. Milsom), Vol 2, Cambridge: Cambridge University Press.

Postles, D.A. (2000) 'Migration and mobility in a less mature economy: English internal migration, c.1200–1350', *Social History*, 25(3): 285–99.

Power, D. (1999) 'French and Norman frontiers in the central Middle Ages', in D. Power and N. Standen (eds) *Frontiers in Question: Eurasian Borderlands, 700–1700*, Basingstoke: MacMillan, pp 105–27.

Power, D. and Standen, N. (eds) (1999) *Frontiers in Question: Eurasian Borderlands, 700–1700*, Basingstoke: MacMillan.

Prestwich, M. (2005) *Plantagenet England, 1225–1360*, Oxford: Oxford University Press.

Razi, Z. (1993) 'The myth of the immutable English family', *Past and Present*, 140(1): 3–44.

Rose, S. (2008) *Calais: An English Town in France, 1347–1558*, Cambridge: Cambridge University Press.

Ruddick, A. (2013) *English Identity and Political Culture in the Fourteenth Century*, Cambridge: Cambridge University Press.

Saul, N. (1997) *Richard II*, New Haven, CT: Yale University Press.

Scales, L. (2007) 'Bread, cheese and genocide: imagining the destruction of peoples in medieval Western Europe', *History*, 92(3): 284–300.

Schmidt, A.V.C. (1992) *Piers Plowman: A New Translation of the B-Text*, trans, with introduction and notes, A.V.C. Schmidt, Oxford: Oxford University Press.

Schofield, P. (2003) *Peasant and Community in Medieval England 1200–1500*, Basingstoke: Macmillan.

Searle, E. (1988) *Predatory Kingship and the Creation of Norman Power*, Berkeley: University of California Press.

Sharma, N. and Wright, C. (2008) 'Decolonizing resistance, challenging colonial states', *Social Justice*, 35(3): 120–38.

Shoemaker, K. (2011) *Sanctuary and Crime in the Middle Ages, 400–1500*, New York: Fordham University Press.

Steinfeld, R. (1991) *The Invention of Free Labour: The Employment Relation in English and American Law and Culture, 1350–1870*, Chapel Hill: University of North Carolina Press.

Summerson, H.R.T. (1979) 'The structure of law enforcement in thirteenth century England', *The American Journal of Legal History*, 23(4): 313–27.

Tout, T.F. (1919) 'Medieval town planning', *The Town Planning Review*, 8(1): 7–36.

Urry, J. (2007) *Mobilities*, Oxford: Polity Press.

Veracini, L. (2010) *Settler Colonialism: A Theoretical Overview*, Basingstoke: Palgrave MacMillan.

Watson, F. (1998) *Under the Hammer: Edward I and Scotland, 1286–1307*, East Linton: Tuckwell Press.

Watts, J. (2002) 'Looking for the state in later medieval England', in P. Coss and M. Keen (eds) *Heraldry, Pageantry and Social Display in Medieval England*, Woodbridge: Boydell Press, pp 243–68.

Wilson, E. (2018) *Homer, The Odyssey*, trans E. Wilson, New York: W.W. Norton & Co.

6

The Aliens Order 1920, the 'Work Permit' and the Making of the National Labour Market

Manoj Dias-Abey

Introduction

The early 20th century was marked by growing attempts to regulate the movement of people across the globe. The preceding period – identified as the 'age of capital' by Eric Hobsbawm in his famous tetralogy – was characterized by growth in mobility and 'money, goods and men moved smoothly and with increasing rapidity' (Hobsbawn, 1975, p 64). The increasing support for restricting the movement of goods and people was very much a global phenomenon, with several countries, including the US, introducing restrictive immigration policies during this period (Timmer and Williams, 1998).

In the British Empire, various pieces of legislation were introduced between 1905 and 1925 which sought to control the entry of 'aliens' to the British Isles. Alien is a legal term of uncertain provenance, but by the 20th century it was taken to mean someone who was not a subject of the Crown.[1] These early attempts at immigration control did not initially apply to the entry of colonial subjects of the British Empire, nor after 1923 to members of the Irish Free State, since these people were not considered aliens at law. This omission from the scope of immigration controls in the case of colonial subjects was likely the result of the small numbers arriving from the peripheries in the early 20th century (Holmes, 1988), while maintaining a Common Travel Area with the Irish Free State was an important aspect of keeping it within the Commonwealth (Ryan, 2001).

The Aliens Order 1920, an Order in Council[2] promulgated under the Aliens Restriction (Amendment) Act 1919, was a particularly important legal intervention in British immigration law. The Aliens Order sought to achieve many objectives, but most crucially, it required any alien coming to the UK with the intention of seeking employment to produce a permit, issued to their employer by the Ministry of Labour. For the duration of the entire interwar period, when high unemployment was an overriding concern, the Ministry of Labour rarely granted such permission. We can think of the Aliens Order 1920 as introducing for the first time into British immigration law the regulatory instrument of the 'work permit', which I define as *the conditional grant of state authorization for a foreigner to participate in the labour market*. The work permit was one of the earliest attempts at aligning immigration with labour market policy and linking immigration to labour market conditions. It went on to have a profound impact on the way that immigration has been thought about, rationalized and regulated ever since.

Curiously, the Aliens Order 1920 has not received a significant amount of academic attention, and the introduction of the work permit even less so. Scholars who have considered the Aliens Order 1920 have tended to focus on some of its other elements, such the medical inspection regime that it consolidated (Taylor, 2016) or the architecture it created for later interventions that regulated the lives of colonial subjects residing in the metropole (Tabili, 1994). One reason for this oversight might be that the Aliens Order is seen simply as one part in a series of escalating immigration controls that started to be introduced in 1905. Collectively, scholars have regarded these interventions as deriving from the legacy of colonialism (El-Enany, 2020) or an ineluctable consequence of the development of the welfare state (Torpey, 2003). Both of these arguments have some explanatory force. It is clear that a colonial mindset that rigidly categorized people according to a racial hierarchy, as well as anti-Semitism in British political culture, combined to create a groundswell of opinion against aliens, who were mostly Jewish migrants seeking refuge from pogroms in Eastern Europe and Russia. This was, at least in the case of the Aliens Act 1905, the proximate reason for its enactment (Holmes, 1988). Similarly, it is plausible that questions of belonging and entitlement inevitably come to the fore when the state turns its mind to provision of social goods. Lending support to this thesis, when several state welfare measures were introduced between 1906 and 1920, many contained prohibitions on unnaturalized aliens accessing entitlements (Cohen, 1985). Therefore, it is reasonable to see immigration controls as a consequence of the development of the social state.

Neither of these explanations, however, provide a persuasive account of why the Aliens Order 1920, and the work permit in particular, were introduced. This chapter shows that high unemployment and rising labour militancy in the post-war period were in fact the more relevant factors when it came to the introduction of the Aliens Order 1920. Together, these form what I term the 'labour market rationale' for the introduction and design of immigration controls, which would go on to have an enormous role in shaping immigration law over the 20th and 21st centuries. Beginning in the late 19th century, unemployment had been growing as an area of sociopolitical concern, and increasingly strident demands were being made for government intervention to reduce its incidence and duration (Harris, 1972; Whiteside, 1991; Whiteside and Gillespie, 1991; Whiteside, 2014). Given this context, the sharp rise in unemployment which occurred in the wake of the Great War led to demands that the government take strong action to manage it (Garside, 1990). In addition, labour militancy was also on the rise in the period following the war and controlling the labour market access of foreigners allowed the government to appease the more nativist wing of the labour movement. The introduction of the work permit gave the appearance that the government was carefully calibrating the access of outsiders to the labour market to suit prevailing economic conditions in Britain, even if, in practice, limiting work opportunities of migrants did little to assist the unemployed.

The second argument that this chapter makes is that the Aliens Order 1920, and the work permit in particular, helped make a distinctly *national* labour market. The work permit could be used as a tool to mould the national labour market by increasing the supply of workers, adding workers with particular skills to the existing workforce and influencing the balance of power between employers and employees. Regulatory instruments can also constitute markets imaginatively. The introduction of the work permit was pivotal in constructing the labour market as a national institution from which those who did not belong to 'Greater Britain' were excluded. Seeing social phenomena at the level of the nation often involves feats of imagination (Anderson, 2006), and a whole range of practices, from collecting national statistics (Tooze, 1998) to applying uniform administrative practices, can help bring into being and reify a *national* labour market.

In the next section, I survey the main forms of immigration control implemented between 1905 and 1916 and show that they laid the legal and institutional groundwork for the Aliens Order 1920. I then provide a history of the two-year period leading up to the introduction of the Aliens Order 1920. To properly understand why the Order came into force, we need to analyse the developments in the British labour market in the aftermath of the Great War, the positions adopted by key actors and the rapidly changing ideas about the extent of permissible government intervention. I follow this by setting out the main features of the Aliens Order 1920, and the Coloured Seamen Order 1925, which came soon after. I also briefly trace the afterlife of the work permit as an important feature of immigration law over the 20th century and the first two decades of the 21st. Finally, I conclude by explaining how the work permit played a prominent role in consolidating a national labour market, amenable to government intercession, over the course of subsequent decades.

Laying the groundwork for the Aliens Order 1920: immigration controls between 1905 and 1916

The first stirrings of the turn to immigration control in the UK began in 1905 with the passage of the Aliens Act. What led to an Empire in thrall to the ideas – if not necessarily always the practice – of free trade, unhindered commerce and liberal toleration to proceed down the path of immigration control in this period? The 1905 Act was clearly a response to the growing chorus of racially charged complaint that was being expressed in the last two decades of the 19th century (Holmes, 1988). Some 150,000 Jews arrived in Britain between 1880 and 1914 – most settling in the East End of London and other industrial centres – and they faced hostility from higher and lower ends of British society (Winder, 2005, p 229). Although the British working class had made great strides in combatting anti-Irish racism over the course of the 19th century, anti-Semitism continued to be a feature of working-class politics (Virdee, 2014, pp 32–55). This anti-Semitism was so potent because it was closely tied up with ideas about racial classification and hierarchy that were commonplace in late Victorian Britain (Malik, 2023, pp 95–116). Several trade union leaders and socialist activists demanded the imposition of immigration controls (Cohen, 1985), and their calls were also supported by influential elites in Parliament and among the intelligentsia. Two of the most notorious in the latter camp were journalist Arnold White, famous for writing several widely read screeds on the topic, and Member of Parliament (MP) for Stepney, William Evans-Gordon, who was one of the founders of the proto-fascist British Brother's League.

The Conservative–Liberal Unionist government responded to this clamour by establishing a Royal Commission on Alien Immigration in 1902. During the proceedings, several grievances were raised, including that the newcomers worked for a pittance, were liable to become a burden on the state, contributed to urban overcrowding and housing squalor, and carried dangerous disease (Royal Commission on Alien Immigration, 1903, paras 37–8). Labour market concerns, including the impact of migration on employment opportunities and working conditions, also featured heavily in the public debate. Despite Britain's position as an imperial power (in which emigration was a vital component), and the relevance of the global political economy, the scale of the debate was very much *national*. Moreover, the Royal Commission found little evidence of these effects, but nevertheless a majority of members recommended that a department of immigration be established and a division of immigration officers be appointed to act as sentries, with these officers to be given the power to exclude 'undesirables'.

The Royal Commission also recommended restricting the settlement of aliens in parts of the country subject to overcrowding. The government's attempt to pass a Bill based on the Royal Commission's recommendations failed, but a weaker version was enacted in the form of the Aliens Act 1905, which required all ships carrying more than 20 immigrant aliens in steerage to disembark at a designated port so that all passengers could be examined by immigration officers (ss 1 and 8). Under the Act, officers were given the power to exclude 'undesirable' aliens, defined as those who lacked the means to support themselves, had been sentenced for a crime, were an 'idiot or lunatic' or had been previously excluded (s 3). Notably, an exception was made for aliens who could prove they were escaping political or religious persecution, and an appeal process was established to provide the opportunity to challenge immigration officers' decision-making. The proposal to place restrictions on where aliens could settle never made it into the legislation. Movement of imperial subjects to the British Isles was unaffected by this statute, but in practice, with the exception of 'lascars' (sailors who were colonial subjects), few other than the very privileged arrived.

Ultimately, because of the limited powers given to the Aliens Inspectorate, the exclusion of political refugees from the scope of the Act and the role of the immigration appeals boards, the Act was unsuccessful in stemming the entry of aliens (Dummett and Nicol, 1990). Notwithstanding, the Aliens Act 1905 was a significant change. First, at the level of ideology, the 1905 statute pierced the consensus about leaving alien immigration unregulated, which led to a series of intensifying legislative interventions over the next decade. Second, the administrative architecture that was established was vital to the operation of future immigration controls. A corps of immigration officers was established, and a civil servant was situated within the Home Office, appointed as 'H.M. Inspector under the Aliens Act', to oversee the new inspection regime (Roche, 1969, p 72).

On the day after the UK declared war on Germany, the government drew on this administrative architecture to implement further immigration controls of a truly draconian nature. Originally intended as a temporary wartime measure, the Aliens Restriction Act 1914 authorized the government to make Orders in Council under broad headings. Orders were to follow that were used to prohibit all aliens from landing, impose severe restrictions on those allowed to enter and provide the government with the power to deport aliens. War hysteria created the cover for these enormously wide-ranging powers, which included the power to control not only the entry of people but also the conditions of their stay as well as their removal without any right of appeal. Several further Orders in Council were made during the Great War, including an Order in 1915 requiring all aliens to hold a passport or other identity document and be subject to inspection by an immigration officer, and an Order in 1916 obliging all those allowed to enter to register with the police. Another piece of legislation, the British Nationality and Status of Aliens Act 1914, was passed during this period which set in statute the process by which an alien could become naturalized as a British subject.

Unemployment and unrest: the context of the Aliens Order 1920

The political economy of Britain when the armistice was signed on 11 November 1918 was radically different from its pre-war form. After the war, it soon became clear that there would be no going back to pre-war economic conditions, as British exports had lost significant market share during the war and domestic consumption was down due to price inflation (Clarke, 1996, p 96). Demobilized soldiers in particular had great difficulty finding work. As the size of the armed forces was reduced from 4.5 million in 1918 to less than a million by 1920, unemployment continued to rise, ending up at 11 per cent by 1921, which equated to 2.2 million people out of work (Weldon, 2021, pp 141–2). This was in sharp contrast to the war years, when one of the critical issues was the availability of workers to produce the massive quantities of materiel (military equipment and supplies) that the war devoured. The labour shortages during the war meant that unemployment receded in importance as a national issue, but it returned as an issue of national prominence when unemployment started climbing upwards following the conclusion of the Great War.

The large numbers out of work caused a significant amount of ferment and this formed the background as the provisions of the Aliens Restriction (Amendment) Bill were being debated in Parliament in 1919. During the war, national trade unions had agreed to suspend strikes in exchange for arbitration for wages and conditions of work (Deakin and Wilkinson, 2005, p 235). Although there had been sporadic labour actions at particular workplaces led by rank and file members, the labour movement as a whole was mostly quiescent. Trade union membership, however, continued to grow over this period, increasing from 4 million in 1914 to 6.5 million at the end of 1918 (Cole, 1948, p 385). After the war, employers took advantage of the economic situation to cut wages and hours, which affected the working conditions of union members. These actions were met with widespread strikes across the entire economy. Whereas an average of 632,000 days had been lost to strike action during the entire period between 1914 and 1918, an average of over two million days per year were lost between 1919 and 1921 (Virdee, 2014, p 78). Given the recent success of the Bolshevik revolution in Russia in 1917, senior members of the government were also paranoid that the idea of radical socialism was animating these strikes (Butler, 2019).

It was predictable that an election called in the immediate aftermath of the war would arouse ugly strains of nationalism. The result was a landslide for the governing Coalition government, comprising Conservatives and Coalition Liberals. In his coruscating text on the victors' attitude towards Germany, *The Economic Consequences of the Peace*, John Maynard Keynes described the elections as being characterized by a lust for vengeance (1920, ch IV, pt 2; cf Morgan, 1979). Another commentator observed that the 'campaign of the Coalition began with the accent on reconstruction; it ended with demands for revenge upon Germany' (Havinghurst, 1979, p 148). The desire for retribution was in evidence in several of the points in the Coalition's manifesto. The Coalition promised to pursue maximum indemnities from the Germans for the costs of the war and seek punishment for those who had committed atrocities. On the domestic front, the Coalition promised, ominously, to create a 'Britain for the British, socially and industrially'. These demands were also coming from some segments of the labour movement who were not always inclined to distinguish between 'enemy aliens' living in Britain, other aliens who had made their home here (for example, Russian Jews) and British subjects from colonies who had contributed significantly to the war effort. As a result, the uptick in working-class militancy during this period was accompanied by violence and discrimination against Jewish people as well as those from the British colonies (Virdee, 2014, p 80).

Renewing the immigration restrictions that had been temporarily introduced at the start of the war provided a means for the newly elected Coalition government to both address the revolt of labour and sate the electors' demand for revenge. In April 1919, the Home Secretary, Edward Shortt, introduced the Aliens Restriction (Amendment) Bill into Parliament to continue the emergency wartime immigration legislation for a period of one year. The Bill proposed to utilize the same mechanism that the Aliens Restriction Act 1914 had introduced: legislative provisions providing the Executive wide-ranging powers to bring into force Orders in Council for the control, management, detention and deportation of aliens (s 1). The government's thinking was that this would give the Home Office maximum flexibility to deal with any exigencies that arose. The Bill also contained express provisions to give the government power to deport those engaged in sedition in the armed forces or among the civilian population, as well as excluding those promoting 'industrial unrest' in an industry in which the accused was not legitimately employed for a period of at least two years prior to the alleged commission of the offence (s 3). In these two provisions, we see clearly distilled the government's aim to assuage anti-German sentiment, clamp down on labour militancy and keep at bay political radicalism. The legislation did not go far enough for some, and a faction of the Home Secretary's Coalition colleagues – known as the Tory 'Die-Hards' – sought amendments to strengthen government's powers to deport enemy aliens and place employment restrictions on *all* aliens (Morgan, 1979, pp 238–9).

During the Parliamentary debate the issue of the employment of aliens featured prominently. The idea that restricting the employment of aliens would materially affect the employment opportunities of native British workers was preposterous, particularly because the industries affected by the downturn were not necessarily those employing aliens in any significant number. However, feeling rather than fact carried the day. When the Aliens Restriction (Amendment) Bill was in the Committee stage, some of the Tory Die-Hards tried unsuccessfully to force an amendment so that all British enterprises employing more than five workers would be restricted from employing aliens at a proportion greater than 10 per cent of their total workforce. To head off any doubts about the fact that the government did not intend to be tough on aliens once the Bill passed, the Home Secretary published a copy of a draft Order in Council that his government expected to promulgate if the Bill was passed. Since the turn of the century, the Home Office had been increasingly playing a role in the drafting of bills and regulations (Pellew, 1982), and it is likely that it had a large hand in the drafting of the Aliens Order. The personnel that were responsible for the Aliens Act 1905 were still in charge a decade and a half later, so continuity in approach was maintained with earlier legislative interventions (Cesarani, 1992).

The draft Order in Council proposed to deal with the issue of employment by restricting the employment prospects of all *future* aliens rather than leaving aliens already in the country without employment and made destitute. The instrument that the government alighted on to achieve this end was the work permit. Under the draft Order in Council, all aliens arriving in the UK and seeking to join the labour market would henceforth be required to produce a work permit issued by the Ministry of Labour granting a specific employer permission to employ the alien. These provisions did not satisfy the Tory Die-Hards and the MP Ronald McNeill (1919) put forward his case most forcefully:

> But we have long ago gone away from that old Free Trade argument, as regards labour at all events, and it is quite well recognised, by nobody so strongly as by Honourable Members opposite, that we cannot allow our own labour to be subjected to the free play of the labour market of the world, and that we must give protection of some sort to it. Therefore, it is quite in line with what has been not only the policy of the Labour party but the policy of practically all parties in this country for a long time past, to restrict in some sense, at all events, the competition coming from abroad into our own labour market. I think the experience of the War convinced the people of this country that they had been going far too much in an easy-going, thoughtless manner with regard to their own nationality and their own

employment, and if we are to have a change in this respect they are resolved for the future to keep employment in this country for our own people to a large extent.

It was also clear during the parliamentary debate that the target of this provision was not simply Germans. The independent MP for Hertford, Noel Billing (1919), told the House of Commons that he wanted to see his country 'saved from the Asiatic'. Despite gaining significant support in the House, the amendment failed with 205 voting against and 130 in favour. In an almost perfect illustration of the constrained contingency of human history, this meant that the path chosen to limit the labour market access of aliens followed the work permit model instead of setting workplace quotas for the employment of aliens.

The Aliens Order 1920 and the Coloured Seamen Order 1925

Under the terms of the Aliens Order 1920, no alien was permitted to land without receiving leave from an immigration officer at an approved port. The immigration officer was required to exclude those who fell into any one of the categories originally set out in the Aliens Act 1905 (s 1(3)). Most significantly for our purposes, any alien intending to join the labour market was required to produce a work permit, issued by the Ministry of Labour, to their intended employer (s 1(3)(b)). The ministry usually granted work permits for a 12-month duration, although it was possible to obtain extensions (Newsome, 1955). The person was required to work exclusively for the employer listed on the work permit and could only change employment with prior permission from the ministry. For those of independent means, the lack of a work permit did not prevent entry unless they were barred for other reasons. Once an alien was permitted entry, s 6 required that they register, in his or her district of registration, with a registration officer. Further, an immigration officer was empowered to impose additional conditions on entry (Scott, 1932, p 34). The Aliens Order took a particularly expansive approach to the issue of deportation by giving the home secretary wide-ranging powers to make an order in a broad range of circumstances. All things considered, the Aliens Order 1920 was a significant milestone in the history of immigration control.

Of course, it did not end there, for 'anti-alien discourse by definition had no boundary: it comprehended everything that was "Other" to British and Englishness' (Cesarani, 1992, p 36). It was already clear during the parliamentary debate that the target of this provision was not simply Germans. From the outset there was pressure applied on the Home Office, as the government department primarily responsible for immigration enforcement, to apply the provisions of the Aliens Order 1920 to the population of colonial British subjects who were living in port cities and working in the maritime industry. The war effort had created significant labour shortages in the merchant shipping industry and employers had recruited widely from the colonies to make up the shortfall. At the end of the war, almost 20 per cent of the British maritime labour force were Indian seamen (Visram, 2002). When returning seamen found themselves competing for jobs with Arab, Asian and Black workers, their response was to demand restrictions on the employment of colonial labour in the shipping industry. Infamously, the period between January and August 1919 was marked by riots and racially motivated attacks in seaports from London to Liverpool to Glasgow (Jenkinson, 2009).

Initially, the Home Office resisted efforts to apply the provisions of the Aliens Act 1920 to seafarers, but the pressure from the National Union of Seamen, local authorities and other government departments, such as the Board of Trade, proved too insistent (Tabili, 1994, p 118). The hope was that the Home Office would force these workers to register under the terms of the Aliens Act 1920 and, eventually, repatriate them to their countries of origin. The nationality of some of those that came to the attention of the Home Office was genuinely in question, but the vast majority were British subjects, a fact which the Home Office was fully cognisant of. There were various efforts by organizations, such as the Indian Seamen's Union and the Seamen's Minority Movement, to organize workers across colour lines and build internationalism, but their actions were not sufficient to challenge the prevailing xenophobia (Visram, 2002).

It was not long before the Home Office issued the Coloured Seamen Order 1925 under Article 2 of the Aliens Order 1920 to resolve this anomaly. Under the terms of this new measure, a 'coloured' seaman who could not provide documentary evidence of their British subject status was deemed to be an alien. In practice, any evidence produced by those targeted was regularly judged to be insufficient. Tabili has argued that the 'enduring result of the Coloured Alien Seamen Order was the codification of a hierarchical definition of British nationality dependent on race, class, and occupation' (1994, p 122). This was one of the early progenitors of what appear on paper to be racially neutral laws (but in practice were racially discriminatory) that would come to characterize immigration law throughout the 20th century.

The afterlife of the work permit

The Aliens Restriction (Amendment Act) 1919 and the Orders in Council passed under its authority were only intended to be in force for a year, yet these powers were continued from year to year until 1971. At various points, more liberally minded MPs sought to seek the repeal of these provisions, but to little avail. The usual catalogue of grievances was aired each time a parliamentary debate on the subject was conducted. As worded in a piece in *The Times* (1924b), repealing the rules would 'open the door to an influx of strangers drawn from the poorest quarters of Eastern Europe'. These warnings had some traction because unemployment remained stubbornly high during the interwar years, hovering somewhere between one million and three million out of work (Garside, 1990). Further, underemployment, even if it was not always counted in the various measures of unemployment that existed at the time, also continued to plague Britain (Whiteside and Gillespie, 1991). This was the context in which the Home Office rarely granted entry to aliens during this period. Even when the Home Office began to relax entry for refugees from Europe between 1937 and 1939 – by administratively resurrecting the distinction between refugee and alien that was contained in the Alien Act 1905 – work permits were seldom granted by the Ministry of Labour (Isaac, 1954, p 13). Any indication that the government was relaxing its attitude to the grant of work permits elicited furious responses, such as in 1924 when the Workers' Union made strong representations to the Ministry of Labour that aliens were being granted permission to work in hospitality (The Times, 1924a). When the Ministry of Labour did positively exercise its discretion, the small number of work permits granted were for entertainers (Newsome, 1955, p 97) or relatively uncontroversial occupations such as *monteurs* (a type of engine fitter) or onion sellers (Roche, 1969, p 108).

During World War II, labour shortages once again began to be felt right across the economy. The government responded by launching various schemes to bring in skilled labour from the colonies. For example, the Overseas Volunteer Scheme allowed men with engineering degrees from the West Indies or skilled tradesmen from India to come to Britain to be trained in government training centres and be placed within industry, such as with aircraft manufacturers (Isaac, 1954). These migrants did not require a work permit, since they were British subjects, and the government could control their entry through the visa system. However, once the war ended, the work permit system was resuscitated and used to allow European migrants, primarily from the north-west of the continent, to enter the UK and work. Close to 136,000 work permits were granted between 1945 and 1950, with the majority going to those doing care work, working in industry, or participating in work experience assignments while studying (Salt and Bauer, 2020, p 15). Notably, the Ministry of Labour required that employers now demonstrate that the wages and conditions of potential migrant employees were no less favourable than those given to British workers in similar work in the relevant trade and district (Isaac, 1954, pp 166–71). When the need for migrant workers increased sharply during the economic boom that marked the post-war period, this demand was met, for the most part, by migration from countries that were former colonies of the British Empire (Castles and Kosack, 1985).

When policy makers were deciding on how they could restrict migration from the new Commonwealth while maintaining the facade of a race-neutral migration policy, a decision was made to apply the work permit system to Commonwealth citizens for the first time. Under s 3(a) of the Commonwealth Immigrants Act 1962, a Commonwealth citizen had to produce a 'voucher' issued by the Ministry of Labour to an immigration officer if he or she wished to work in the UK. The Ministry of Labour issued three categories of work voucher: 'Category A' for those with a specific job offer; 'Category B' for skilled workers; and 'Category C' for unskilled workers (the latter was subject to various quotas; Hansen, 2000, p 110). For all intents and purposes, the work voucher was still a work permit, though they were not time limited, and Category B and C vouchers allowed for a measure of labour market mobility.

After the UK joined the European Economic Community in 1973, the principle of free movement meant that it became unnecessary for Europeans from member states to seek work permits altogether. This, however, did not herald the end of the work permit system. After Thatcher's Conservative government introduced the British Nationality Act 1981, citizens of the former colonies lost their privileged access to the UK. For the next two decades, work permits were issued only in very limited numbers for highly skilled jobs in sectors such as finance and IT, and those granted work permits were primarily from Australia, India, Japan and the US (Salt and Bauer, 2020, p 21). The immigration reforms implemented by the Labour government in the early 2000s extended work permits to cover both high skilled occupations and areas facing specific labour shortages, and today the work permit system continues to be the mainstay of the post-Brexit immigration system (Dias-Abey, 2022).

The making of the national labour market

The claim that the work permit contributes to the making of the labour market operates at two distinct levels. The first sense in which the work permit makes the labour market is that it controls the size of the market by increasing or decreasing the supply of workers as circumstances necessitate (Davies and Freedland, 1984). The work permit system allows government actors to influence not only the size but also the make-up of the (legal) labour market. By adding various conditions for the grant of a work permit – for example, salary and training requirements – those administering the system can choose to introduce workers with certain human capital endowments into the labour market. The work permit also constitutes particular power relations within a labour market. At most points in its hundred-year history, a work permit has only been granted to a worker with a specific job offer, and then only for a limited time. It has remained within the discretion of the Ministry of Labour (and its later incarnations) to allow an extension or a transfer from one employer to another. This means to be able to renew their permit and continue to work, a permit holder is dependent on their existing employer to offer ongoing work or, if they are to change employers, on another employer to make a new job offer. The work permit hence provides employers with another mechanism of control and shifts power decidedly in their favour (Anderson, 2010).

The second sense in which the work permit has made the labour market is that it has helped consolidate a vision of the labour market at a national scale. Over the course of the 20th century, Britain went from being a globally oriented, free trading, world hegemon to a conventional nation state, albeit one made up of four 'nations' with distinct identities and governing structures. Historians disagree on the precise point at which Empire gave way to the nation state, with some seeing the end of World War II as a pivotal moment (Edgerton, 2018) and others positioning the end of the British Empire several decades later (Darwin, 2009). The introduction of the work permit in 1920 suggests nationalizing tendencies within the labour market were operating earlier. Adam Tooze has argued that the national economy is a 'product of a dramatic process of imaginative abstraction and representational labour' (1998, p 214), and we could say much the same about the national labour market. The labour market is of course an abstraction we use to describe the sum totality of the contractual relationships between those who buy and sell their labour power. In such abstract conceptualizations, the geographical scale at which the labour market operates remains underspecified (Peck, 1996). What the work permit helps communicate is a vision of the labour market as coterminous with the physical boundaries of the British Isles, because the administrative arrangements around the work permit presupposes state actors – officials at the Ministry of Labour and immigration inspectors at ports of landing – acting as guardians preventing external parties accessing the national labour market.

To claim that the national labour market is a feat of imagination does not mean that it does not operate as such. Beginning in the early 20th century, a national labour market was coming into being as a result of two main reforms. First, the creation of national labour exchanges in 1908 aimed to encourage those out of work to seek opportunities further afield. Second, the formation of the Ministry of Labour in 1916 inaugurated a national field of vision among policy makers, because departmental officials were required to collect and publish national statistics about 'manpower' and industrial relations issues, and to devise and implement solutions that were national in scope (Ince, 1960). Although in most cases workers still acquired their jobs through local channels, a national labour market was beginning to take hold because of increasing worker mobility and increasing centralized bureaucratic control.

Once a labour market is imagined at a national scale, it becomes an object of knowledge and politics that creates the conditions for further intervention. We can see this process clearly at play if we focus on the factors that led to the introduction of the work permit and the chain reaction that its introduction set in motion. In the aftermath of World War I, the labour market was characterized by widespread unemployment and labour militancy, including by colonial subjects and aliens. These two facts of the labour market were front and centre in the minds of legislators and policy makers, and this resulted in a decision to control the labour market access of aliens and, later, the small number of colonial subjects working in Britain. The very fact that government intervention in this form was contemplated was the result of two previous developments. First, the legislation introduced between 1906 and 1914 to address unemployment had already constructed the labour market as an object of knowledge and politics capable of being shaped by government action. Second, the capacity to operationalize the work permit rested on an institutional architecture, such as the body of immigration inspectors with expertise to monitor those entering at ports, which was the result of the earlier Aliens Act 1905. Once the work permit had been implemented, it only reinforced the idea that the national labour market could be shaped and moulded through government action. Over the course of the next few decades, this new conceptualization of the labour market enabled much more radical forms of government action to achieve labour market outcomes. We can see that a variety of labour market interventions, such as labour law, income policy, social welfare entitlements and, most relevantly, immigration controls, were implemented in the post–World War II period based on newer ideas about the labour market and its malleability.

Conclusion

When policy makers look at a problem and seek to devise solutions, they cannot but help reaching back into the past. In the case of migration, the history that is commonly referenced is the wave of migration from the former colonies that took place in the period 1950–70 (see, for example, Patel, 2021). There is no doubt those who migrated in this period have changed the face of British society in profound ways. Three snippets illustrate the significance of this period. Until very recently, the UK's government was led by Rishi Sunak, a prime minister who is a direct descendant of people that came to the UK in this wave of migration, as are several other members of his Cabinet, including current and previous holders of the office of the home secretary (see Chapter 11 in this volume). Some of those who bore the brunt of the government's 'hostile environment' policies introduced in

2012 were members of the 'Windrush generation'. And across England and Wales, among the 'non-White' population who constitute almost one fifth of the population, the vast majority can directly trace their lineage to migrants who entered in the post-World War II period. Thus, the migration in this period is highly relevant to understanding Britain today.

Nonetheless, if we want to understand the rules that govern migration, the regulatory infrastructure and our conceptual frameworks informing the regulatory design of the migration system, we need to cast our minds back to an earlier period: 1905–25. The history of migration regulation in the early decades of the 20th century deserves its moment in the limelight of notoriety. For it was in this period that the UK first started to impose immigration controls on those who were seeking to enter its territory. The first legislative intervention, the Aliens Act 1905, sought to limit the entry of aliens by creating a corps of immigration officers who were empowered to turn away 'undesirable' migrants as defined in the legislation. In practice, this legislation achieved very little other than to shatter the consensus against immigration controls that had held sway throughout the 19th century. Next came the Aliens Restriction Act 1914, enacted at the start of World War I, which led to an almost total bar on alien entry, hastened the widespread usage of passports and resulted in the development of a deportation structure. When the Aliens Restriction (Amendment) Act 1919 was passed, it gave authority to the government to promulgate the Aliens Order 1920. Under that Order, the government started to closely connect migration with labour market conditions in its thinking and, in terms of practice, to treat entry as separate to the *privilege* of labour market access. A mere five years later, the application of the Aliens Order 1920 was extended to colonial subjects as a result of a new Order in Council, the Coloured Seamen Order 1925, thereby creating a system of racial stratification of which today's segmented labour market still bears traces. These developments are absolutely key to understanding how and why the UK regulates migration in the way it does today.

Notes

[1] Under the common law, an 'alien' was understood to mean 'one who is born out of the faith and allegiance of the King of England, and of parents owing no obedience to him' (C. Okey, cited in Rawlings, 2021, p 2). Section 27 of the British Nationality and Status of Aliens Act 1914 defined an alien simply as a 'a person who is not a British subject'. See also Smith, this volume.

[2] This was an order made by the Monarch on the advice of the Privy Council and authorized under statute or the Crown's prerogative powers and not subject to Parliamentary debate.

References

Anderson, B. (2006) *Imagined Communities: Reflections on the Origin and Spread of Nationalism*, London: Verso Books.

Anderson, B. (2010) 'Migration, immigration controls and the fashioning of precarious workers', *Work, Employment and Society*, 24(2): 300–17.

Billing, N. (1919) 'Aliens Restriction Bill', Hansard: House of Commons debates, 22 October 1919, vol 120 col 86. Available from: https://hansard.parliament.uk/Commons/1919-10-22/debates/4846bacd-a12b-4cb0-b466-692d8e3cc48e/CommonsChamber (accessed 19 May 2024).

Butler, W. (2019) '"The British soldier is no Bolshevik": the British Army, discipline, and the demobilization strikes of 1919', *20th Century British History*, 30(3): 321–46.

Castles, S. and Kosack, G. (1985) *Immigrant Workers and Class Structure in Western Europe* (2nd edn), Oxford: Oxford University Press.

Cesarani, D. (1992) 'An alien concept? The continuity of anti-alienism in British society before 1940', *Immigrants & Minorities*, 11(3): 24–52.

Clarke, P. (1996) *Hope and Glory: Britain 1900-1990*, London: Allen Lane.

Cohen, S. (1985) 'Anti-semitism, immigration controls and the welfare state', *Critical Social Policy*, 5(13): 73–92.

Cole, G.D.H. (1948) *A Short History of the British Working Class Movement, 1789–1947* (4th edn), London: George Allen & Unwin Ltd.

Darwin, J. (2009) *The Empire Project: The Rise and Fall of the British World-System, 1830–1970*, Cambridge: Cambridge University Press.

Davies, P. and Freedland, M. (1984) *Labour Law: Text and Materials* (2nd edn), London: Weidenfeld & Nicolson.

Deakin, S. and Wilkinson, F. (2005) *The Law of the Labour Market: Industrialization, Employment, and Legal Evolution*, Oxford: Oxford University Press.

Dias-Abey, M. (2022) 'Path dependent policymaking in the post-Brexit United Kingdom: what's new about the "points-based" labour migration system?', 3(1): 720–32.

Dummett, A. and Nicol, A. (1990) *Subjects, Citizens, Aliens and Others: Nationality and Immigration Law*, London: Weidenfeld & Nicolson.

Edgerton, D. (2018) *The Rise and Fall of the British Nation: A Twentieth-Century History*, London: Penguin Books.

El-Enany, N. (2020) *Bordering Britain: Law, Race and Empire*, Manchester: Manchester University Press.

Garside, W.R. (1990) *British Unemployment, 1919–1939: A Study in Public Policy*, Cambridge: Cambridge University Press.

Hansen, R. (2000) *Citizenship and Immigration in Post-War Britain: The Institutional Origins of a Multicultural Nation*, Oxford: Oxford University Press.

Harris, J. (1972) *Unemployment and Politics: A Study in English Social Policy 1886–1914*, Oxford: Clarendon Press.

Havinghurst, A.F. (1979) *Britain in Transition: The Twentieth Century*, Chicago: University of Chicago Press.

Hobsbawn, E. (1975) *The Age of Capital, 1848–1875*, London: Weidenfeld & Nicolson.

Holmes, C. (1988) *John Bull's Island: Immigration & British Society, 1871–1971*, London: MacMillan.

Ince, G. (1960) *The Ministry of Labour*, London: George Allen & Unwin Ltd.

Isaac, J. (1954) *British Post-War Migration*, Cambridge: Cambridge University Press.

Jenkinson, J. (2009) *Black 1919: Riots, Racism and Resistance in Imperial Britain*, Liverpool: Liverpool University Press.

Keynes, J.M. (1920) *The Economic Consequences of the Peace*, New York: Harcourt, Brace and Howe.

Malik, K. (2023) *Not so Black or White: A History of Race from White Supremacy to Identity Politics*, London: C. Hurst & Co.

McNeill, R. (1919) 'Aliens Restriction Bill', Hansard: House of Commons debates, 22 October 1919, vol 120, cols 67–8. Available from: https://hansard.parliament.uk/Commons/1919-10-22/debates/4846bacd-a12b-4cb0-b466-692d8e3cc48e/CommonsChamber (accessed 19 May 2024).

Morgan, K.O. (1979) *Consensus and Disunity: The Lloyd George Coalition Government 1918–1922*, Oxford: Clarendon Press.

Newsome, F. (1955) *The Home Office* (2nd edn), London: George Allen & Unwin Ltd.

Patel, I.S. (2021) *We're Here Because You Were There: Immigration and the End of Empire*, London: Verso.

Peck, J. (1996) *Workplace: The Social Regulation of Labour Markets*, New York: Guilford Press.

Pellew, J. (1982) *The Home Office, 1848–1914*, London: Heinemann Educational Books.

Rawlings, P. (2021) '"An absurd and humiliating kind of legislation": Oscar Levy and the Alien Acts', *SSRN*. Available from: https://papers.ssrn.com/sol3/papers.cfm?abstract_id=3969886 (accessed 19 May 2024).

Roche, T.W.E. (1969) *The Key in the Lock: A History of Immigration Control in England from 1066 to the Present Day*, London: John Murray.

Royal Commission on Alien Immigration (1903). Report of the Royal Commission on Alien Immigration, Cd 1741, London: HMSO.

Ryan, B. (2001) 'The Common Travel Area between Britain and Ireland', *Modern Law Review*, 64(6): 855–74.

Salt, J. and Bauer, V. (2020) *Managing Foreign Labour Immigration to the UK: Government Policy and Outcomes Since 1945*, London: UCL Migration Research Unit. Available from: www.ucl.ac.uk/geography/sites/geography/files/mru_report_js_1.pdf (accessed 19 May 2024).

Scott, H.R. (1932) 'The control of aliens', *The Police Journal*, 5(1): 24–48.

Tabili, L. (1994) *'We Ask for British Justice', Workers and Racial Justice in Late Imperial Britain*, Ithaca, NY: Cornell University Press.

Taylor, B. (2016) 'Immigration, statecraft and public health: the 1920 Aliens Order, medical examinations and the limitations of the state in England', *Social History of Medicine*, 29(3): 512–33.

The Times (1924a) 'Aliens in the catering trade', 27 May, p 24.

The Times (1924b) 'Undesirable aliens', 15 December, p 15.

Timmer, A.S. and Williams, J.G. (1998) 'Immigration policy prior to the 1930s: labor markets, policy interactions, and globalization backlash', *Population and Development Review*, 24(4): 739–71.

Tooze, J.A. (1998) 'Imagining national economies: national and international economic statistics, 1900–1950', in G. Cubitt (ed) *Imagining Nations*, Manchester: Manchester University Press, pp 212–28.

Torpey, J. (2003) 'Passports and the development of immigration controls in the North Atlantic world during the long nineteenth century', in A. Fahrmeir, O. Faron and P. Weil (eds) *Migration Control in the North Atlantic World, The Evolution of State Practices in Europe and the United States from the French Revolution to the Inter-War Period*, New York: Berghahn Books, pp 73–91.

Virdee, S. (2014) *Racism, Class and the Racialized Outsider*, Basingstoke: Palgrave Macmillan.

Visram, R. (2002) *Asians in Britain: 400 Years of History*, London: Pluto Press.

Weldon, D. (2021) *Two Hundred Years of Muddling Through: The Surprising Story of Britain's Economy from Boom to Bust and Back Again*, London: Little, Brown.

Whiteside, N. (1991) *Bad Times: Unemployment in British Social and Political History*, London: Faber and Faber.

Whiteside, N. (2014) 'Constructing unemployment: Britain and France in historical perspective', *Social Policy and Administration*, 48(1): 67–85.

Whiteside, N. and Gillespie, J.A. (1991) 'Deconstructing unemployment: developments in Britain in the interwar years', *The Economic History Review*, 44(4): 665–82.

Winder, R. (2005) *Bloody Foreigner: The Story of Immigration to Britain*, London: Abacus.

7

The Production and Negotiation of the 'Good' and the 'Bad' Migrant

Angelo Martins Junior

The final group I want to talk about today are illegal immigrants. [...] We've got to be so much better at finding these people and getting them out of our country. How do we know when we are getting immigration right? It's when we are getting the right people we need for our economy ... and when all those who come here do so for genuine reasons and join with the rest of society in making our country stronger, richer and more secure.

David Cameron, then UK Prime Minister, 2011

I think that the people coming here illegally do possess values which are at odds with our country. We are seeing heightened levels of criminality when related to the people who've come on boats, related to drug dealing, exploitation, prostitution. We need to ensure that we bring an end to the boat crossings. It is becoming a notable feature of everyday crime-fighting in England and Wales. Many people are coming here illegally and they're getting very quickly involved in the drugs trade, in other forms of exploitation.

Suella Braverman, then UK Home Secretary, 2023

Introduction

This chapter explores the role of the state in the production and negotiation of difference in a 'world on the move'. In particular, it is concerned with the consequences of the divide between the 'legal' and 'illegal' migrant, at both a material and symbolic level, for how Brazilians live and structure their lives in London.

Although political discourse about immigration often works to homogenize the 'migrant' as a symbolic figure in opposition to the 'citizen', immigration policies also work to split migrants into different types according to reason for entering the country (student, family reunion, refugee, temporary worker, highly skilled and business migrant) or legal status ('legal', 'illegal'). Yet categories employed by the state for its own administrative purposes are volatile and do not map onto the realities of the lives of people who move (Anderson, 2013). Most people classed as 'migrants', for instance, enter a country or remain in it for several reasons simultaneously (Martins Junior, 2020a). Nevertheless, the earlier excerpts from both the 2011 speech of then UK Prime Minister David Cameron and the 2023 speech of then UK Home Secretary Suella Braverman illustrate how these administrative migration categories are often taken as fixed, natural, neutral and descriptive, reflecting person's identity (the 'illegal', the 'bad migrant', the 'criminal'), rather than referencing and shaping particular types of relation with the law (Anderson, 2013; Goldberg and Giroux, 2014). As Goldberg and Giroux (2014) observe, this is done within a context of neoliberal policies that criminalize and racialize migration through discourses that deny social structures and individualize the issue of 'illegality'.

This chapter explores how administrative (and moral) categories, the 'legal' and the 'illegal' migrant, impact on how people can live and plan their lives, what rights they have, how they imagine themselves and what forms of sociality they construct in their daily lives. Drawing on empirical research that combines an 18-month ethnography in places of leisure with 33 in-depth interviews with Brazilians in London, the chapter examines the material and symbolic consequences of institutionalized illegality (De Genova, 2002) on the ways in which migrants navigate their lives in London. It is argued that due to the stigma against the 'illegal' migrant, as well as to the exploitation and symbolic violence facilitated by the production of (il)legality, legal categories of migration help to instil perceptions of conflict and division inside the Brazilian population in London, not solidarity derived from common ethnic/national ties – 'ethnic solidarity' (Light and Gold, 2000).

Denaturalizing the state and its (moral) categories

Because of Brazil's history of 'race', class and nation, Brazilians are a particularly interesting lens through which to examine migrants' experiences of legal statuses and their socialities. After the abolition of slavery in 1888, Brazil, influenced by eugenic racial assumptions, embarked on a Whitening project and incentivized European immigration in order to 'civilize' the new nation by 'improving' its mixed 'blood' (Schwarcz, 1993). A new population of European (and Japanese) migrants was encouraged, concentrated almost entirely in the south and south-east of Brazil. These were regions that, since independence, had acquired a central position in the national economy, initially thanks to the production of coffee and, later, industrialization. At the same time, without access to land or any form of state compensation, an entire class of Black and 'mixed' people – the formerly enslaved and their descendants – as well as lighter-skinned poor Brazilians (often from the north-east) were marginalized both in the configuration of urban space and in the labour market, facing daily exclusion, discrimination, degradation and state violence. This has given a historical spatial feature to the intertwined configuration of 'race' and class in Brazil. (Guimarães, 2002).

Today, Brazil's colonial and racial histories play an important role in determining whether and how journeys are undertaken by Brazilians in Europe. The middle-class, lighter-skinned descendants of European participants in Brazil's Whitening project enjoy greater freedom of movement in Europe than others, since their ancestry means they can acquire European Union passports. Thus, alongside the legislative framework at the time of their arrival, nationality and 'race', as well as the volume and composition of their capital, differently shapes Brazilian migrants' arrival in the UK. Speaking English (cultural capital), having money to pay for a student visa (economic capital), having a partner/family visa or a contact who provides an invitation letter (social capital), having a European passport (national and 'racial' capital), for instance, all shape the social, legal and economic conditions of their journey and stay.

Bourdieu (2014, p 115) draws attention to an 'amnesia of genesis' in which we tend to 'dehistoricize' and naturalize the state and its internal mechanisms. Within these processes, the state – as well as its categories – are taken as 'an object that seems to exist by itself or that was created by nature' (Sayad, 2004, p 280). Such a naturalizing and dehistoricizing process results from the continuous reproduction in our everyday life of what Bourdieu (2014, p 108) calls 'state thought'. This is a form of thought that reflects the mental structures that the state has produced and inculcated in each one of us. This mode of naturalized dehistoricized thought is inscribed within the line of demarcation that in Brazil, for instance, divides lighter and darker-skinned people, and across the world separates nationals from non-nationals, 'legals' from 'illegals', citizens from non-citizens.

'Illegal migration', for instance, is understood by the Home Office as:

> a collective term for many forms of abuse of the immigration rules. It may be entering the country illegally – by attempting to get through the controls we have overseas, or at our border through fraudulent or clandestine entry – or by breaking the immigration rules in the UK – by

working full time having been allowed in to study, or by failing to leave at the end of their stay. (Home Office, 2007, p 8)

In this sense, as Gutierrez-Garza (2013, p 88) states, the term 'illegal migrant', for the Home Office, constitutes an alien-like subject who, by virtue of their 'lack' of proper documentation to enter, stay and work in the country, commits a criminal offence. As a consequence, 'illegality' is framed and naturalized as absence of status (Anderson, 2010). And, yet, as many scholars have shown, 'illegality' is produced by the state through legal frameworks that construct different statuses within immigration categories, and this institutionalized production of 'illegality' has direct consequences for how people can live their lives (Coutin, 2000; De Genova, 2002, 2004; Anderson, 2010). Besides having to deal with exploitation and restricted physical and social mobility due to legal constraints, being categorized as 'illegal' also means being subjected to a symbolic violence that sequesters migrants in 'a space of forced invisibility, exclusion, subjugation and repression' (Coutin, 2000, p 30). This is because 'legal' migrant and 'illegal' migrant are part of a system of differential social judgments and opportunities, consecrated by the state, as well as referencing legal standing (Sayad, 2004). The state – and the law – has the power to create social divisions and a symbolic system of classification that generates moral values and functions based on representations (signs and objects), which places people in differential positions in social space, some of which are heavily stigmatized (see Sayad, 2004; Loyal, 2014).

But immigration law and its categories are in constant flux, changing alongside shifts in the broader social, economic and ideological context. In this sense, '(il)legality', both as a legal category and as social representation, is historically produced within specific contextual power struggles to define what is 'legal' and 'illegal', and in relation to the value that those representations carry (see De Genova, 2002; Loyal, 2014). As the remainder of the chapter shows, the stories of my Brazilian research participants contribute empirical grounding for the effort to denaturalize the institutional divide between the 'legal' migrant and the 'illegal' migrant, in line with Bourdieu's (2014, p 114) broader project of historicizing the state and its categories.

Differential inclusion structuring lives

Drawing on the cases of those who have experienced long periods without regular documentation, the institutional production of the '(il)legal' migrant has differential consequences, both material and symbolic, for Brazilians' lives in London. Some are integrated with different levels of rights, while others are marginalized as 'illegals' without rights. In this sense, border control and immigration policies more generally play an important role in the legal and cognitive production of difference, since they allow both the establishment of taxonomies and the conceptual hierarchies – such as 'legal' migrant and 'illegal' migrant – that structure the movement of people and thought. Thus, they are centrally involved in the production of symbolic domination and symbolic violence (Bourdieu, 1987), as physical and political borders are designed to divide the 'other' from the 'citizen', fuelling tensions and projecting as threats those who are – or should be – on the other side of the 'wall' (Goldberg and Giroux, 2014, p 140). Yet, borders, as well as immigration law, are intended to be porous and do not stop all people entering state territories. Rather than putting an end to 'illegality', porous borders result in a (classed and racialized) differential inclusion, leading to differential material distribution and access to goods and services, (re)producing relations of domination, exploitation and subjection, power and resistance (Foucault, 1975; Balibar, 2002; Mezzadra and Neilson, 2012; De Genova 2013). The journeys of Brazilians without a European passport and with lower economic and cultural capital are an excellent illustration of such differential inclusion (see Martins Junior, 2020a).

The space of possibilities to enter the country 'legally' is considerably more restricted for those lacking economic capital, who in the case of Brazilians tend to be darker-skinned people without European ancestry. Relying on their social capital and the limited amount of money at their disposal, most try to enter the country as tourists, and information provided by social networks plays a pivotal role in making this attempt successful. As Mezzadra and Neilson (2012, p 69) argue, a constellation of other actors – such as labour brokers, migration agencies, NGOs and go-betweens (including personal friends and relatives) – work along the hierarchized boundaries between 'legality' and 'illegality', profiting, often through exploitation, from the process. These actors are important for these migrants both in the process of border crossing and after they have entered, as they help them develop and employ tactics to live and, sometimes, to regularize their situation in their destination country.[1] But these social networks are directly involved in producing as well as alleviating the multiple personal and economic precarities migrants face once in the country. This can be seen in the case of Brazilians without regular documentation in London, who experience inclusion through multiple layers of precarity.

The differential status of migrants, created by the state, is directly reflected in the stratification of the labour market, which produces different levels of precariousness and exploitation. In particular, as Anderson notes, a cheap and flexible workforce is 'structurally produced by the interaction of employment and immigration legislation' (2010, p 311). Among Brazilians, this precariousness is often realized in interactions with their co-nationals. Unable to obtain formal work because of their lack of regular documentation and low economic and cultural capital (such as the inability to speak English), some Brazilians must rely on their social capital to find informal work and survive. This, however, can result in a variety of forms of exploitation, including labour exploitation but also exploitation of social reproductive necessities. Take the situation of Adriano, a 44-year-old Black working-class man from São Paulo who arrived in the UK without regular documentation.

> I lost too much money in this city because I didn't have documents. I was cheated and exploited at houses – paying a deposit and then later they wouldn't give it back to me, by working for people who never paid me, and being robbed. The first one who exploited me was my cousin. I called him after I arrived in London. He told me a friend had a room for me, £90 a week, plus a deposit of two months' rent. Later my housemates said they were robbing me – the room was £60 per week and two weeks' deposit. Then, a Brazilian guy, who was the landlord in my second house, offered me a job helping him to refurbish the house. I worked for him for two weeks, non-stop. He said my work was worthy of only one week's rent and did not give me any money. From the contacts at this house, I got a few other jobs and was exploited again. I helped a guy who had a van and worked moving people around London. After two weeks of work, he gave me £100 and said he would give me more later. Of course he didn't. As I was illegal, I kept quiet, better to not pressure. Then I paid a Brazilian guy who told me he would manage to open a bank account for me, without documents, for £150. Later a Brazilian guy who works for a British bank said his bank open accounts for people for free, and I didn't need a visa.

Adriano's journey without regular documentation brings up several analytical points regarding the ambiguous legal production of 'illegality' and its multiple consequences for those subjected to immigration control.

First, we can see that besides being fundamental to entering the country, social capital continues to play a critical role in migrants' lives in London (Tilly, 1990; Portes, 1995). It is through their contacts that they acquire the skills to navigate in the city, find jobs, buy 'fake' documents needed to find work, open bank accounts and access goods and services. Nevertheless, this does not result in a 'generalised reciprocity', as Putnam (2001, p 21; see also Putnam, 1995) calls it, between Brazilians, in which members help each other because they see 'themselves as belonging to the same group of people, who are "in the same ship", and have to co-operate to "survive" in the strange and maybe "hostile" environment they have migrated to' (Den Butter et al, 2007, p 49). Often, the access provided by social networks comes with exploitation and precariousness. As Adriano said, since entering the UK, he has been constantly working for people who don't pay him, receiving far less than the minimum wage and having to accept it because he does not have documents.

Second, the production of hierarchical migratory statuses is consequential not only for the positioning of migrants in the labour market, but also the creation of exploitative conditions in other spheres of migrant life, such as personal relations. Adriano 'was cheated and exploited' by his cousin, by landlords and by people who got him work and documents. Thus, being subject to immigration control becomes an important structuring element in the ways that Brazilians without documentation interact with their co-nationals in London.

'Illegality' also produces lack of solidarity, isolation and fear. Brazilians without regular documentation tend to say they do not trust Brazilians in London, since those with more experience and access to goods and services frequently exploit undocumented newcomers. Thus, instead of talking about 'ethnic solidarity', they talk about the *lack* of solidarity among Brazilians, and about isolation, not community. Adriano told me:

> Life here showed me that I can't trust people until they prove the contrary. I had to develop a defensive mechanism here: not involve myself with Brazilians. I have become a very isolated person. When you are illegal, you are always inferior, so when a Brazilian knows you don't have documents, they automatically feel superior to you. They exploit and threaten you and you can't do anything because you don't have rights. Last month, a Brazilian girl who used to work with me said she wanted to see me. I met her in Elephant and Castle; she took me to a building saying a friend lived there. When I got there, there were four men waiting for me. They punched me and put a knife to my neck. They took my cards and I gave them the pin numbers. I lost £1,500. They let me go after that, but I couldn't do anything, because I don't have documents.

Being an irregular migrant places Adriano in a 'rightless condition' (De Genova, 2010, p 116), in which he cannot access any kind of state protection. This allows him to be easily exploited by others. Thus, being 'legal' or 'illegal' results in a perception of hierarchy inside the Brazilian population, and those positioned on its bottom rung see no solidarity among Brazilian migrants in London. Rather, they speak of Brazilians preying on their vulnerability and subjecting them to violence and exploitation. Becoming isolated is Adriano's way of dealing with the vulnerabilities that result also from the 'production of illegality'. As this production results in social differences that are also inscribed in the symbolic order, through discourses and cognitive classifications, it exercises symbolic, as well as physical, violence (Bourdieu, 1987; Loyal, 2014) on those subjected to migration control. Moreover, as Willen (2007, p 9) argues, 'illegality does not only affect the external structure of migrants' worlds but also shapes their subjective experience of time, space, embodiment, sociality and self'. One of the primary examples of such symbolic violence shaping the subjective experience of irregular migrants is the constant fear of being deported.

Fear of deportation facilitates subjection and exploitation, exposing irregular migrants to high levels of abuse and humiliation in every sphere of their lives. As we have seen with Adriano's journey, migrants who are without regular documentation tend to accept any kind of working conditions without complaint, as the threat of denunciation and deportation always hangs over their heads. They live in a constant state of 'deportability', as De Genova (2004) calls it, and fear of denunciation facilitates their subordination as a docile and highly exploitable workforce. Another research participant, Guilherme described how he felt in the years he lived in London without regular documentation as follows:

> I was illegal for four years, living in a cage, taking many injustices and being quiet, leaving my house in the morning to go to work not knowing whether I would return or not. It is a horrible sensation – you can't trust anyone. All the time you hear about cases of Brazilians denouncing Brazilians. You live in constant fear – at home, work, on the train. You see police officers, even if they don't look at your face, even if they don't know you're there, you are afraid of them.

For Guilherme, this kind of continuous symbolic violence structures his whole life. His comment about 'living in a cage' vividly captures his sense of 'ever-present vulnerability' (De Genova, 2004, p 178), be it on the train, at work or at home.

This vulnerability creates a continual uncertainty. Guilherme's description of leaving home not knowing if he would be coming back expresses not only a feeling of constant vigilance but also a feeling of temporariness. The fear of deportation traps migrants 'in a vacuous present fraught with anxiety and question marks about tomorrow' (Ahmad, 2008, p 315). This leads to the pressure of having to maximize the 'now', whatever the current opportunities might be, 'taking ... injustices and being quiet'. Being exploited and living with constant fear, in turn, reinforces the perception of isolation and the undercurrent of distrust, since 'Brazilians denounc[e] Brazilians', as Guilherme said. But though migrants' criminalized documental status has profound consequences for their lives, they do not necessarily contest the 'state thought' that produces it.

Negotiating the 'good' migrant and the 'bad' migrant

In order to deal with and distance themselves from the stigmatized representation of the 'illegal' or 'bad' migrant, Brazilians tend to legitimate the state thought which decontextualizes and naturalizes the 'legal'/'illegal' dichotomy and frames it as a matter of individual or class morals. As previously discussed, state categories are more than legal categories; they are part of a symbolic system, which imbues them with moral values and functions and that social agents must constantly negotiate. Citizenship, for example, has historically been a nebulous concept connected to an idea of civility, and its blurry boundaries are not simply defined by law but shaped also by notions of 'race', class and gender (see Mezzadra, 2005; Anderson, 2013).

For Anderson (2013, pp 2–5), modern states do not portray themselves only as collections of people hanging together by a common legal status, but also as an imagined 'community of value', composed of people who share common ideals and exemplary patterns of behaviour, expressed through ethnicity, religion, culture or language. The community of value is populated by 'good citizens', law-abiding and hard-working members of stable and respectable families, who feel they must protect it from those who aren't 'good'. The community of value is defined from the outside by the 'non-citizen' (migrant), who may be associated with a particular legal status, and, from the inside by the 'failed' citizen, individuals and groups imagined as incapable of or failing to live up to liberal ideals, such as criminals, benefit 'scroungers' and others. Thus, not all formal (legal) citizens are 'good' citizens, and the 'non-citizens' or the 'failed' citizens are not properly modern (civilized) compared to the 'good' citizens.

Anderson (2013, p 7) further observes that there is a strong tendency to naturalize stigmatized categories (such as racialized and classed categories) through 'genetic' or 'cultural' explanations. This allows the 'good' citizen and the state to reproduce individualizing discourses of 'success' and 'failure' that do not take into account structural constraints. Such individualizing accounts are also often used by Brazilians to justify the mass of people living as pariahs or 'sub-citizens' in the urban poor peripheries and slums of the country's southern cities (Guimarães, 2002), often represented as a 'criminal class'. When moving to London and finding themselves faced with the possibility of being framed as the pariah of British society, the 'bad'/'criminal' migrants, Brazilians in London tend to also draw on individualizing explanations to negotiate British categories and hierarchies, and my data suggest it is not only the state and 'good' citizens that deploy and reproduce stigmatized categories and the associated moral discourse; in order to deal with stigmatized representations of migrants, Brazilians with regular documentation to live in the UK tend to reproduce the oversimplified and individualizing binary distinction between the 'legal' and the 'illegal'. This is particularly true of those who enter the country with a student visa and later manage to qualify for indefinite leave to remain and/or British citizenship. Fernando, a 39-year-old lighter-skinned middle-class Brazilian man proudly told me:

> I am the living proof that you can get a British passport without doing anything dodgy, like these Brazilians do – buying a marriage and so on. There are some days that I open my drawer and grab my passport and look at it. I feel so happy, proud, I can't describe it. I get emotional when I hold it. This is why I always tell people, 'Come here as a student, get a job, make yourself indispensable to the company, and that's it. You get it.' I didn't do anything dodgy and I got it.

Despite the fact that his own journey is both structured by privilege and full of 'illegalities', he still insists that anyone can be legal 'without doing anything dodgy', following his example. Fernando had decided to come to London in 2004 to study English for one year, a skill crucial to his career development given he had graduated in marketing. Fernando arrived in London with a one-year student visa and accommodation paid for two months. With the help of a friend living in London, Fernando started working as a kitchen porter in his second week in the city, as soon as he had received his national insurance. In the first two months, Fernando managed to go to school in the morning and work in the afternoons and evenings. However, like many other 'good migrants', after a while he stopped attending classes: 'In my third month, I had already decided to stay longer, so I got a second job to be able to work to renew my visa'.

The first time I met him in a pub in south London, Fernando, who was with his friend, continually emphasized that he would never 'do anything dodgy or stay here illegally'; hence he kept renewing his visa. Yet in order to do so, he had to work more than the maximum number of hours permitted by his student visa. By working long hours in 'sub-jobs' that he 'would never do in Brazil', such as cleaning and catering, Fernando managed to stay on a student visa for four years – two years taking English courses and two years on a marketing course. After this, and through a contact made in London, he secured employment in a marketing company that provided him with a work visa.

Though Fernando had graduated with a BA in marketing in Brazil, he took an MBA in graphic design and interior decoration before coming to London. The company that sponsored his work visa informed the Home Office that he met its need for a graphic designer who specialized in interior decor. However, Fernando told me: 'my qualifications did not actually matter for the job, but it was the only way the company could justify the need for my work visa. I worked hard there. They needed me. Also, the manager had become a good friend of mine, so he helped me a lot with this'. In 2014, Fernando was entitled to apply for indefinite leave to remain, which later allowed him to apply for and eventually be granted British citizenship.

Fernando's story is similar to others I heard when talking to people who would be considered 'good' migrants, here for 'genuine' reasons and helping to make the country stronger and richer, and who viewed themselves as 'good' and upright people who would never 'do anything dodgy'. But the tactics that Fernando used to 'legally' stay and acquire 'citizenship' – studying, working and paying tax – were dependent on his economic, social and cultural capital. He had money to pay for a student visa;[2] contacts in the company that employed him helped him with his work visa; and he used his academic qualifications to make his case in the visa application. Furthermore, his tactics to maintain his 'legality' were often technically 'illegal'. He broke rules around the maximum working hours for those present on a student visa, and the company that provided him with a work visa invented the fact that they specifically required a graphic designer specializing in interior decor. His journey thus troubles the notion of a naturalized, 'fixed' distinction between the 'good' ('legal') and the 'bad' ('illegal') migrant. It is also important to recognize that the 'good' migrant's legality depends on the 'repertoire of possibilities' that the system offers (Bourdieu, 2014). Fernando was only able to effectively deploy his tactics because of the legal context in which he arrived and lived in the UK, which enabled him to apply for British citizenship after living in the country for ten years. Timing played an important role in Fernando's journey to citizenship and, thus, his capacity to see himself and be seen as a 'good' migrant.

The student visa route to entering the country legally, which Fernando took, was also used by many other 'good' migrants. Nevertheless, from 2009, with the implementation of the points-based system and the increasingly strict immigration laws, things began to change (Allen and Sumption, 2015; Davies, 2015). The new immigration rules meant that access to student visas was now limited to people with the economic resources to stay in the country without paid work. In 2009, English-language students were allowed to work up to a maximum of 20 hours per week; in 2011, they were no longer allowed to work. The renewing of student visas was also prevented in order to continue in the country regularly, many people would have to obtain a work visa and complete the ten-year residency required for requesting indefinite leave to remain, as Fernando did. Brazilians who arrived after these changes in the law or those who, before the law changed, had not been in the country long enough to apply for indefinite leave to remain had a different experience. Indeed, changes to immigration law since 2008 have increasingly restricted the possibilities for 'good' migrants to remain so on their journeys in the UK. This did not necessarily result in them leaving the country; rather, they have had to develop other tactics to try to maintain their 'legal' status, even if this means entering into situations they thought they never would.

Fernando's meritocratic 'self-made man' understanding of his own 'legality' is a clear example of how the dominant neoliberal discourse, which stresses individual self-responsibility alongside a denial of the social, is reproduced, confirming the legitimacy of the established order in the eyes of those subjected to the power of the state (Bourdieu, 2014). Fernando's lack of self-critical reflection on the conditions that made it possible for him to obtain his British citizenship exposes the mechanisms of a symbolic power that dehistoricizes and naturalizes 'legalities' and 'illegalities' by reducing everything to the individual's will and actions.

Burying the contradictory and structural dependency of his 'legality' and legitimating state thought by emphasizing that he acquired his citizenship in 'the right way' is a way for Fernando to distance himself from his previous stigmatized condition as 'migrant' and 'non-citizen' and move as close as possible to what Anderson (2013) calls the 'good citizen'. This move also means distinguishing himself from other Brazilians, who may have also acquired citizenship, but did so through 'dodgy' means and thus 'fail' to measure to the ideals of citizenship. The impulse to divide other Brazilians into the 'good' and the 'bad' is shared by many other research participants, and the moral boundaries tend to be drawn according to context, in class and regional terms.

Brazilians in London often negotiate '(il)legality' as a classed and racialized (moral) category. Research in Amsterdam (Roggeveen and Meeteren, 2013) and some cities of the US (Oliveira, 2003) has found that Brazilian migrants often discuss 'illegality' in classed terms, associated with skills and morality. Roggeveen and Meeteren (2013) shows how most documented Brazilian migrants describe their undocumented peers as 'vulgar' people with whom they do not wish to be associated. As such, these authors divide Brazilians in Amsterdam into two groups:

> From now on, we shall refer to these two groups as regular and irregular immigrants. [...] Regular migrants are usually higher educated and from upper middle class or middle class families. Respondents from the second group are lower-educated, from lower middle class families, and they have an irregular residence status or they have a history of irregular migration. (Roggeveen and Meeteren, 2013, pp 1085–6)

Thus, for Roggeveen and Meeteren, the migrant from the lower classes is 'irregular', and those with 'regular' status are from classes further up the hierarchy and hold this status whether or not they have a history of irregular migration. Yet this blunt correlation between class and (ir)regularity is problematic. As already argued, the 'legal'/'illegal' binary does not always sustain itself empirically. Many middle-class Brazilians stay in London with irregular documentation for a while or keep their regular status through irregular means. Moreover, representations of these categories are classed and racialized in ways that go beyond the issue of actually being regular or irregular, allowing people to avoid classifying themselves as 'illegal' even when they experience a situation of irregular documentation, as is the case for many middle-class Brazilians in London.

Those from the middle class who use irregular tactics, such as arranged marriage, to acquire European/British citizenship, tend to justify their own 'bad'/'illegal' actions in two ways. First, they blame structural conditions and deny their own responsibility. Second, by talking about class, they differentiate themselves from 'other' (inferior) Brazilians, whose acts always lack 'good faith'. This was the explanation given to me by Priscila.

Coming from a White upper-middle-class background and with a BA in business, Priscila came to London in 2007 to study English for one year. Like many others, she stayed longer than planned. In 2011, when I interviewed her for the first time, her narrative was similar to Fernando's. She was proud of being in the country 'legally', as she had always renewed her student visa, and she distinguished herself from 'those Brazilians' who were here 'illegally'. However, unlike Fernando, Priscila had not been in the country long enough to acquire permanent leave to remain before the law changed. Thus, in order to try to keep her situation of 'legality' and continue to see herself as 'good' migrant, she had to navigate differently within the new immigration legislation. Thus, when I last met Priscila, in 2011, she was applying to renew her visa with the help of a Brazilian lawyer. The lawyer's idea was to try to renew her student visa knowing the Home Office would refuse, then keep appealing, which would give her a few more years in the country 'legally'. However, after receiving £5,000 from Priscila to renew her visa, the lawyer disappeared with the money. Being left without regular status prompted Priscila to do something she had previously told me she would never do: get married for a visa.

> I am doing it, but it is with someone that I trust. I wouldn't do it if I weren't in this situation, but I am only in this situation because of that idiot who stole from me [the Brazilian lawyer] and because the law changed and I couldn't renew my visa anymore. I am not doing it like these illegal Brazilians who come here to save money and buy a piece of land in Brazil. They get here and the first thing they do is pay a stranger to get married and that's it. I always did everything right, always spent a lot of money renewing my visa, but things changed.

As we can see, even though she does something 'illegal' by arranging a marriage for a visa, Priscila still sees herself as a 'good' migrant, justifying her actions by saying the situation is not her fault. She is only doing this because the lawyer defrauded her and because 'the law changed'. Thus, when talking about her personal contravention of the law, she uses social constraints as mitigating factors. This is in direct contrast to the way she judges the 'illegal' situation of other people, which she assumes is simply a matter of individual will. Thus, in the end, she retains the individualizing logic to distance herself from 'the other Brazilian' – the 'bad' migrant – who does not come to the UK for 'genuine reasons', as David Cameron put it in 2011.

Moreover, Priscila uses class to distance herself from 'these illegal Brazilians' who also acquire European citizenship but lack the moral qualifications to become 'good' citizens. As discussed elsewhere (Martins Junior, 2020c), middle-class Brazilians differentiate their own pursuit of cultural capital from 'other' migrant Brazilians' (assumed) pursuit of economic capital as a way to remake class boundaries and distinguish themselves from the 'economic migrant', who lacks civility, is morally inferior and would do anything for money. Priscila moralizes the class boundary when she stresses that, even though she is getting married to acquire European citizenship, she did not come to London with the intention of 'paying a stranger to get married' for her own financial gain. Seeing herself as a 'good migrant', with a 'genuine reason to be here', she does not consider that her use of 'illegal' means to achieve 'legality' makes her a 'bad migrant', or a criminal. This is not least because Priscila views herself through the Brazilian lens that has historically constructed her as 'good citizen', someone who belongs to the 'community of value' and so is quite the opposite to the poor and racialized Brazilian bodies who form the 'criminal class' and who constitute the real 'illegals' in the UK. Again, difference moves with the Brazilian migrants.

However, working-class Brazilians without regular documentation also reproduce state thought and try to morally differentiate themselves from stigmatized 'others' when discussing their co-nationals in London. This is done by negotiating 'illegality' through individual and regional morality. After telling me about his experience without regular documentation in London, Adriano explained that he was living in more fear due to the recent changes in policy on 'illegality', yet he understood and supported the government's stricter and more punitive immigration controls because

> they give everything to people here, the quality of life here is very good, and the government here has the country in hand, the way that they want it to be. So they need to keep order by coercing and curbing these illegals who come from all parts of the world wanting to take advantage of the country. These people don't come with good intentions. They come to get the money, the benefits. There are a lot of Brazilians here who are tricking the system, so the government needs to get these guys and send them out, because they are tricking the system and destroying these countries, like a lot of goianos[2] here. This is why I don't mix with them.

It is important to note that like Priscila, Adriano reproduces state thought while simultaneously differentiating himself from the 'illegals' who are 'tricking the system' and 'destroying [the country]'. Because he comes from a working-class background and migrated, in large part, to improve his economic capital, and because he is racialized as Black, he cannot use class or 'race', as Priscila does, to try to distinguish himself from the stigma of the 'illegal'. The option that Adriano has is to play with Brazilian regional differences, and he therefore uses the figure of the goiano to crystallize the representation of the inferior 'other' Brazilian in London.[3]

More generally, my conversation with Adriano highlights how the fear and subjection people experience when living irregularly can be accompanied by a certain validation of the established order. Even after telling me all the precarities in his life, caused by not having regular documentation, Adriano expresses support for the government's immigration policies. Following Loyal (2014), we can see here how the legal and cognitive classification of '(il)legal migrant' is part of a symbolic system in which 'arbitrary relations of power are masked, disguised and exercised with the complicity of those over whom it is exercised'.[4] Adriano's comments highlight the durability of state thought on migration. Here we see that its constancy and repetition (Bourdieu, 2014) can make even those who are the most affected by its real and symbolic violence imagine the 'legal'/'illegal' divide as a matter of individual choice.

Conclusion

In this chapter, I analysed how the production and negotiation of difference in a globalized world are shaped by the state creating and imposing social divisions through legal categories, namely those of the 'legal' and 'illegal' migrant. When examining the divide between 'legal' and 'illegal' migrants empirically, some important analytical points emerge. '(Il)legality' is strongly dependent on structural constraints that open opportunities for some which are foreclosed to others. Those with lower economic and cultural capital, for instance, have a more restricted space of possibilities through which to enter and live in the country 'legally'. This results in a classed differential inclusion in which some individuals are integrated with varied levels of rights, while others are only marginally included as 'illegals', without rights. Within this marginal inclusion, many migrants are exposed to high levels of exploitation in the labour market and in their personal relations. They narrate experiences of fear and isolation in which the Brazilian population in London is seen as not just 'lacking in solidarity' but also, in some cases, predatory and treacherous. Nevertheless, despite the differential inclusion and symbolic violence resulting from immigration law, state thought, which naturalizes and individualizes 'illegality', is frequently legitimized by Brazilians. This is especially evident when Brazilians try to distance themselves from the (classed/racialized) representation of the 'bad', 'illegal' migrant. As a consequence, 'being legal', as well as being a 'good citizen', becomes a (racialized/classed) aspiration of the self. And yet the ways in which migrants are able to negotiate this representation are also circumscribed by structural constraints, such as class and region. Engaging with stigmatized representations of 'illegal' migrants is one way in which Brazilians in London reinforce social differentiations among the migrant population.

Notes

1   For tactics developed by Brazilian migrants to enter in the country and then formalize their situation, see Martins Junior (2014, 2020b).
2   'Goiano' refers to someone from the centre-western state of Goiás. The figure of the goiano is generally referenced by Brazilians in London as the most 'inferior' element of their population. This crystallized figure of 'the Brazilian other' is then managed, by both goianos and non-goianos in London, through markers of class, 'race', gender, documental status and space (see Martins Junior, 2020b).
3   For further discussion on regional differences among Brazilians in London, see Martins Junior (2020b).
4   It is important to remember that in some cases, immigrant groups do organize resistance, such as the mass mobilizations of migrants in the US stating: '"¡Aquí Estamos, y No Nos Vamos!" [Here we are, and we're not leaving!]' (De Genova, 2010).

References

Ahmad, A. (2008) 'Dead men working: time and space in London's (illegal) migrant economy', *Work, Employment and Society*, 22(2): 301–18.

Allen, W. and Sumption, M. (2015) 'UK migration policy since the 2010 general election', *Full Fact*, 28 April. Available from: https://fullf act.org/immigration/migration_policy_since_election-41297 (accessed 19 August 2022).

Anderson, B. (2010) 'Migration, immigration controls and the fashioning of precarious workers', *Work, Employment and Society*, 24(2): 300–17.

Anderson, B. (2013) *Us and Them? The Dangerous Politics of Immigration Control*, Oxford: Oxford University Press.

Balibar, E. (2002) 'What is a border?', in E. Balibar (ed) *Politics and the Other Scene*, New York: Verso, pp 75–86.

Bourdieu, P. (1987) 'The force of law: towards a sociology of the juridical field', *Hastings Law Journal*, 38(5): 814–53.

Bourdieu, P. (2014) *On the State: Lectures at the College de France 1989–1992*, Cambridge: Polity Press.

Braverman, S. (2023) 'Home Secretary Suella Braverman claims people arriving in the UK on small boats have "values at odds with our country"', *LBC*, 26 April. Available from: www.lbc.co.uk/news/suella-braverman-migrant-values/ (accessed 29 August 2023).

Cameron, D. (2011) 'David Cameron immigration speech in full', *Politics. co.uk*, 10 October. Available from: www.politics.co.uk/comment-analy sis/2011/10/10/david-cameron-immigration-speech-in-full (accessed 28 November 2013).

Coutin, S.B. (2000) *Legalizing Moves: Savadoran Immigrants' Struggle for US Residency*, Ann Arbor: University Michigan Press.

Davies, J. (2015) *Migration Policies and Migration Streams: A Case Study of Brazilian Immigration to the UK*, Master's dissertation, King's College, Brazil Institute, London.

De Genova, N. (2002) 'Migrant "illegality" and deportability in everyday life', *Annual Review of Anthropology*, 31: 419–47.

De Genova, N. (2004) 'The legal production of Mexican/migrant "illegality"', *Latino Studies*, 2(2): 160–85.

De Genova, N. (2010) 'The queer politics of migration: reflections on "illegality" and "incorrigibility"', *Studies in Social Justice*, 4(2): 101–26.

De Genova, N. (2013) 'Spectacles of migrant "illegality": the scene of exclusion, the obscene of inclusion', *Ethnic and Racial Studies*, 36(7): 1180–98.

Den Butter, F., Masurel, E. and Mosch, R. (2007) 'The economics of co-ethnic employment: incentives, welfare effects and policy options', in L.P. Dana (ed) *Handbook of Research on Ethnic Minority Entrepreneurship*, Northampton, MA: Edward Elgar, pp 42–60.

de Oliveira, A.C. (2003) 'O Caminho sem Volta – classe social e etnicidade entre os brasileiros na Flórida', in A.C.B. Martes and S. Fleischer (eds) *Fronteiras Cruzadas: Etnicidade, Gênero e Redes*, Petropolis, Brazil: Editora Paz e Terra, pp 115–38.

Foucault, M. (1975) *Discipline and Punish: The Birth of the Prison*, New York: Random House.

Goldberg, D.T. and Giroux, S.S. (2014) *Sites of Race: Conversations with Susan Searls Giroux*, Cambridge: Polity Press.

Guimarães, A.S. (2002) *Classes, raças e democracia*, São Paulo: Editora 34.

Gutierrez-Garza, A. (2007) *Enforcing the Rules: A Strategy to Ensure and Enforce Compliance with Our Immigration Laws*, London: Home Office.

Gutierrez-Garza, A. (2013) *The Everyday Moralities of Migrant Women: Life and Labour of Latin American Domestic and Sex Workers in London*, PhD thesis, London School of Economics and Political Science.

Home Office (2007) *Enforcing the Rules: A Strategy to Ensure and Enforce Compliance with our Immigration Laws*, London: Home Office.

Light, I. and Gold, S.J. (2000) *Ethnic Economies*, San Diego, CA: Academic Press.

Loyal, S. (2014) 'From the sanctity of the family to state sovereignty: the Irish supreme courts changing role in maintaining national sovereignty', *Critical Sociology*. doi: 10.1177/089692051454

Martins Junior, A. (2014) *Lives in Motion: Notebooks of an Immigrant in London*, Copenhagen: Whyte Tracks.

Martins Junior, A. (2020a) '"Differentiated journeys": Brazilians in London beyond homogenising categories of "the migrant"', *PLURAL – Revista de Ciências Sociais*, 27(1): 114–44.

Martins Junior, A. (2020b) *Moving Difference: Brazilians in London*, London: Routledge.

Martins Junior, A. (2020c) '(Re)fazendo diferenças de classe em movimento: a classe média brasileira em Londres', *RevIISE – Revista De Ciencias Sociales Y Humanas*, 16(16): 165–80.

Mezzadra, S. (2005) 'Citizen and subject: a postcolonial constitution for the European Union?', *Situations*, 1(2): 31–42.

Mezzadra, S. and Neilson, B. (2012) 'Between inclusion and exclusion: on the topology of global space and borders', *Theory, Culture and Society*, 29(4–5): 58–75.

Portes, A. (1995) 'Economic sociology and the sociology of immigration: a conceptual overview', in A. Portes (ed) *The Economic Sociology of Immigration*, Princeton, NJ: Russel Sage Foundation, pp 1–41.

Putnam, R.D. (1995) 'Bowling alone: America's declining social capital', *Journal of Democracy*, 6(1): 65–78.

Putnam, RD. (2001) *Bowling Alone*, New York: Simon & Schuster.

Roggeveen, S. and van Meeteren, M. (2013) 'Beyond community: an analysis of social capital and the social networks of Brazilian migrants in Amsterdam', *Current Sociology*, 61(7): 1078–96.

Sayad, A. (2004) *The Suffering of the Immigrant*, Cambridge: Polity.

Schwarcz, L. (1993) *O Espetáculo das Raças*, São Paulo: Cia das Letras.

Tilly, C. (1990) 'Transplanted networks', in V. Yans-McLaughlin (ed) *Immigration Reconsidered: History, Sociology, and Politics*, New York: Oxford University Press, pp 79–95.

Willen, S.S. (2007) 'Toward a critical phenomenology of "illegality": state power, criminalization, and abjectivity among undocumented migrant workers in Tel Aviv, Israel', *International Migration*, 45(3): 8–38.

PART 3

Transformative Representations

Introduction

Nariman Massoumi, Florian Scheding and Juan Zhang

Our chapters, which make up Part 3 of this book, concern two principal areas, both broadly defined. The first is the dialectics of envoicement and unvoicement. Who shapes discourses on migration? Who has access to participating in these debates, and who is excluded from them? Who has the terminological power to label someone a 'migrant'? We draw on existing debates in migration studies across disciplines and connect these with frequent use of the term 'voice' in humanitarian and refugee campaigns. We highlight the importance of access to debates and discourses surrounding migration, mobility and citizenship, and we interrogate the extent to which these enable or disempower the multiple (and often cacophonic) migrant voices. Second, we are concerned with representation. How are migratory voices mediated? Who does the representing, who listens to the representations, and how are they framed? What is the role of media in framing and labelling migration? Our chapters consider traditional and social media, film and music, among other sources, and we seek to remind readers that media representations are not mere commentary from the sidelines. Rather, they are crucial and transformative, central to shaping discourses and creating our imaginary of what migration is.

While our focus lies on border crossing, we do not lose sight of the nation. Indeed, an engagement with nationalism looms large in all three contributions to Part 3. We recognize that, in the cases that inform our focus, national ideologies play central roles in labelling people as migrants and in representing migration as problematic. That said, the nation is not the sole determinant of migration's terminology or ontology. All three chapters point out that neither national borders themselves nor the physical crossing of state borders are the primary factors in constructing and representing migration. Further, our chapters highlight the fragility of nationalist belonging and the debates about access to national identity and citizenship. National borders shift in times of war, mobile citizens are vilified during crisis, and artistic responses to upheaval can become ideological devices for negotiating the dialectics of inclusion and exclusion.

It is worth noting that we, like most of the contributors to this volume, might all be labelled 'migrants'. We have migrated at various points in time, along different trajectories, and for varied reasons. By sheer coincidence, we are employed by the same institution and live in the same city. In some ways, we are similar. We inhabit what is called the Global North and Global West. Our employment affords us access to cultural, social and financial capital denied to much of the world's population, including many of the people discussed in this book's chapters. By little more than coincidence, we have the ability to cross national borders without much difficulty, travelling at the forefront of queues, in comfort, and staying in pleasant hotels, as welcome visitors. And yet, significant differences persist. We hold different gender, ethnic, and racial identities resulting in uneven experiences of belonging and inclusion within systems of power. The nation states that define our identities as citizens or migrants — whether British, Iranian, Chinese or German — restrict and regulate our presumed freedoms to move in unequal and irregular ways. Our language backgrounds are different, as are the cultural experiences of our upbringings that shape our views of the world.

In Chapter 8, focusing on politicized constructions of citizenship, Juan Zhang explores how overseas Chinese citizens returning home during the COVID-19 pandemic were branded as threats, accused of fleeing disease hotspots and labelled as culprits for spreading the virus. Blamed for 'spreading the virus for a thousand miles', international mobility during the pandemic quickly became stigmatized, creating new biopolitical borders based on public health and civic responsibility. Overseas Chinese faced a double stigma, battling COVID-19-related xenophobia abroad while being branded toxic suspects when returning to China. Based on digital research and interviews, Zhang examines the imagined toxicity of international mobility and how it was used to blame returning nationals. Negative representations portrayed them as selfish and irresponsible, but a counter-narrative emerged among traveling migrants, emphasizing their compliance with rules and civic responsibility and justifying their right to return. Zhang explores what became termed as 'unethical returns', with returnees represented as opportunistic for returning only after the worst of the pandemic was over. This chapter delves into the dilemmas of overseas Chinese, who viewed their return as a moral right, countering toxic discourses of exclusion by showcasing their responsible behaviour during travel and quarantine.

In Chapter 9, Nariman Massoumi delves into the impact of films portraying migrant and refugee experiences and highlights their potential to both combat and perpetuate racism. He focuses on Marjane Satrapi's autobiographical animated film *Persepolis* (2007) which recounts her life during the Iranian revolution, her migration to Vienna and her eventual move to France. Drawing on Hamid Naficy's (2001) theory of diasporic films as 'accented cinemas', Massoumi problematizes how *Persepolis* ideologically represents migration and mobility. The film constructs the idea of home as an enclosed middle-class family world, starkly contrasting with the turmoil of the Islamic revolution and migration. Nostalgic of a pre-revolutionary Iran, *Persepolis* portrays Muslims as hostile outsiders in post-revolutionary society, implying cultural superiority over lower social classes. The chapter questions the film's universality and argues that it racializes Satrapi and her family as progressive and European while portraying poor Muslim characters as backward and violent. The film's underlying representational strategy thus aligns with what Zia-Ebrahimi (2016) terms 'dislocative nationalism', connecting Iran to Europe geographically while displaying hostility towards Arabs and Islam. This simultaneously reproduces French neo-republican perspectives on 'good' citizenship, with Satrapi's family sharing a similitude with a racialized French national identity defined in contradistinction to essentialized Muslim or Arab 'outsiders'. Representations of family dynamics in diasporic films like *Persepolis* can thus serve as both inclusionary and exclusionary ideological devices, shedding light on complex racial and cultural identities within the context of migration.

In Chapter 10, Florian Scheding explores musical responses to the 2022 Russia–Ukraine war, focusing on three key events: the Eurovision 2022 winning song 'Stefania' by Kalush Orchestra, Pink Floyd's collaboration with Andriy Khlyvnyuk, 'Hey hey rise up', and the Concert for Ukraine organized by British broadcaster ITV. These case studies raise questions about sonic access and migratory representations, examining the envoicement and silencing of migrant voices. Despite their intentions to support refugees and anti-war causes, the musical examples inadvertently contribute to the exceptionalization of migration and reinforce nationalist narratives. All three case studies are prestigious and well funded, and they reached millions of audience members. They demonstrate music's ability to build communities and protest border restrictions, yet they also strengthen nationalist ideologies. The ITV concert largely excluded Ukrainian musicians and took place amid British Right-wing anti-migration politics. The Eurovision Song Contest blends transnational identity politics with nationalist constructions of belonging, while 'Hey hey rise up' promotes militarism and patriotism, revealing divisions among Pink Floyd's members regarding the war. By shifting the focus to sound and music, Scheding challenges methodological nationalisms, offering a rich perspective on migration and mobility. He reminds us that migration is inherently sonic, though this is often overshadowed by visually and textually dominant media. In an era of border closures and refugee debates, this approach provides a valuable alternative to crisis-driven narratives.

Questions of voice and representation have animated debates on migration, identity and media for some time. Voicing, literally and figuratively, is often evoked as a liberating form of agency and a response to systems of domination through the implication that 'being heard' functions as a self/ collective representative act against marginalization and subordination. All three chapters here are interested in understanding the complexities of voice as self-representation in the context of mobility across physical and imaginative borders. If, as Spivak suggests, representation requires both speaker and listener, then our chapters are interested not only in which voices are heard but, more importantly, *how* they are listened to and the extent to which these fall within or outside the 'lines laid down by the official structures of representation' (Spivak, 1996, p 306). So, while Chinese nationals are labelled as bearers of disease and infection and racialized as foreign in the process, voicing claims of responsibility in response as an act of self-representation can constitute an appeal to belonging that still follows the logic of deserving or undeserving. Similarly, *Persepolis'* autobiographical response to anti-migrant racism engages in a definition of the self that is predicated on the identity of the presumed listener(s) (European, Western, secular), thereby excluding co-nationals in its appeal to belonging. Meanwhile, the Kalush Orchestra's nationalist appeals of motherland rely on folkloric self-orientalizing strategies encased in cultural patterns familiar to Western ears, whether in the form of a hip-hop backing track or Eurovision's narration of nationhood.

Our chapters thus employ specific case studies to contribute to wider debates. Sharing common themes, the actual cases we focus on are very different. These dialectics of verisimilitude and difference cut to the heart of debates in thinking about migration. How can we, as scholars of migration, and as migrants ourselves, narrate migration? On a basic level, we argue that migration is inherently diverse. Every story of migration is unique. Part 3, much like the rest of the volume, advocates for attention to these differences and to individual stories of mobility. It is important to listen to these stories and not dismiss them. On the other hand, specific case studies also risk the danger of myopia and need to respond to the fact that migration is not only a mass phenomenon but also part of the human condition. We aim to highlight the overlap between migration's ontology and phenomenology, between what migration might be and how it manifests itself in the world. We suggest that it is worth listening to how migration and mobility are voiced and to consider the ways they are represented. We argue, in other words, that a foregrounding of voice and representation is crucial to migration studies today, as representations of mobility and migration hold transformative power.

References

Naficy, H. (2001) *An Accented Cinema: Exilic and Diasporic Filmmaking*, Princeton, NJ: Princeton University Press.

Spivak, G.C. (1996) *The Spivak Reader: Selected Works of Gayatri Chakravorty Spivak*, edited by D. Landry and G.M. MacLean, New York: Routledge.

Zia-Ebrahimi, R. (2016) *The Emergence of Iranian Nationalism: Race and the Politics of Dislocation*, New York: Columbia University Press.

8

Why Can't Chinese Citizens Go Home? Spoiled Citizenship and Stigmatized Returns in Pandemic Times

Juan Zhang

Introduction

In March 2020, a topic on China's largest social media platform Weibo titled '#Returning international student responding to public criticism during quarantine' went viral, capturing the attention of millions. Within days, it amassed 260 million views and tens of thousands of comments. What triggered this maelstrom of online reaction was a vlog created by a Chinese student named Yang, who was returning to China from Italy, at that time the epicentre of the coronavirus outbreak in Europe. This vlog chronicled Yang's arduous 30-hour journey, marked by anxiety and multiple stop-overs due to the sudden cancellation of direct flights. It concluded with his eventual safe arrival in the city of Shanghai – just one example of the efforts of international students to return home in the face of challenges during the early stages of the global health emergency.

What could have been an ordinary international journey home took a remarkable twist, fuelled by the intense paranoia that existed at the onset of the COVID-19 pandemic. Yang's story immediately drew online criticism, not just towards him as an individual but also towards 'overseas Chinese' as a whole, who were perceived collectively as a potential threat. Tens of thousands were making efforts to return from various disease hotspots in Europe and the US, where COVID-19 death tolls were steadily rising. Many of these Chinese returnees, including students and working professionals, were reported to be fleeing the Global North in large numbers during the early stages of the outbreaks (Fifield, 2020; Weale, 2020). However, their 'shock mobilities' – sudden movements in response to acute anxiety and disruptions (Xiang et al, 2023) – ignited new social tensions as returnees found themselves scapegoated as the people responsible for reintroducing COVID-19 back into China. Although China was the country where the SARS-CoV-2 virus was initially detected as the cause of the COVID-19 pandemic in December 2019, by March 2020, when the outbreak began spreading to the rest of the world, the first wave of infections in China had been brought under control. The Chinese government had declared a victory in containing and effectively 'eliminating' COVID-19 within the country's borders. Consequently, from March 2020, Chinese citizens were led to believe that subsequent COVID-19 cases and domestic outbreaks were primarily a result of the virus being 'imported'; it was believed to have re-entered China through imported goods and individuals travelling into the country. Consequently, negative sentiments quickly emerged in Chinese public discourse, with condemnations directed at the mobility and return of overseas Chinese (Yuan, 2020). Migrant returnees were accused of being 'the least involved in contributing to the motherland', and the phrase 'the most capable of spreading the virus for thousands of miles' (*jianshe zuguo ni buzai, qianli songdu ni zuixing*) gained immediate traction and popularity in China (Figure 8.1).

Figure 8.1: Accounts of the phenomenon of *qianli songdu* proliferated across Chinese social media

Note: The image is a screenshot taken from Phoenix Weekly's WeChat public account featuring headlines that read (top) 'The case of "imported viral infection" gained prominence following public criticism: while you were absent in contributing to the homeland's progress, you were the quickest to spread poison from thousands of miles away' (被骂上热搜的 "境外传毒"事件: 家乡建设你不在，万里投毒你最快）and (bottom) '"Recklessly seeking refuge in China and infecting 123 people by spreading the virus from a distance." Your shamelessness is truly ugly!' ("回国避难还撒泼，千里投毒感染123人": 你们不要脸的样子，真丑!).

Source: www.ifengweekly.com/detil.php?id=9279

The term *qianli songdu*, meaning 'spreading the virus for a thousand miles', vividly encapsulated the stigmatization of mobility in the midst of an uncontrolled pandemic. It marked a period when both internal and international movements were closely regulated and policed in line with the logic of a 'crisis regime of mobility' (Salazar, 2021), which classified movements along 'essential' and 'non-essential' axes. International travel for health precautions and disease avoidance, under such circumstances, was not only deemed non-essential but also viewed with suspicion and considered potentially harmful. Public criticism directed at travelling individuals, who allegedly 'spread the virus for a thousand miles', therefore fortified new biopolitical borders that were justified on the grounds of public health and civic responsibility. The word *du*, in its most literal translation, did not directly refer to the virus itself but rather to a 'poison' or 'toxin' that could have fatal consequences if it came into contact with a healthy body and caused infection. Individuals carrying such toxicity were perceived as potential carriers of danger and harm, with returning migrants increasingly blamed for allegedly 'poisoning China' and sabotaging the country's previously successful pandemic response. Critics voiced their grievances that returning migrants were selfishly benefiting from China's defence efforts without actively contributing and that they were also burdening China's public health system, which relied on the tireless efforts of tens of thousands of volunteers who dedicated months to safeguarding health borders and defending Chinese lives. As a result, returning Chinese faced heightened scrutiny during their journeys home, as they were viewed as jeopardizing the nation's hard-won progress in the fight against the virus.

The association of 'toxicity' with international mobility shed light on the 'spoiled citizenship' of Chinese nationals abroad. Compromised by imaginations of infection, they were denied the right to return, and due to fears about contagion, their intentions were deemed irresponsible. Overseas Chinese thus found themselves subjected to a double stigmatization resulting from both COVID-related xenophobia and the discriminatory Othering of mobile bodies. While abroad, they faced intense racism and attendant anxiety fuelled by discourses surrounding the 'China virus'. Yet, on contemplating their return, they were labelled as 'toxic suspects' (*daidu xianfan*), feared as potentially carrying the virus back to their families and communities.

Much has been written on migrants as carriers and transmitters of infectious diseases, ranging from tuberculosis to HIV (for example, Grove and Zwi, 2006), Ebola (Thomas, 2019) and the more recent COVID-19 (O'Brien et al, 2021). The notion of the migrant body as 'diseased' has long been a familiar trope, evoking a particular image of the migrant as either a threatening figure coming from the outside (Su, 2020) or an individual with heightened vulnerability in need of separation from native citizens (White, 2020). However, when the 'migrant' in question is a returning citizen, someone ostensibly 'one of us', the grounds for fear become less stable and the dynamics of differentiation reveal great ambiguity. One's citizenship status, in the context of pandemic-era China, did not guarantee automatic inclusion and trust, unless individuals could demonstrate belonging through acts of solidarity, demonstrating deservingness. The disease stigma attached to 'foreigners' and 'migrants' also tarnished the identity of returning citizens, whose claims to full recognition and formal rights were often heavily discounted. Drawing on Erving Goffman's (1963) notion of stigma and 'spoiled identity', it is important to consider how 'spoiled citizenship' could rewrite social relations when COVID-19 became a powerful attribute according to which bodies were stigmatized and discredited, social surveillance was reinforced and a particular moral regime was upheld. Spoiled citizenship brings to the fore how one's deservingness – signifying moral worth – can be separated from entitlement as legal and formal rights (see Willen, 2012). It also underscores how citizenship as both a status and a web of relationships involves not only physical and metaphorical boundaries but also the various sites and practices that imbue it with meaning (Staeheli, 2011).

This chapter aims to offer a preliminary analysis of the imagined and embodied 'toxicity' of international mobility and how it became an attribute of spoiled citizenship when it was used to validate a discourse of blame directed at travelling and returning citizens. The toxicity of mobility justified a new moral regime of containment that actively stigmatized moving bodies and things while creating a distinct category of citizenship tainted by an Other identity. Within this moral regime of containment, Chinese citizens residing abroad found themselves effectively barred from exercising their right to return home. Negative representations in both popular and official media portrayed them as selfish and irresponsible individuals, casting them as 'underserving citizens' bringing risk home. In this light, returning home became both undesirable and unethical. Simultaneously, a counter-narrative emerged among travelling migrants asserting their 'right to go home'. Many defended their mobility decisions by invoking the same ethical framework of responsibility, contending that their adherence to regulations and vigilance against infection risks had earned them the right to return. They also distanced themselves from other 'irresponsible' returnees, who voiced complaints and resisted regulations (for example, demanding the right to outdoor activities during quarantine), and in doing so reinforced a moral discourse on immobility that imposed restrictions on their movements.

Moralizing pandemic immobility

Since the beginning of the COVID-19 pandemic, the curtailment of cross-border movement due to successive travel restrictions, national lockdowns and border closures has been well documented. Fears of contagion and the imperative to contain and control viral transmission have shaped a new 'mobility regime', an intersecting system of mobility control through cultural norms and policies, previously theorized by scholars such as Shamir (2005) as well as Schiller and Salazar (2013). This Covid-19 mobility regime was characterized by a pervasive sense of 'stuckedness' (Hage, 2009), particularly evident during the first two years of the pandemic worldwide. In certain regions, stringent border controls have led to prolonged immobility.

Recent research has shed light on how border closures and travel restrictions effectively trapped migrants in place, exacerbating their vulnerabilities with the loss of employment, lack of care, disease stigma and destitution (Ullah et al, 2021). Temporary migrant workers and undocumented migrants suddenly found themselves jobless and homeless, and many were compelled to undertake 'extreme mobility', with tens of thousands embarking on arduous journeys home on foot (Nayar, 2020). Scholars have observed how this new mobility regime under COVID-19 restricted 'the physical mobility of some, while granting highly conditional mobility to others, resulting in situations of enforced and permanent temporariness and ontological insecurity' (Brandhorst et al, 2020, p 263). Immobilities triggered by COVID-19 have prompted scholars to question the problematic restrictions on freedom of movement (Mezzadra and Stierl, 2020) and the pathological control of transnational flows (Lin and Yeoh, 2021).

Prior to examining 'pandemic immobilities' (Adey et al, 2021), migration scholars had already been offering a renewed critique of the long-held mobility bias, considering non-movement, interruptions, stops and stasis as crucial processes in need of theoretical engagement (Schewel, 2019). Scholars such as Bélanger and Silvey proposed an 'immobilities turn' to shift focus on the 'constraints, regulations, and limits simultaneously placed on migration, everyday mobility, and border crossings at multiple scales' (2019, pp 3429, 3425). While, previously, studies on migrant immobilities portrayed the roles played by nation states with their pervasive regulatory and disciplinary structures underpinning who could move and who ought to stay (for example, Bigo, 2002; Johnson, 2015), migrant subjective experiences and their agency in rationalizing and regulating (non)-movements are now receiving more attention in this immobilities turn (Tan et al, 2022; Zhang and Wang, 2023).

The expanding body of literature on pandemic-induced (im)mobilities offers a crucial analytical framework for delving into the lived experiences, migrant aspirations and evolving imaginaries of borders and movements. Nevertheless, two aspects warrant further discussion. First, the pandemic-specific mobility regime necessitates contextualization within an evolving moral framework, where various movements, decisions, and bodies are ascribed differing values and claims to legitimacy. The COVID-19 pandemic has revealed that the 'elementary freedom to move' can be curtailed in the name of 'the greater good', with mobility itself subjected to scrutiny based on made-up criteria of essentiality (Mezzadra and Stierl, 2020). Forced immobility, particularly during the pandemic, has become normalized and moralized through shifting public discourses surrounding responsibility, deservingness and national (health) security. Mobility, especially when perceived as non-essential, is now closely intertwined with notions of contagion and risk (and increasingly with discourses around climate change), making it highly susceptible to containment and delegitimization.

Second, the emerging (im)mobility regime also introduces a distinct categorization process where assumed boundaries between self and Other are redrawn. The migrant, as demonstrated in existing studies (see, for example, Nail, 2015), constitutes the 'perfect Other', in most cases as an ambivalent figure delineating national borders that separate domestic citizens from 'outsiders'. Returning nationals, who have resided outside of the country, embody a unique 'migrant' identity that further complicates the nationalized imagination of 'we-ness'. Do returning citizens still constitute a part of the national 'we'? Or are they categorized differently, mirroring shifting perceptions of belonging, especially when the broader society has grappled with health-related threats?

Focusing on Chinese nationals residing overseas who sought to return home during the COVID-19 pandemic, this chapter illustrates how their homecoming was stigmatized within the moral regime of pandemic immobility. They were disproportionately represented by the Chinese public discourse as the culprit for domestic transmission. This stigmatization served a broader political agenda aimed at regulating mobility within China, where the curtailment of citizens' everyday movement could occur with minimal resistance against COVID-19 control. Furthermore, this chapter explores how returning Chinese nationals cultivated an image of themselves as responsible and patriotic returnees, countering the prevailing stigma and discrimination. In doing so, they inadvertently reinforced the same moral underpinning of immobility that hinged on conditions of deservingness.

Difficult returns during COVID-19

When the COVID-19 pandemic first broke out, it prompted a global wave of panic and the declaration of a worldwide 'war' against the coronavirus (New York Times, 2020). This was followed by border closures and travel restrictions, while the media's proliferation of 'outbreak narratives' (Wald, 2008) fuelled xenophobia, fear and even acts of violence (Elias et al, 2021). Race-based hate crimes driven by coronavirus-related fears began to surge, particularly targeting individuals with an Asian appearance. Headlines recounting incidents of verbal harassment and physical assault intensified the prevailing sense of fear, particularly among Chinese residents in Europe and North America, who were already anxious due to rising infection rates. In France, for instance, the French media used phrases like 'Chinese virus' and 'yellow alert' when referring to the pandemic, while words such as 'pangolin' and 'bat' were frequently mentioned to implicate China as the outbreak origin (Wang et al, 2020). In the UK, Chinese nationals feared not only the virus itself but also potential racist attacks triggered by widespread 'maskaphobia'. One student in Manchester voiced their concerns, stating: 'We are not only afraid of coronavirus, but the violence brought by racism is also much more scary now. I have got the feeling I am an outsider in the UK. And now I finally find we are not welcomed by British people. Diversity sounds like a joke' (Weale, 2020).

It was also during this time of acute panic and uncertainty, when tens of thousands of Chinese citizens sought to leave Europe and return to China for safety, that returning home was no longer a straightforward option. Effective from 29 March 2020, the Civil Aviation Administration of China implemented the 'Five One' (*wu ge yi*) policy, capping international flights at an extremely low level. This policy put in place stringent limitations, allowing only one flight per week on one specific route to one country. In the first week of the Five One policy, a mere 108 flights were authorized to land in China, each flight operating at only 75 per cent capacity, which amounted to just 1.2 per cent of the usual flight volume compared to pre-pandemic levels (Caijing, 2020).

The Five One policy was enforced at a juncture when China had already successfully contained widespread domestic transmission and declared triumph in its 'people's war against COVID'. By March 2020, signs of economic recovery were emerging in China, while the rest of the world was just beginning to grapple with the chaos induced by COVID-19. This proclaimed victory gave rise to a strong nationalist narrative asserting that China was managing the pandemic better than any other country in the world (de Kloet et al, 2020). This narrative bolstered the defensive stance around China's hard-earned 'immunity' against viral infection. Consequently, China's pandemic response shifted towards preventing 'foreign imports' at its border and imposing mandatory quarantine measures at designated national entry points.

Despite the heightened travel restrictions, for tens of thousands of Chinese seeking safety with their families, the desire to return home proved to be strong. As a consequence, air travel costs skyrocketed and flight availability plummeted. Chinese in the UK and across Europe found their prebooked flights cancelled at the last minute. Many were forced to purchase multiple tickets in anticipation of such cancellations, and a fortunate few resorted to chartering private jets for their journey home (Zhang and Lampert, 2020). During the initial wave of the pandemic, an estimated 1.4 million Chinese remained overseas; for many of them, staying put was often not a matter of choice (Xia, 2022).

From the early months of 2020 through to December 2022, a substantial number of Chinese nationals residing abroad found themselves unable to return to China. The expenses associated with travel remained exorbitant and flight availability was capped to a minimum. In order to maintain a 'COVID-free bubble' within China, stringent border control measures were tightened further with a rigorous COVID-19 testing protocol and an extended compulsory quarantine period for international arrivals, which could extend to 56 days. These measures persisted throughout 2021 and 2022, with only minor adjustments made by the Chinese authorities, such as modifications to testing requirements or the duration of mandatory quarantine. It was not until the close of 2022 that these restrictions were lifted as a result of the Chinese state's rash decision to abandon its 'zero-COVID' policy (Ling and Zhang, 2023).

The 'foreignness' of COVID-19

Although COVID-19 first broke out in the Chinese city of Wuhan, over the course of the next two years Chinese authorities vehemently rejected accusations regarding the virus' origin. Instead, they asserted that the US was to blame for introducing the virus to China (Nie, 2020). An elaborate conspiracy theory targeted at the US in particular and the West in general (effectively, politicizing the pandemic) quickly gained traction among Chinese citizens, who came to believe that the coronavirus was a 'foreign' entity and that China had been victimized by West-engineered 'biological warfare' but had dealt with the threat responsibly and successfully. Misinformation and fearmongering spread widely within China, fuelling a new wave of xenophobia alongside a growing sense of nationalism (Elias et al, 2021). African migrants residing in Guangzhou, for example, were targeted for COVID-19 testing and contact tracing, and many were forcibly evicted from their accommodation for no good reason other than people's fear of infection (see, for example, Castillo and Amoah, 2020; Ma, 2020). Anti-Black discrimination was acutely symptomatic of the deep-seated racism in China, compounded by a disease paranoia reminiscent of earlier epidemics related to HIV/AIDS and Ebola (Ouassini et al, 2022).

The xenophobic reactions during COVID-19 mirrored China's approach to previous infectious outbreaks, notably the SARS outbreak in 2003 and the H1N1 influenza outbreak in 2009. Katherine Mason (2015) observes the racialization of viruses and infections, where highly infectious viruses were depicted as 'White' and 'foreign', but not Chinese. During the H1N1 outbreak, for example, Chinese public health experts repeatedly emphasized to Mason that H1N1 was 'not a Chinese virus' and that its 'Euro-American genes' were uniquely predisposed to infect Euro-American populations.

These experts 'cast H1N1 as a Euro-American disease and diverted any blame for the spread of foreign viruses inside China' (Mason, 2015, p 501).

COVID-19, in a similar vein, has been recast as a foreign virus imported from the 'outside' shortly after the initial outbreak in Wuhan was contained. As Chinese authorities began to insinuate the pandemic's potential origins in the US, they effectively 'raced' the virus to be 'White' (or 'Black') and foreign so as to refute the blame and avoid it being characterized as a 'Chinese virus'. This manufactured 'foreignness' of COVID-19 also served the purpose of creating distance between China and the prolonged threat of (re)infection. As long as public health authorities could prevent the virus from re-entering China's borders, this narrative might explicitly absolve China from responsibility.

Stigmatized returnees and spoiled identity

Once COVID-19 was framed as a foreign threat, especially as an 'American virus' originating from outside China, individuals attempting to enter the country were viewed with suspicion as potential virus carriers. Chinese nationals, particularly those residing in the US or Europe, found themselves in a new identity category that fell into an ambiguous space between being Chinese and wholly foreign. Returning Chinese bodies, consequently, became a source of particular concern due to this ambiguity. Once these returnees crossed Chinese borders, they were not as easily identifiable and traceable as Black or White foreigners. This raised the risk that the virus could be reintroduced by these travelling bodies, potentially breaching the racialized boundaries that had been established as a frontline defence against the pandemic.

Not only was the coronavirus 'raced' to create essential separation from being called Chinese, but returnees were also 'raced' as a separate from ordinary citizens living inside China. Their increased exposure to the West and the virus itself spoiled their identity as fully Chinese citizens, and their bodies were associated with unknown risks of deception and contagion. As Mason states, the 'racialisation of foreign, immigrant, or ethnic minority populations' has long been utilized as 'a means to separate out the infectious from the non-infectious' (2015, p 502). Mobile individuals, in particular, have often been the 'target of racialisation discourses aimed at keeping them from crossing boundaries guarded by those in power' (Mason, 2015, p 502). The racialization of Chinese nationals in the context of COVID-19 occurred in two interconnected realms, both closely associated with the virus. Outside China, their presence served as a reminder of the devastating 'Chinese virus' that wrecked lives; within China, they symbolized an 'imported infection' that posted a threat to public health in the country.

This dual process of racializing Chinese nationals living overseas introduced new dimensions to their identities and transnational movements. It also gave rise to a distinct ambiguity that resisted any kind of stable categorization. The mobility of bodies and the potential for contagion complicated the meanings of being Chinese as they crossed borders, particularly during a period when a deadly virus – a strong signifier of disease and impurity and a familiar trope in bioterrorism and biothrillers (Mayer, 2007) – registered unprecedented perceptions of threat. The virus, described as 'a trope of interrelation, mix-up, complication, subtlety and subversion' (Mayer, 2007, p 1), implicated invisible harm brought back by the transnational return journeys of Chinese nationals. These journeys, consequently, were imagined as pathways for the 'foreign' virus to infiltrate and breach the containment measures that had protected China.

On 19 March 2020, news broke regarding a man named Guo Weipeng from Zhengzhou city, Henan Province, who travelled to Milan to watch an Italian Serie A football match on 1 March 2020, right in the midst of the coronavirus outbreak. A few days later, on his return to China, Guo was found to be infected with the virus (Sina News, 2020). In the two days following his return, Guo continued his regular activities, including going to work, grocery shopping and visiting a pharmacy, until he started showing symptoms. Guo became the first confirmed case of COVID-19 in Henan Province, which has a population of 96 million. To the alarm of the local Centre for Disease Control in Zhengzhou City, nearly 40,000 individuals could have potentially come into contact with him within three days of his return, as he had been to various public places. Furthermore, some of his family members and several colleagues had already tested positive for the virus. This incident sparked immediate public panic in China, and Guo was given the pejorative nickname 'virus king' (*duwang*). Chinese authorities not only disclosed Guo's detailed travel itinerary through multiple media platforms but also shared his personal information, including his address and current employment status. By the time the news spread, Guo had already been apprehended by the police and charged with 'endangering public safety by dangerous means', a crime carrying severe penalties, including the possibility of life imprisonment.

The official announcement containing Guo's personal information and travel itinerary circulated widely on Chinese social media, eliciting public outrage directed toward Guo himself as well as other returning Chinese citizens, who were regarded as endangering tens of thousands of lives. The itemized itinerary provided a traceable record that portrayed Guo's trip to Italy as the source of mass infection. Guo's personhood disappeared in this public scandal when his identity became overwhelmingly entangled with the virus. Accused of being the 'virus king', Guo's spoiled identity cast him as a stigmatized figure, an Other within his own country and a national being 'out of place'. Guo, along with many others in similar situations, became the coronavirus personified, appearing to enter China from beyond its borders and disrupt and cause harm.

Guo's incident occurred simultaneously with several similar cases that went viral on social media platforms. These incidents all followed a similar pattern: Chinese returnees concealing their travel histories and subsequently testing positive after having possibly transmitted the virus and spread infection during their journeys back home. In a matter of days, online forums and social spaces were filled with criticism and growing resentment towards these Chinese returnees (Xia, 2022). Students in particular were referred to as 'giant babies' (*juying*) or 'spoiled brats' who had the economic means 'to flee China's brutal educational competition and then return home to reduce their coronavirus risk' (Jing, 2021, p 2). A few Chinese students studying in the US told the BBC that they were 'getting the short end of the stick from both sides' and felt like they were 'being kicked like a ball between the two countries'. They lamented how 'America wants to kick us out, while China doesn't allow us to return' (Feng, 2020).

On 23 May 2020, a Chinese student posted a vlog titled 'Foreign students' heart-breaking return in 2020, on the Five One Policy' on the popular video-sharing platform Bilibili (the equivalent of YouTube in the Chinese social media space). The video quickly garnered 10,000 views within days.[1] The vlogger, known as 'Elephant Susan', was a Chinese student in the US who shared her experiences of being stranded abroad due to multiple cancelled flights resulting from the Five One travel restrictions. She expressed feelings of helplessness and despair, describing the Five One policy as a 'fatal blow' (*zhiming de daji*) to overseas Chinese who needed to return home. Comments under this video showed a mix of strong sympathy and harsh criticism. One comment, for instance, read 'Stay out of China! Do you want to oppress (*pohai*) people back home? Are you returning to "poison" (*toudu*) us? We are already in a miserable situation, just give us an opportunity to live' (comment by 'pulushi chifei', posted 25 May 2020, Bilibili).

In addition to being stigmatized as 'virus carriers' (or even as the 'virus' itself), returning Chinese nationals were also labelled as 'pandemic refugees', adding another layer of separation intended to diminish any sense of entitlement or rights that Chinese returnees might assert. Chenchen Zhang (2020) observes a growing hostility in recent years aimed at immigrants, Muslims, feminists and asylum seekers within Chinese society, particularly in its online spaces. This trend mirrored the rise of Right-wing populism in Europe and North America. Chinese netizens picked up the vocabulary of the populist Right during the 2015 European refugee crisis and the 2016 US presidential election, becoming familiar with the overwhelmingly anti-refugee and anti-liberal rhetoric. Within the Chinese popular media landscape, immigrants and refugees, together with Muslims and Black individuals, were consistently portrayed as 'lazy, crime-prone and self-entitled', reinforcing an image of the ethno-racial Other as a stark contrast to the perceived Chinese self (that is, hard-working and high achieving; Zhang,

2020, p 101). The COVID-19 pandemic exacerbated this xenophobia and unapologetic racism, so much so that even Chinese nationals returning from abroad could not escape these extreme forms of Othering or avoid being stigmatized or verbally assaulted.

Online discussions claimed 'China is not a refugee camp' (Phoenix Weekly, 2020) and urged returning nationals to reconsider their actions so as not to strain China's public health system. On Zhihu, China's largest question-and-answer forum, akin to Quora, the following question was raised: 'What are your views on the verbal abuse by Chinese netizens directed at international students who returned home during the pandemic?'[2] This question attracted over 11 million views and received more than 4,500 responses. A notable reply, posted by 'Huli Chenxi' – a prominent influencer with nearly 400,000 followers on Zhihu – likened Chinese returnees to 'pandemic refugees':

> Our country certainly will never abandon any compatriot who holds Chinese citizenship or uses a Chinese passport. We cannot turn away those who wish to return driven by a sense of compatriot sentiments. However, they need to get a better grip of who they are and be realistic with where they stand. They need to realise that escaping the plague outside China is still an act of fleeing, and people need to act accordingly and approach it with humility. Do not expect that after studying abroad for a few years, or having obtained a Green Card and permanent residency, they will be treated as VIPs on their return, entitled to special treatment and privileges. (Huli Chenxi, 18 March 2020)[3]

The 'refugee' status associated with returning Chinese nationals, while temporary, consolidated a sense of Otherness. In Hélène Joffe's examination on risk and the Other, she explains how the Other was often defined in terms of 'difference and inferiority in relation to normative values in an ongoing sense' and notes that the 'representations that arise at times of crisis intensify this distinction' (Joffe, 1999, p 23). Mary Douglas (1966) previously demonstrated how a clear divide between the righteous 'us' and the transgressive 'them' could effectively create in-group solidarity and uphold the system of moral values that 'we' have established for ourselves. Chinese returnees, labelled as 'COVID refugees', symbolized both the chaos and failures symptomatic of the problems with the 'outside' world and China's safety and strength on the 'inside'. This stark contrast not only legitimized the 'contagion discourse' by reinforcing fortified borders and even stricter control over mobility, but also affirmed a sense of Chinese exceptionalism and biopolitical nationalism in the global war against COVID-19 (de Kloet et al, 2020).

Becoming deserving Chinese again

To return or not to return became a profound moral dilemma that overseas Chinese students grappled with in the weeks and months of the subsequent waves of the pandemic. Many ultimately chose to 'stay put', viewing this not just as an act of self-sacrifice to protect others but also as a means to regain recognition as legitimate, deserving Chinese citizens after the immediate crisis subsided. Staying in place was rationalized as a duty and obligation, as voluntary immobility was seen as the opposite of 'spreading the virus' or 'sending harm from afar'. By keeping the threat of infection at a distance from Chinese borders, would-be returnees believed they were serving their nation by alleviating the strain on infection control efforts and not 'bringing chaos to the nation' (*gei guojia tianluan*), thus supporting the work of Chinese public health workers and authorities. Many overseas students were personally swayed by these arguments, including 'Elephant Susan', who decided not to pursue their 'selfish' desires to return in order to safeguard the 'COVID-free bubble' maintained by China's fortified biopolitical borders. Convinced that China was 'the safest place in the world' (RFI, 2020), students credited the colossal efforts of the Chinese state in implementing draconian control measures even if it meant they themselves were prevented from returning home.

For those who made the decision to return, in an effort to counter the stigmatizing discourse representing returnees as irresponsible, transgressive and selfish, Chinese nationals developed their own framework of responsibility. Many diligently practised self-protection as they travelled across numerous airports and train stations, check-points and quarantine facilities, meticulously adhering to every safety guideline on final arrival and cooperating fully with authorities. Being recognized as a 'responsible returnee' on the way home was therefore a reward for good behaviour and a recognition of one's deservingness. B.L. (2023) details the tedious yet necessary 'rituals' that Chinese students undertook in preparation for their return. According to her account, in 2022 some students took rapid antigen tests daily for two months leading up to their departure in order to maintain a COVID-free status. Others engaged in extended pre-departure self-isolation, even when it was not required by either UK or Chinese authorities. To ensure they could travel COVID-free, some Chinese students in the UK, at a time when almost all COVID-19-related restrictions were lifted in the city where they resided, voluntarily limited their social activities and refrained from going out unless absolutely necessary. Their voluntary quarantine might have seemed excessive in the UK context when self-isolation was not even required for those testing positive for COVID-19.

These additional preventative measures bore a resemblance to the expected practices in China under the prolonged 'zero-COVID' (*qingling*) regime.

While the rest of the world had, to some extent, transitioned back to more 'normal' lives, in China, people continued to live under the coercive biopolitical apparatus institutionalized by the state in pursuit of zero infection targets three years into the pandemic (Yerushalmy, 2022). Within China's borders, it was nearly inconceivable to go anywhere without a negative COVID-19 test. Contracting the virus could trigger instant stigmatization, with infected individuals often blamed for being careless or irresponsible (Ling and Zhang, 2023). Chinese citizens remained apprehensive about both the disease itself and about the associated culpability and stigma that came with it.

In a curious way, prospective Chinese returnees found themselves aligning their daily practices with China's zero-COVID-19 norms and adhering to extended restrictions even while living abroad. As argued by B.L. (2023), overseas Chinese nationals planning to return to China 'constructed their identities as liminal subjects and separated themselves from the existing social structures' well in advance of their intended journeys. It was as if they had to lead parallel lives across time-space – while physically residing in the UK, they had to pre-emptively adjust to synchronize with Chinese temporal rhythms and Chinese moral social codes. Returning as COVID-19-free citizens meant that they would be acknowledged as innocent and harmless, as responsible returnees deserving reintegration into the Chinese 'we group'. Their commitment to self-discipline and compliance while living abroad showcased their capacity and willingness to be 'model citizens', effectively distinguishing themselves, as deserving compatriots, from the less deserving Other.

Conclusion

In a discussion of media portrayals of Ukrainian labour migrants during the pandemic, Tymezuk (2021) highlights how Ukrainian nationals were often blamed for 'bringing the virus back home'. He observes that while Ukrainian labour migrants were considered part of the national 'we', their presence 'in the dangerous outside excludes them from the imagined immunity' (Tymczuk, 2021, p 928). In a similar way, Chinese nationals embodied this ambiguity. Blamed for transmitting COVID-19 back home when the coronavirus was imagined to be a 'foreign virus' in Chinese society, returning nationals were recast as outsiders, as contaminated national subjects whose return would penetrate and weaken China's 'imagined immunity'.

On Chinese social media, the question of whether overseas Chinese should return for safety elicited divided opinion. In relation to the Zhihu post mentioned earlier, a comment with thousands of upvotes encapsulated the ambiguity around the identity of Chinese returnees: 'With a Chinese passport or ID card, you are indeed a Chinese citizen (*zhongguo gongmin*); however, this does not mean you are one of the Chinese people (*zhongguo renmin*)' (comment by 'eAGp87', posted 15 March 2020). This distinction between a 'Chinese citizen' and a member of the 'Chinese people' illustrates how blunt boundary making within the 'we group' continued to separate self from the Other.

Chinese citizens faced difficulties returning home as they were not considered integral to the national identity amid the global health crisis. Stigmatization, fuelled by the perception of Chinese returnees as potential carriers of the coronavirus, eroded their sense of belonging. Such stigmatization resulted in their classification as 'foreigners', essentially a form of racialization that served to differentiate and exclude, due to not only the fear of the virus but also the politicization of pandemic nationalism. The movements and transnational journeys of Chinese individuals were viewed as perilous and transgressive, as their ambiguous mobility could compromise the biopolitical borders and jeopardize China's public and social health. Citizen returnees were therefore framed as unethical and selfish, and their prolonged immobility and commitment to self-discipline became a moral decision reflecting a distinct form of COVID-19 'ethopolitics' (Rose, 2001).

Notes

[1]   The original video was quickly banned by Bilibili, on 24 May 2020, and 'Elephant Susan' reposted the same video on YouTube, attracting over 53,000 views. The video is available at: https://youtu.be/RwZ2CHmoeXE (accessed 20 April 2023).

[2]   The question and responses are available at: www.zhihu.com/question/378706911 (accessed 20 April 2023).

[3]   The original quote in Chinese is: '我们的国家当然不会放弃任何一个同胞。只要还是中国国籍，拿着中国护照，基于同胞情分，当然绝不可能拒绝，但也希望他们明确一下自己的身份，摆正一下自己的位置：逃避瘟疫也是逃难，逃难就要有逃难的觉悟。别以为去国外念了几年书，或者是拿了绿卡永居权，就真把自己当作回来做客的贵宾，当成必须要享受特殊待遇的人上人了' (available at www.zhihu.com/question/378706911, accessed 20 April 2023).

References

Adey, P., Hannam, K., Sheller, M. and Tyfield, D. (2021) 'Pandemic (im)mobilities', *Mobilities*, 16(1): 1–19.

Bélanger, D. and Silvey, R. (2019) 'An im/mobility turn: power geometries of care and migration', *Journal of Ethnic and Migration Studies*, 46(16): 3423–40.

Bigo, D. (2002) 'Security and immigration: toward a critique of the governmentality of unease', *Alternatives: Global Local Political*, 27(1): 63–92.

B.L. (2023) 'Embodied border control on the move: elf-management of Chinese returnees under the zero-COVID regime', *HAU: Journal of Ethnographic Theory*, 13(2). doi: 10.1086/726622

Brandhorst, R., Baldassar, L. and Wilding, R. (2020) 'Introduction to the special issue: "transnational family care 'on hold'? intergenerational relationships and obligations in the context of immobility regimes"', *Journal of Intergenerational Relationships*, 18(3): 261–80.

Caijing (2020) 'What obstacles need to be addressed for the 1.42 million overseas students stranded abroad to return home by charter flights?' (142万留学生滞留海外，包机回国需要解决的阻碍是什么), *Caijing News*, 31 March. Available from: https://news.sina.cn/2020-03-31/detail-iimxxsth2898231.d.html (accessed 14 March 2023).

Castillo, R. and Amoah, P.A. (2020) 'Africans in post-COVID-19 pandemic China: is there a future for China's "new minority"?', *Asian Ethnicity*, 21(4): 560–5.

de Kloet, J., Lin, J. and Chow, Y.F. (2020) '"We are doing better": biopolitical nationalism and the COVID-19 virus in east Asia', *European Journal of Cultural Studies*, 23(4): 635–40.

Douglas, M. (1966) *Purity and Danger: An Analysis of the Concepts of Pollution and Taboo*, London: Routledge.

Elias, A., Ben, J., Mansouri, F. and Paradies, Y. (2021) 'Racism and nationalism during and beyond the COVID-19 pandemic', *Ethnic and Racial Studies*, 44(5): 783–93.

Feng, Z. (2020) 'Being a Chinese student in the US: "neither the US nor China wants us"', *BBC*, 4 August. Available from: www.bbc.co.uk/news/world-us-canada-53573289 (accessed 15 April 2023).

Fifield, A. (2020) 'Chinese citizens abroad seek refuge from the coronavirus pandemic—at home', *The Washington Post*, 17 March. Available from: www.washingtonpost.com/world/asia_pacific/chinese-citizens-abroad-seek-refuge-from-the-coronavirus-epidemic--at-home/2020/03/17/836140f8-67f2-11ea-b199-3a9799c54512_story.html (accessed 15 March 2023).

Goffman, E. (1963) *Stigma: Notes on the Management of Spoiled Identity*, Englewood Cliffs, NJ: Prentice-Hall.

Grove, N.J. and Zwi, A.B. (2006) 'Our health and theirs: forced migration, othering, and public health', *Social Science & Medicine*, 62(8): 1931–42.

Hage, G. (2009) 'Waiting out the crisis: on stuckedness and governmentality', in G. Hage (ed) *Waiting*, Melbourne: Melbourne University Press, pp 97–106.

Jing, Y. (2021) 'Caught in the middle? Chinese international students' self-formation amid politics and pandemic', *International Journal of Chinese Education*, 10(3): 1–15.

Joffe, H. (1999) *Risk and 'the Other'*, Cambridge: Cambridge University Press.

Johnson, M. (2015) 'Surveillance, pastoral power and embodied infrastructures of care among migrant Filipino Muslims in the Kingdom of Saudi Arabia', *Surveillance & Society*, 13(2): 250–64.

Lin, W. and Yeoh, B.S.A. (2021) 'Pathological (im)mobilities: managing risk in a time of pandemics', *Mobilities*, 16(1): 96–112.

Ling, M. and Zhang, J. (2023) 'Introduction: zero-COVID was forever, until it was no more', *HAU: Journal of Ethnographic Theory*, 13(2). doi: 10.1086/726456

Ma, X. (2020) 'Unemployment and xenophobia persist for migrant workers as China's lockdown is lifted', *MMB Blog*, 23 June. Available from: https://migration.bristol.ac.uk/2020/06/23/unemployment-and-xenophobia-persist-for-migrant-workers-in-china-as-lockdown-is-lifted/ (accessed 27 October 2023).

Mason, K.A. (2015) 'H1N1 is not a Chinese virus: the racialisation of people and viruses in post-SARS China', *Studies in Comparative International Development*, 50(4): 500–18.

Mayer, R. (2007) 'Virus discourse: the rhetoric of threat and terrorism in the biothriller', *Cultural Critique*, 66: 1–20.

Mezzadra, S. and Stierl, M. (2020) 'What happens to freedom of movement during a pandemic?', *Open Democracy*, 24 March. Available from: www.opendemocracy.net/en/can-europe-make-it/what-happens-freedom-movement-during-pandemic/ (accessed 25 October 2021).

Nail, T. (2015) *The Figure of the Migrant*, Stanford, CA: Stanford University Press.

Nayar, P.K. (2020) 'The long walk: migrant workers and extreme mobility in the age of corona', *Journal of Extreme Anthropology*, 4(1): E1–E6.

New York Times (2020) 'It's like a war', 17 March. Available from: www.nytimes.com/2020/03/17/podcasts/the-daily/italy-coronavirus.html (accessed 22 June 2021).

Nie, J.B. (2020) 'In the shadow of biological warfare: conspiracy theories on the origins of COVID-19 and enhancing global governance of biosafety as a matter of urgency', *Journal of Bioethical Inquiry*, 17(4): 567–74.

O'Brien, M.L. and Eger, M.A. (2021) 'Suppression, spikes, and stigma: how COVID-19 will shape international migration and hostilities toward it', *International Migration Review*, 55(3): 640–59.

Ouassini, A., Amini, M. and Ouassini, N. (2022) '#ChinaMustexplain: global tweets, COVID-19, and anti-Black racism in China', *The Review of Black Political Economy*, 49(1): 61–76.

Phoenix Weekly (2020) 'Why is it that when Chinese people return to their own country, they are labelled as "spreading poisoning from afar"?' (中国人回个国，怎么就成了'万里投毒'), 23 March. Available from: www.ifengweekly.com/detil.php?id=9279 (accessed 15 April 2023).

RFI (2020) 'China has become the safest place in the world, but overseas students, you should hold off on returning for now' (中國成了世界上最安全的地方但是留學生們你先別回來), 9 March. Available from: https://rfi.my/5a3G (accessed 20 April 2023).

Rose, N. (2001) 'The politics of life itself', *Theory, Culture & Society*, 18(6): 1–30.

Salazar, N.B. (2021) 'Existential vs. essential mobilities: insights from before, during and after a crisis', *Mobilities*, 16(1): 20–34.

Schewel, K. (2019) 'Understanding immobility: moving beyond the mobility bias in migration studies', *International Migration Review*, 54(2): 328–55.

Schiller, N.G. and Salazar, N.B. (2013) 'Regimes of mobility across the globe', *Journal of Ethnic and Migration Studies*, 39(2): 183–200.

Shamir, R. (2005) 'Without borders? Notes on globalization as a mobility regime', *Sociological Theory*, 23(2): 197–217.

Sina News (2020) 'How was Guo Weipeng, the virus king of Zhengzhou, discovered? Having come into contact with 39,373 people, what punishment did he receive?' (郑州毒王郭伟鹏是怎么被发现的？接触39373人，受到什么惩罚), 19 March. Available from: https://k.sina.com.cn/article_7032887726_1a33159ae00100lmev.html?from=news (accessed 14 March 2023).

Staeheli, L.A. (2011) 'Political geography: where's citizenship?', *Progress in Human Geography*, 35(3): 393–400.

Su, A. (2020) '"No Blacks": evicted, harassed and targeted in China for their race amid coronavirus', *Los Angeles Times*, 16 April. Available from: www.latimes.com/world-nation/story/2020-04-16/china-coronavirus-black-african-evictions (accessed 15 April 2023).

Tan, Y., Li, W. and Tsuda, T. (2022) 'Cross-border im/mobility of skilled migrants from the U.S. to China: a capital-mobility framework', *Journal of Ethnic and Migration Studies*, 49(13): 3327–47.

Thomas, K. (2019) *Global Epidemics, Local Implications: African Immigrants and the Ebola Crisis in Dallas*, Baltimore, MD: Johns Hopkins University Press.

Tymczuk, A. (2021) 'Bringing the virus back home: media representations of Ukrainian labour migrants in a time of pandemic', *East European Politics and Societies and Cultures*, 36(3): 913–34.

Ullah, A.K.M.A., Nawaz, F. and Chattoraj, D. (2021) 'Locked up under lockdown: the COVID-19 pandemic and the migrant population', *Social Sciences & Humanities Open*, 3(1): art 100126. doi: 10.1016/j.ssaho.2021.100126

Wald, P. (2008) *Contagious: Cultures, Carriers, and the Outbreak Narrative*, Durham, NC: Duke University Press.

Wang, S., Chen, X., Li, Y., Luu, C., Yan, R. and Madrisotti, F. (2020) '"I'm more afraid of racism than of the virus!": racism awareness and resistance among Chinese migrants and their descendants in France during the COVID-19 pandemic', *European Societies*, 23(1): 721–42.

Weale, S. (2020) 'Chinese students flee UK after "maskaphobia" triggered racist attacks', *The Guardian*, 17 March. Available from: www.theguardian.com/education/2020/mar/17/chinese-students-flee-uk-after-maskaphobia-triggered-racist-attacks (accessed 23 June 2021).

White, A.I.R. (2020) 'Historical linkages: epidemic threat, economic risk, and xenophobia', *The Lancet*, 395(10232): 1250–1.

Willen, S.S. (2012) 'How is health-related "deservingness" reckoned? Perspectives from unauthorized im/migrants in Tel Aviv', *Social Science & Medicine*, 74(6): 812–21.

Xia, Z. (2022) 'Resentment in China against those studying abroad during COVID-19 is a symptom of larger social problems', *South China Morning Post*, 18 May. Available from: www.scmp.com/comment/opinion/arti cle/3178036/resentment-china-against-those-studying-abroad-during-covid-19?module=perpetual_scroll_0&pgtype=article&campaign=3178 036 (accessed 15 March 2023).

Xiang, B., Allen, W.L., Khosravi, S., Kringelbach, H.N., Ortiga, Y.Y., Liao, K.A.S. et al (2023) 'Shock mobilities during moments of acute uncertainty', *Geopolitics*, 28(4): 1632–57.

Yerushalmy, J. (2022) 'Zero-COVID policy: why is China still having severe lockdowns?', *The Guardian*, 29 November. Available from: www.theguard ian.com/world/2022/nov/29/china-zero-covid-policy-what-is-it-and-why-lockdowns-quarantine-protests (accessed 20 April 2023).

Yuan, L. (2020) 'Trapped abroad, China's "little pinks" rethink their country', *New York Times*, 24 June. Available from: https://cn.nytimes.com/china/20200624/china-nationalist-students-coronavirus/dual/ (accessed 15 March 2023).

Zhang, C. (2020) 'Right-wing populism with Chinese characteristics? Identity, otherness and global imaginaries in debating world politics online', *European Journal of International Relations*, 26(1): 88–115.

Zhang, J. and Wang, B. (2023) 'Nearly mobile: pandemic im/mobilities and lockdown strategies amongst Asian migrant professionals in England', *Journal of Ethnic and Migration Studies*, 49(19): 4964–83.

Zhang, Y. and Lampert, A. (2020) 'Chinese students fleeing virus-hit U.S. pay $20,000 for seats on private jets', *Reuters*, 25 March. Available from: www.reuters.com/article/us-health-coronavirus-china-students-idUSKBN21C 0SF (accessed 14 March 2023).

9

The Family Idyll, Exclusion and Ideology in *Persepolis*

Nariman Massoumi

Introduction

In 'giving voice' to marginalized or under-represented communities, autobiographical films about migration might be considered as challenging or, offering opposition to, anti-migrant discourse. Rarely is attention given to instances where such films (despite, perhaps, the stated intentions of their makers) do precisely the opposite – that is, when they contribute to anti-migrant perspectives by (re)producing exclusionary stereotypes or ideologies. Furthermore, while diasporic cinema has challenged the methodological nationalism of the 'national cinemas' paradigm (Higson, 2000; Ezra and Rowden, 2006), scholarship in this area has tended to ignore how mobility across borders can imaginatively or discursively reinforce (and not necessarily simply challenge) nationalist perspectives, except more broadly in the prelapsarian or nostalgic representations of an idealized homeland. Focusing on the widely celebrated French–Iranian diasporic autobiographical animation *Persepolis* (2007) by Marjane Satrapi and Vincent Paronnaud and adapted from the former's celebrated graphic novels, this chapter examines the film's construction of community identity and how precisely through its appeal for belonging and inclusion of one kind of migrant (namely, secular, middle-class Iranians), the film denies the belonging and inclusion of others.

Persepolis chronicles Satrapi's formative childhood years in Iran against the backdrop of the turmoil of the Iranian revolution and the Iran–Iraq War (1980–88), her migration to Vienna for secondary education and her subsequent return to Iran during her teens, concluding with her eventual decision to move to France. The migration and resettlement of Iranians around the globe in the aftermath of the Iranian revolution (1979) and the Iran–Iraq War was matched by a rise in Iranian films, filmmakers and audiences outside the territorial boundaries of Iran (Naficy, 2008, 2012). For Naficy, these media forms have 'spoken' for displaced Iranians and shaped their experiences, allowing them to navigate and make sense of their migration, reconstruct their past and form new cultural identities (Naficy, 2012, p 384).

Persepolis is arguably the most high profile and celebrated of Iranian diasporic autobiographical films. It won the Jury Prize at Cannes (2007) and was nominated for an Oscar for Best Animated Feature (2008). The film is adapted from the four-volume French graphic novels (Satrapi, 2000–03), published in two volumes in English (Satrapi, 2003–04), to widespread acclaim. It is one of the few films depicting the experience of secular Leftist Iranians in the diaspora. In 'speaking for' Iranian migration (as Naficy claims of Iranian diasporic films), *Persepolis* brings attention to Spivak's distinction (mentioned in the introduction of this book) between representation as *Vertretung* – that is, 'speaking for' or standing for – and *Darstellung* – a representation or portrait.

Published in the context of the war on terror and hostile relations between Iran and the West, Satrapi's graphic novels belonged to a flurry of autobiographical memoirs emerging from Iranian women during this period. Their commercial success, Negar Mottahadeh (2004, p 2) notes, cannot be coincidental. As Whitlock argues, in surfacing 'a long history of fascination, mourning, obsession', Iranian life narratives 'occupy a specific subculture that is shaped by their origins in a turbulent period of Iranian history and culture and by the geopolitical grid of the war on terror that determines their production and reception as valued commodities' (2007, p 16).

Satrapi's decision to adapt the novels using animation over live action was partly motivated by a desire to humanize Iranians and Middle Easterners against negative representations shaped by this context, with Iran's designation by then US president George Bush as one of the countries on the 'axis of evil'. While live action 'would have turned into a story of people living in a distant land who don't look like us', Satrapi claims, the abstraction of animation allows for 'a universal story' (Satrapi, 2007, pp 5–6). This chapter is interested in the meaning of 'us' in the film and its implications for Satrapi's intentions of challenging misrepresentations.

Satrapi's novels have been the focus of energetic academic debate, with broad agreement on their status as a feminist text challenging rigid distinctions between West and East (Malek, 2006), resisting Brown girl rescue narratives (Gilmore and Marshall, 2010) and challenging simplistic representations of the veil (Naghibi and O'Malley, 2005). However, other authors have also questioned the novels' orientalism in relation to the war on terror (Ezzatikarami and Ameri, 2019). While some critics (for example, Hamid, 2007) note the lack of nuance and complexity in the animated adaptation, the film has not received the level of critical attention afforded the novels.

This chapter seeks to contribute to our understanding of the racialized representations in the film, beyond the contexts of orientalism and the war on terror (albeit acknowledging the relevance of these framings), by focusing instead on two significant yet neglected aspects: the centrality of the family as a trope in the construction of identity and belonging; and the film's position as a French film about the Iranian revolution and its aftermath. As Whitlock argues, it is the work of criticism to 'decipher the imaginative weaving together of "here" and "there"' for there is a tendency in analysis of exilic memoir to efface 'the historically specific conditions of production, dissemination, and reception' (2007, p 162).

My interest lies not in rehearsing existing debates on the film or novels, but rather in a closer reading on hitherto overlooked aspects of the film relevant to the representation of migrants. Focusing on several scenes narrating the revolution and post-revolutionary society, I show how *Persepolis* reproduces French neo-republican views on legitimate statehood or 'good' citizenship within an Iranian domestic setting. Satrapi's family are constructed as French citizens-in-waiting, sharing a commonality to a racialized idea of French national identity defined in contradistinction to an essentialized Muslim or Arab identity, in turn coded as alien or threatening to this 'community of value' (Anderson, 2013). The film's depiction of domestic family scenes in pre- and post-revolutionary Iran, I argue, are equally, if not more, relevant to *Persepolis'* status as a film about migration than the scenes charting her relocation from Iran to Europe. The chapter considers then how the 'I' in the autobiographical *Persepolis*, pluralized to a collective 'us' or 'we', is reliant on the exclusion of a 'them'.

An accented family

One of the pioneering contributions to the study of migrant cinemas is Hamid Naficy's (2001) theory of 'accented cinemas', where the linguistic analogy of the accent is applied to frame stylistic commonalities between exilic and diasporic filmmakers.[1] As Naficy argues, an accent in film functions as both an accent and dialect in linguistics by penetrating at a deep structural level. Exilic and diasporic accented films inflect the components of a classical or dominant cinema language by their displaced cultural origins and traditions. Society's dominant form of cinema, Hollywood, is *the* standardized 'accent'. Much like the official accent of newsreaders on television news, Hollywood's accent is considered 'standard, neutral and value-free' (Naficy, 2001, p 23). What distinguishes the accents in exilic or diasporic films is their displacement and deterritorialization due to their position within the 'interstices' of social formations and cinematic practices. Naficy (2001, p 4) identifies a range of components that are typical of the accented style, including open and closed forms; epistolary form; nostalgic structures of feeling; interstitial and collective modes of production; and self-inscription of the filmmakers dis/location. Through a linguistic frame of reference, Naficy demonstrates 'the sense of a different cultural *voice* contained in a permanent dialogic relationship with the dominant host culture' (Philips, 2003, p 344).

We can see how *Persepolis* might be 'accented' by its interstitiality between Western, French and Iranian cultural influences. Its hand-drawn black-and-white two-dimensional animation, developed from the original graphic novel illustrations, has clear influences of German expressionism and Italian neo-realism in its rendering of revolution and war, as Satrapi herself has stated (see Satrapi, 2008). Floating jasmine flowers and minarets in the opening credits recall formal aesthetics of both Persian miniature art and the French–Belgian *bande dessinée* (comic strip) tradition to which the graphic novels belong. While motion does not allow for the concentration afforded by the graphic comic panel, the movement, sound, voice-over and temporality enabled in animated film allow for a speed and fluidity in the representation of life events – these features have their limitations (Hamid, 2007, p 62) and, I would add, potential. Satrapi chose animation over live action partly to maintain 'cohesion and consistency' (Satrapi, 2007, p 6) between reality and dream/fantasy and partly to work at a level of abstraction when it came to the setting and location. The playful fluidity between dream and reality aligns with the coming-of-age story structure and the perspective of the child central protagonist, while rendering traumatic events experienced, such as repression and violence during the Iran–Iraq War, accessible (Warren, 2010).

This formal hybridity, however, does not extend more literally and audibly to the film's spoken voices, despite accented cinemas being mostly characterized as 'bilingual, multilingual or multi-accented' (Naficy, 2001, p 24). Unlike the graphic novel, animated film allows for an original language and its accents (their tonality, cadence, inflections and so on) to be *heard* while they are simultaneously translated into another language via subtitles. *Persepolis*, however, adopts the language of the host country (French), with characters voiced by famous French actors, including generations of illustrious French female stars as lead women: Chiara Mastroianni as Marjane; Catherine Deneuve[2] as her mother; and Danielle Darrieux – whose eight-decade career embodies quintessential French female stardom – as Marjane's grandmother. In the English-language version, Mastroianni and Deneuve retain their roles but speak in French-accented English.

Cristina Johnston claims the recounting of an exile story through iconic French women is a deliberately subversive strategy for 'giving voice to a generation of Iranian women' (2015, p 111). But it is difficult not to regard it as an erasure, or domestication of, cultural difference through a liberal humanist universality – an example of 'they are like us' rather than 'we are like them' (Naghibi and O'Malley, 2005, p 226). Satrapi's background is relevant here. Coming from a middle-class family of political dissidents, she was educated in Le Lycee Razi, a French-language school in Tehran, attended a French Catholic boarding school during her time in Vienna and completed her master's degree in Iran before attending university at Haute école des arts du Rhin in Strasbourg.

From the outset, the melancholic exile story places France as the 'primary point of reference' with Marjane's perspective as a French citizen (Hamid, 2007, p 62). An adult Marjane, reluctantly wearing a hijab (preparing for travel to Iran), sits despondently in Paris' Orly airport unable to bring herself to board the flight. The scene is rendered in colour to represent the present day, yet as Marjane sits smoking, a monochrome energetic younger 'Marji'[3] appears before her, signalling our entry into childhood memories. We track[4] with Marji as she runs to embrace her cousin Nioucha (not wearing the hijab), who is returning to Tehran from a trip to Paris in 1978 – Marji bombards her with questions about her trip, forging an imaginative connection with France as a desirable destination. The film mostly takes place in the monochrome flashback but returns to the present–day airport briefly a further three times, reiterating Marjane's ambivalence to her homeland and ending with her decision not to return.

From the beginning of the flashback, Marjane's immediate family – parents, uncle and aunt, and grandmother – are centralized, pictured as a unit in one frame like a family portrait, as they greet Nioucha. Families feature prominently in diasporic cinema through narratives of separation and reunion or as a site where cultural identities and generational conflicts can be explored (Berghahn, 2013, p 40). A powerful concept in 'domestic genealogies' of race and nationhood (Gilroy, 1993; McClintock, 1995), the family as nation (for example, 'motherland') offers a neat rhetorical device in cinema, a universal reach that can speak to the macro politics of inclusion and exclusion within an intimate frame. However, its cultural heterogeneity means the diasporic family is sometimes perceived as undermining the singular identity imposed by nationalism (Berghahn, 2013, p 44) by resisting its containment into the 'imagined community' of nationhood (Anderson, 1983). To the contrary, *Persepolis'* hybridity, I would suggest, fuses ideas of imagined nationhood in two different countries (France and Iran) that reinforce, rather than challenge, dominant nationalist discourses in each.

To illustrate this point, Mikhail Bakhtin's concept 'chronotope' is useful. For Bakhtin, the chronotope (literally time-space) is a 'unit of analysis' for identifying the interconnectedness of space and time in literature, where 'time thickens, takes on flesh, becomes artistically visible' and 'space becomes charged and responsive to the movements of time, plot and history' (1981, p 84). The inextricability of space and time renders the chronotope relevant to cinema and diaspora 'by the temporal component of memory and the spatial component of dislocation', which are 'constitutive of diaspora consciousness', but also the 'dialectical tensions between two places, the "here" and "there", coalesce with the tensions between the present and the past' (Berghahn, 2013, p 64).[5]

The family is one historical permutation of the *idyll* chronotope, defined by Bakhtin as a folkloric experience of time and space, 'an organic fastening-down, a grafting of life and its events to a place, to a familiar territory' (1981, p 225). Life and events are 'inseparable from this concrete, spatial corner of the world where the fathers and grandfathers lived and one's children and their children will live' (Bakhtin, 1981, p 225). As a limited 'little world', the idyll is 'sufficient unto itself, not linked in any intrinsic way with other places, with the rest of the world', but where 'a sequence of generations is localized that is potentially without limit' (Bakhtin, 1981, p 225). Emerging in the provisional and classic family novel, against the backdrop of capitalist modernity, the idyll was 'radically reworked' on the 'soil of the bourgeois family' (Bakhtin, 1981, p 231).

One of the defining characteristics of the family idyll relevant to *Persepolis* is the temporary mobility of its characters into the confusing and hostile 'cold, hard alien world' outside, before returning to the 'warm little corners of human feeling' (Bakhtin, 1981, p 233) and stability of the family home. Repeatedly, Marjane's experiences outside the family home are mired in danger, fear, failure, rejection and disappointment, and she continually returns for security, continuity, stability, education and understanding, most evident in Marjane's isolated experience as a migrant adolescent in Vienna, which ultimately ends in disappointment and return home. For Berghahn, the circularity and the cyclicity of the family idyll is threatened by the unpredictability of migration, or the linearity of the 'road chronotope', which is 'characterised by progress, random encounters with strangers and unexpected occurrences' and the reason why families rarely feature in the road movie genre (2013, p 65). My interest lies in how the family idyll (and threat of its destruction) structures Marji's experience of revolution and its aftermath, the viewer's access to knowledge and understanding of these events, and how this comes to define the Satrapi family's identity against others.

Early in the film, Marji's blissful childhood is disrupted by the revolutionary turmoil under the Shah's dictatorship, which permeates her family home through Marji's encounters with family or friends. Marji processes challenging and traumatic events in the adult world through a combination of rebellion, curiosity and childhood play. The witnessing of everyday violence is an important theme here, carried successfully from the novels, with a 'radical disjuncture' between the minimalist animation and the 'complicated traumatic events they depict: harassment, torture, execution, bombings, mass murder' (Chute, 2008, p 99). After hearing the account of a family friend, Siamak, who experienced torture in prison, Marji and her friends seek vengeance against a classmate, believing his father worked for the Shah's secret police. While represented comically, the fervour of the pursuit points to how 'impressionable young minds … can easily be converted to the belief systems of the adults around them' (Warren, 2010, p 122). In an earlier scene, a cosy domestic encounter between Marji and her grandmother (as Marji's mother cooks) is interrupted by shouts of 'Down with the Shah', leading the three of them to witness the protests through the window. Marji's father runs up the stairs to report enthusiastically that the Shah has fallen. Domestic spaces (living room, kitchen, bedroom), thresholds (windows, doors, stairs) and activities (watching television, cooking) become transitional conduits to Marji's witnessing and understanding political developments outside her childhood world. For Palmer (2011), the significance of the relationship between Marjane and her mother and grandmother and the reproductive space in particularizing history challenges the silencing of women and connects motherhood politically to a cultural and national narrative.

Marji's childhood innocence relies on her family members' explanations of these events and their history. It is useful to distinguish here between Marjane Satrapi as the underlying narrator of narrative events[6] and the textual presence of Marjane in the film as the two character narrators – an adult reflecting on her past (mostly in voice-over) and a child/teenager whose experiences are being narrated and depicted in graphic form. The viewer's encounter with historical events is shaped through this hierarchy of knowledge: the child's view – how Marji sees, experiences, interprets and responds to revolution and war – and the adult Marjane, addressing us directly, lending explanation to unfolding events from a reflective distance. As adults who explain historical events to Marji (but who are not always aware precisely how they will unfold), Marjane's family members adopt a pedagogical authority, both with Marji and with an audience presumed to be unfamiliar with the political history.

When, for example, Marji expresses the view of the Shah's divine right to rule ('He was chosen by God'), her father explains 'what really happened' by offering her a quick and humorous history of Mohammad Reza Shah's father, Reza Shah, his overthrow of the Qajar dynasty and the establishment of a dictatorship with the help of the British. This account is represented as a marionette-style puppet show, drawing on French and Persian traditions of puppetry and oral storytelling. Visually, the hand-drawn animation constructs a fluidity between childhood fantasy and historical reality, as Marji takes pride in learning of her grandfather, a Qajar prince turned communist, and his imprisonment by Reza Shah. One of Marji's closest connections is with her revolutionary Uncle Anouche, who recalls, in the form of a bedtime story, his Uncle Fereydoun's involvement in declaring independence of Azerbaijan province, his subsequent execution and Anouche's own persecution and exile to Russia before returning to Iran. Anouche's later imprisonment and execution under the Islamic republic has a profound impact on Marji's emotional and intellectual development.

While the idyll is determined by an intrinsic *disconnection* from the outside world, in placing generations of Satrapi family members 'who had lived in the same place, under the same conditions, and who had seen the same things' (Bakhtin, 1981, p 225) at the centre of unfolding political events in a histography of Iran, external events are accommodated into the idyll's structuring logic. The Satrapis are defined as a secular family with a set of democratic ideals and dissident tradition at the centre of Iranian history. However, this fusion of the familial with the historical is highly selective through its idyllic structure. There is little indication of the class antagonism driving the Iranian revolution, particularly the pivotal role of oil workers' strikes and the *shohras* (workers councils), which for a Leftist or communist dissident family would be of significant interest. *Persepolis* draws on the family idyll's 'concealed logic of abandonment' and 'self-justifying narrowing of the human community', which, as Dave (2006, p 51) argues,[7] makes it a serviceable form in capitalist societies as it denies class while simultaneously making claims on universal human experience.

Persepolis and dislocative nationalism

Persepolis takes its title from the name of the ceremonial capital of the Persian Empire, a key referent in Aryanist discourses within Iranian nationalism. In her study of Satrapi's graphic novels, Hamidi (2022) shows how Satrapi approaches the Aryanist myth critically. For example, her father's explanation of Reza Shah Pahlavi's rise challenges Marji's uncritical adoption of the Pahlavis' myth-making – also present in the film and mentioned earlier. However, Satrapi still adopts a version of the Aryanist perspective, albeit a liberal human rights counter-narrative (Hamidi, 2022, p 243). The graphic novels' introduction is particularly revealing, celebrating the purity of Persian culture, its Aryan roots and how it 'withstood' invasions from the outside and changed the invaders who were assimilated by its, presumably irresistible, allure.[8]

Zia-Ebrahimi (2016) identifies a dominant ideological current in Iranian nationalism that he has coined 'dislocative nationalism'. This views Iran as an Aryan nation adrift from the 'rest of its fellow Aryans (read: Europeans)' and characterized by a longing for a pre-Islamic grandeur and glory, inspired by pre-Islamic forms and symbols (Zia-Ebrahimi, 2016, p 5). Through an imaginative operation, Iran is dislodged 'from its empirical reality as a majority-Muslim society situated—broadly—in the "East"' (Zia-Ebrahimi, 2016, p 5). Dislocative nationalism has a set of core ideas: it views Iran as 'a primordial nation that has been in uninterrupted existence for 2,500 years' and considers its 'essence and glory is to be found in its pre-Islamic golden age' (Zia-Ebrahimi, 2016, pp 2–3). As a body of thought and set of discursive practices, it is a modern ideology, a popular form of nationalism, rooted in Iran's troubled encounter with Europe and characterized by the view that Iran's history after the arrival of Islam was one of 'a long process of degeneration' and 'ethnicized into an "Arab invasion"' (Zia-Ebrahami, 2016, pp 1–2).

The significance of this emerges in the film's depiction of the post-revolutionary government's arrival. Over black, a radio voice announces the election of an Islamic republic in a referendum by popular vote. Fading in and out, each family member appears as an individual vignette against black, reflecting on the turn of events. The vignettes visually imply the spotlight of being under interrogation, while indicating the fragmentation of the formerly cohesive family unit or the destruction of the idyll. Uncle Anouche demonstrates naive hope ('Every revolution goes through a period of transition'), while others speak of friends leaving or fears of political repression. Attempting to reflect the arrival of a new oppressive government and the difficult choices many Iranians were confronting, the scene might be defined in narrational terms as a 'surprise-shock' (Buckland, 2021, p 45), where information that may help explain a narrative event is withheld from the viewer. Unlike the historical background given for the Pahlavi dynasty, the imperial powers and Satrapi's radical heritage, there are no explanations, historical or otherwise, for the emergence of the Islamic republic. Put simply, it arrives from nowhere. Unlike the widely available documentaries and news footage on the Iranian revolution, the revolutionary scenes give little indication of the mass participation of Muslims or the presence of Islam as a political force in the revolutionary upheaval. A repressive Islamic authoritarianism materializes unexpectedly from without, threatening the unity and temporal continuity of the family's world, which until now has accommodated political and historical events into its cyclical and circular logic. Like the arrival of Islam in Iran in dislocative nationalist discourse, the Islamic republic appears as an imposition from the outside, not one emerging from the political dynamics of the revolution or the complexities of Iran as a Muslim and Middle Eastern country.

Dislocative nationalism's views of Iranians' similitude with European subjects and their country's geographical dislocation by historical accident become particularly significant to the film's representations of the aftermath of the revolution and the early post-revolutionary period. The scenes chart the Satrapi family's experience of early 1980s Iran following the consolidation of the Islamic revolution and Khomeini's grip on power.[9] Rebellion against the new Islamic government and the family's desire for freedom is explored, not through any explicit political activity but through their attempts to maintain a secular cultural identity through everyday activities, either putting them into direct conflict with new repressive state restrictions or leading them to avoid punishment by performing these activities secretly. Most evident is the imposition of the mandatory hijab and restrictions on women, and Marjane's and her mother's experiences in navigating, challenging or being subjugated by these.

Marjane's opposition to restrictions on her freedom is fused with her adolescence and growing rebelliousness. She openly ridicules, with her schoolfriends, state propaganda or the ideology of martyrdom during the Iran–Iraq War. Much like the graphic novels, the monochromatic aesthetic underlines a critique of the rigidity and control of the post-revolutionary society – the stark black and white intensifying the cultural uniformity of young women wearing the chador. But as has been frequently noted, Marjane's rebellion develops through her embracing of Western pop culture forms. In one well-known scene, she is confronted by two Islamic women officials wearing chador, who take issue with her trainers ('punk shoes') and her jacket with a Michael Jackson badge ('that symbol of Western decadence'). Arguably, Marjane's adoption of Western culture is, as Typhaine Leservot argues, a strategy 'for resisting the dominant paradigm of Islamic rule', a counter-discourse to the restrictions placed on Iranians by their government (2011, p 127). However, unlike the graphic novels, where Satrapi is shown to engage with Marx and Descartes, Satrapi's occidentalism in the film is less nuanced. Importantly, for an Iranian Leftist secular family, there are no instances displaying Marjane's or her family's appreciation of Iranian cultural traditions, such as the poetry, cuisine or music, other than the subtle influence of elements in visual form of the animation, musical motifs or the film's title. Nor can we discount the influence on identity of the characters' French voices, mentioned earlier. Presumably this is all part of the intention to make the family appear 'like us', whoever that might be, but inevitably it leaves an impression 'that Marjane is already a French citizen merely awaiting her final reunion with her true Western self and mother country' (Hamid, 2007, p 62).

A reading of the Satrapi family as a temporally and spatially dislocated French family sheds some light on the film's racialized politics. Modern states represent themselves as a 'community of value', defined as a group of people brought together who share 'common ideals and (exemplary) patterns of behaviour expressed through ethnicity, religion, culture, or language' (Anderson, 2013, p 2) – that is, sharing values rather than simply sharing the same legal status. The idea of a community 'facilitates a seamless switch between scales, between the imagined national community and the imagined local community' (Anderson, 2013, p 3), and this localism underlines the significance of everyday practices to the patriotic notion of a national identity. Watching cricket or drinking pints of beer in a pub might be considered distinctive virtues of being English, for example. A community of value is populated by hard-working, law-abiding 'good citizens', and a key component of this construction of belonging is the importance of protecting core values against outsiders, which translates on a national level to foreigners (or immigrants, migrants), whose outsider-ness is defined by not sharing these 'right' values.

In *Persepolis*, the Satrapi family is depicted as upholding certain values which need protecting from those who do not uphold them or threaten them. The need to maintain them is underlined by the structuring logic of the family idyll and the racial and cultural differences associated with French national identity. For example, about a third of the way into the film, Madame Nasrine, the family's domestic worker, sits unveiled at the kitchen table, with Marji and her mother, with a key in hand, explaining how her son received it at school with the promise it would unlock 'food, women, and they'd live in houses of gold and diamonds' in paradise. The scene follows a horrifying depiction of the martyrdom of young men in the battlefield. Madame Nasrine, worried about her son, questions her religious faith despite having 'worn the veil and obeyed' her whole life. Their conversation is interrupted by the arrival of Marji's father sharing news of neighbours arrested for alcohol consumption. The film then cuts to a cowered Madame Nasrine, who has swiftly donned a hijab. Asked why by Marjane's mother, Madame Nasrine points to Marjane's father: 'That's how I was brought up'. The scene ends with the family around the kitchen table dissolving into a night-time scene with Marji's mother and father patiently talking to Madame Nasrine's son and Madame Nasrine (veiled) looking concerned. In voice-over, Marjane explains: 'Thanks to my parents, Mrs Nasrine's son never went to the front'.

Madame Nasrine's son appears easily convinced by the lure of a sexual encounter with women, and Madame Nasrine clearly lacks knowledge and agency for parenting her son and convincing him otherwise. Her religious conviction is a potential source of her inability to find a solution. Marjane's family, conversely, as rational subjects, not only convince Madame Nasrine's son of his errors but probe Madame Nasrine's devotion to her religious practice and expose its irrationality. Whereas Marjane's family's hierarchy of knowledge has been a key narrational device in the film, here it functions to produce superiority over characters on the margins of the family circle, bringing them into their community but with a clear distinction in status. Through the secure locale of the family idyll, the Satrapi family have a set of secular, liberal values and virtues that resist the irrational and violent character of religious extremism of the outside world. Yet while this may position them as repressed or dissident political subjects in the Islamic republic, it produces them as 'good citizens' of the French republic.

In recent decades, debates about French citizenship have shifted towards questioning the 'authenticity' of Muslims' and migrants' French identity, resulting in a narrow, nationalist political field (Wolfreys, 2018, p 3). While Islamophobia is a global phenomenon, in France this has dovetailed with a persistent narrative, with roots in France's colonial history that predates 9/11 and the war on terror, focusing on the integration of migrants and their descendants (Wolfreys, 2018, p 2). The paradise key story aligns with the moral panics during the period of *Persepolis'* production about impressionable young Muslim men in danger of religious radicalization and terrorism and the denigration of North African migrants and their decedents who bear a 'licentiousness and misogyny that has traditionally characterized depictions of the savage "other" in the colonial imagination' (Wolfreys, 2018, p 4).

Persepolis was produced in 2007, between the legislation and implementation of hijab bans in 2004 and 2010 in France – that is, at the same point when an intolerant form of nationalist secularism began to be deployed to restrict the practices of Muslims. From the late 1980s, the 'transformative narrative' of French republicanism, associated with the Left, increasingly shifted Right with demands for allegiance to republican values and a distorted version of *laïcité*, a previously open form of secularism, which was weaponized by the political elite as a tool to scrutinize Muslims and migrants (Chabal, 2015). The questioning (or perhaps policing) of Madame Nasrine's veiling in the intimacy of Satrapi's secular idyll and the veiling mandated by a repressive government outside the home becomes highly charged, a direct inversion of the public restrictions and private practices of secularism and veiling taking place in contemporary France.

This inversion is reinforced in scenes which depict a clandestine family party. Marjane's Uncle Taher appears in a basement surrounded with wine-producing equipment and wearing a white laboratory coat and taste-testing his product.

We cut to a close-up of feet stamping on grapes before a wide shot reveals Madame Nasrine wearing her hijab, skirt raised, in a bathtub, stomping the fruit and repeating 'God forgive me. God forgive me', as Marjane explains in voice-over how 'her uncle's cleaning lady' helped crush the grapes. Madame Nasrine is the target of humour, the 'joke' being that despite her religious conviction she is a key part of the labour process in producing wine for family parties. Her activity is both physically demanding and humiliating, whereas Marjane's uncle's labour underscores his cultural 'taste' and scientific expertise. In the privacy of the bathroom, Madame Nasrine would be away from unrelated men and not needing to wear a headscarf, so the purpose is to underline the joke of a Muslim woman sinfully helping to produce wine. Moreover, the crushing of wine is a pastoral image which, for Bakhtin (1981), represents the bond between human beings, life events and the natural world. It is part of the agricultural cycle in rural idyllic life where people consume the products of their labour, including food and drink (Bakhtin, 1981, p 227). Wine cultivation and consumption are central to French provincial life and symbolic constructions of national identity – a valued part of what it means to be 'French'. Madame Nasrine, of course, is not taking part in the partying and is only responsible for the labour required for the Satrapis to conduct those secret activities. She is thus positioned as socially and culturally inferior, a domestic worker who is the subject of ridicule. If we read the Satrapis as a middle-class French family, Madame Nasrine might represent the low-income Muslim, Arab or 'migrant' (regardless of immigration status) population of domestic workers. Notably, discussions of the film's feminist politics rarely take into account the representation of Madame Nasrine or other Muslim women in the film and the implications these have for the film's resistance to dominant narratives of gender and power. Social class was an important factor in experiences of the Iranian revolution. The mandatory veil restricted freedoms for many women, but it facilitated the participation of religious women from working-class or low-income backgrounds in work, education and public spaces (Poya, 1999; Dad Mohammadi, 2016). *Persepolis* elides these complexities.

If there was any doubt about the film's position on these matters, it is re-emphasized in the next scene, which portrays Marjane's Uncle Taher on a ventilator and in need of heart surgery, making a visual link to the wine equipment in the previous scene. Exasperated by the refusal of the hospital director to send him to England for an urgent operation, Marjane's aunt proclaims: 'That incompetent window-cleaner grew a beard and put a suit on. And now he's the director! My husband's fate now lies in the hands of a window-cleaner!' There seems to be no awareness that the 'great unwashed who mistreat [Marjane Satrapi] and her family' might be as 'motivated by class antagonism as they are by Islamic revolutionary ideology' (Golsorkhi, 2008). The Muslim characters' class status becomes instead a partial explanation for their susceptibility to backward ideas or uncritical adherence to government propaganda. Satrapi and her family are depicted as a victimized secular minority, controlled by people depicted as less educated and, ostensibly, lower in social hierarchy under the previous regime. Therefore, a certain class superiority underlies the family's despair with their predicament. Differences in accent reflect 'social and class origin, religious affiliation, educational level, and political grouping' as well as regional, national or cultural characteristics (Naficy, 2001, p 23). *Persepolis'* accent, in other words, is also determined by Satrapi's middle-class status.

While these scenes may seek to show the plight of a secular family against the cruelty of a new repressive government, they also define Satrapi's family's values through their *contradistinction* to the values of Muslim, poor or working-class characters. Through black-and-white animation, Satrapi claimed to avoid ethnic divisions, but despite these claims to universality, there are clear cultural and racial markers of difference. Marjane and her family are distinguished by their cultural similitude to Western and French subjects through secular beliefs, cultural consumption, knowledge and tastes. While the monochrome avoids variations in skin tone, Muslim subjects are physically coded and identified as non-White by beards or strictly observed veils or chadors, thereby coding the Satrapis as 'White'. These markers are interlinked with the Muslim characters' intellectual simplicity, religious zealotry, aggressive and oppressive attitudes and irrational worldviews, thereby ensuring 'ideological and religious difference is visually coded as a racial, almost organic division' (Hamid, 2007, p 62). Analogous to its monochromatic aesthetics, *Persepolis* draws equally stark black-and-white dichotomies between good and evil, veiled and unveiled, secular and Muslim, progressive and backward, modern and traditional.

Persepolis has also been noted for its representations of racism during Marjane's time in Europe. In an early Vienna scene, Marjane experiences racism at a boarding house when a nun describes Iranians as 'lacking manners', in reference to Marjane eating out of a pot. Later, when Marjane pretends to pass as French when meeting a guy at a bar, she is exposed as a fraud and mocked by his sister and friends. Marjane is described as backward and uncultured or racialized as non-White through these encounters. While the response ends in her challenging the racists and reclaiming her identity, these scenes need to be seen in the context of the depictions of Muslim characters discussed earlier. Neda Maghbouleh (2020) has shown how Iranian American migrants' racialization is continually shifting between categories of White and non-White, which is relevant to secular Iranian identity formation elsewhere. In navigating contradictory identities and the experience of discrimination and racism, the Aryan myth, romanticization of the Persian Empire and exclusion of Islam from Iranian history and identity has remained an influential narrative of racial superiority over religious and ethnic groups. Despite the success in 'calling out xenophobic attitudes toward her and other Iranians in Europe', *Persepolis* problematically reproduces some of this 'rhetoric of whiteness against non-Persians/Iranians' (Hamidi, 2022, p 254). These racialized representations are not only shaped by and feed into a dislocative nationalism that views Muslims and Arabs as inferior or alien to Persian racial purity, but also, I would argue, engaging in an Islamophobic, anti-migrant discourse driven by narrow constructions of a secularist French national identity.

Satrapi's representation of her experience of racial stigma is therefore, in this context, better defined as a reflection of *misracialization*. Marjane is advised by her grandmother to be proud of her country, but there is little understanding of what this 'highly abstracted ideal' might mean (Hamid, 2007, p 63). In fact, the corrective to the racist narrative of Iranians being uncivilized, as we have seen, is the Satrapis' progressive, modern and cultural (read: French/European) values, which continue to be defined against the uncivilized values of Islam. We can see further evidence of this in the opening scenes at Orly airport where Marjane fixes her hijab in the mirror (to be able to board the flight to Iran) and the woman beside in the bathroom looks at her with disdain. The suggestion is that Marjane being perceived as Muslim is what puts her into the purview of a racist. Marjane's experience of racism is therefore due to her misassociation with an identity and set of values that the film shows ultimately belong to Muslim or non-White characters. In short, *Persepolis* makes an appeal for the Satrapis' inclusion into France's imagined community as good citizens who are mischaracterized as Muslim or non-White through their country's unfortunate, accidental and incorrect association with Islam. 'We are like you', the film seems to say, 'despite our association with them'.

Conclusion

Alongside the themes of childhood, the representational strategies of animated abstraction, geographical non-specificity and childhood subjectivity, the family operates as a key structuring principle in *Persepolis'* so-called universality. This chapter has sought to problematize its universal claims by considering how the family produces a narrow universal appeal that, combined with ideological constructions of national belonging, is exclusionary. Like the idea that Whiteness is 'beyond ethnicity', the Satrapi family is defined as 'normal' or 'ordinary'. The film supposedly shows, to repeat Satrapi's quote, how Iranians are 'like us', and this, we are told, humanizes Iranians or Middle Easterns. Yet this humanization is predicated on a set of presumptions about what constitutes 'us'. It requires neutralizing the Satrapis' upper-/middle-class status and seeing their Frenchness or Western cultural tastes as value-free or 'unaccented'. A large part of *Persepolis* is concerned with the threat of outside forces to Satrapi's idyll, with the idea of Muslims or the poor wielding power being the most dangerous. Nowhere in *Persepolis* is Islam or a Muslim character represented in positive or nuanced terms, nor is the complexity of religiosity and secularity in contemporary Iran touched on.

Liberal, feminist autobiographical texts have been criticized by scholars for generalizing the experiences of Western, middle-class elites and, through their connections to their co-nationals, constructing 'Islam and Muslims – whether traditionalist or revivalist – by employing recycled Orientalist tropes cast in the insider's voice' (Nash, 2012, p 26). In *Persepolis* these racialized constructions are produced not only from the Western country in which it was produced but by the ideological current of racial purity in Iran.

Persepolis has been described as a film about a liminal subject with an identity crisis who cannot find a home. But the search for belonging is constructed by an idea of cultural similitude to a narrowly defined French or Western community of value, to which Muslims or those 'like them' do not belong. The idyllic family structure is crucial here, as it operates as a terrain for nationalist ideological perspectives that dislodge Iran from its geographical or historical specificity, its deep and rich Islamic roots, and cast it onto the landscape of French neo-republican secularism, which views Muslim and Arab identities as alien to the national body.

Filmmakers from minority or marginalized backgrounds must constantly negotiate the 'burden of representation', with self-representations or autobiographical work often laden with the responsibility of representing a group identity or taken to be allegorical for the community at large. *Persepolis* reminds us that while the family in migrant cinema may not be contained by the imagined community of nationhood, it can still reinforce hegemonic ideas of nationhood, ones that may overlap between 'host' and 'home' countries and operate in excluding those who are defined as outsiders regardless of their status as migrant or citizen.

As a lauded film for charting the Iranian experience of revolution, war and migration to Europe, *Persepolis* stands as an important example of the problems of self-representation in migrant cinema. Calls for 'giving voice', 'speaking for oneself' or celebrating self-representation dominate contemporary discussions on the representation of migrants and refugees. This relies on an uncritical form of standpoint epistemology, where 'envoicement' of migrants or refugees (and/or their self-representations) is regarded as a necessary and an essential end in itself, superseding the political character of what may or may not be said, the positionality from which such voices may speak, the implications of what is expressed on marginalized others and, most importantly, the need to question the terms by which such voices will be listened to or heard.

Notes

[1] Originally, Naficy (2001) distinguished three modalities of accented filmmakers: exilic, diasporic and postcolonial/ethnic. More recently, and specifically in relation to Iranian accented filmmakers, he locates five types: exilic, diasporic, émigré, ethnic and cosmopolitan – each correspond to a different relationship to displacement, placement and production (Naficy, 2012, p 393).

[2] Mastroianni's biological mother.

[3] Marji is the name used in the film to refer to Marjane's child character.

[4] Although *Persepolis* is a hand-drawn animation and therefore does not use camera movements, it draws on these conventions as part of its signification of cinematic realism. I therefore draw on filmic terminology (for example, 'track', 'close-up', 'cut to', 'wide shot') for clarity of description where necessary.

[5] Naficy (2001) proposes 'closed chronotopes', expressing the claustrophobia of exile, 'open chronotopes' (derived from Bakhtin's 'idyll'), reflecting the nostalgia for homeland and characterized by boundlessness and timelessness, and 'thirdspace chronotopes', articulating the journeying and in-betweenness of the diasporic condition.

[6] Marjane Satrapi is not only the writer and director but also the graphic artist responsible for the hand-drawn depictions and whose autobiographical experiences are being drawn on (literally) and fictionalized. Satrapi even performed the movements of the

characters for the animation construction, so her body is, in some ways, also present in the work.

7   Dave is writing with reference to the middle-class idyll constructed in the film *Notting Hill* (1999).

8   'In the second millennium B.C., while the Elam nation was developing a civilization alongside Babylon, Indo-European invaders gave their name to the immense Iranian plateau where they settled. The word "Iran" was derived from "Ayryana Vaejo," which means "the origin of the Aryans." [. ...] Iran was rich. Because of its wealth and its geographic location, it invited attacks: From Alexander the Great, from its Arab neighbors to the west, from Turkish and Mongolian conquerors, Iran was often subject to foreign domination. Yet the Persian language and culture withstood these invasions. The invaders assimilated into this strong culture, and in some ways they became Iranians themselves' (Satrapi, 2008, Introduction).

9   Neither Khomeini nor any other political figures are depicted or made reference to, unlike the depiction of the Shah and the Pahlavi dynasty in pre-revolutionary scenes.

References

Anderson, B. (1983) *Imagined Communities: Reflections on the Origin and Spread of Nationalism*, London: Verso.

Anderson, B. (2013) *Us and Them? The Dangerous Politics of Immigration Control*, Oxford: Oxford University Press.

Bakhtin, M. (1981) *The Dialogic Imagination: Four Essays*, ed and trans M. Holquist, Austin: University of Texas Press.

Berghahn, D. (2013) *Far-Flung Families in Film: The Diasporic Family in Contemporary European Cinema*, Edinburgh: Edinburgh University Press.

Buckland, W. (2021) *Narrative and Narration: Analyzing Cinematic Storytelling*, New York: Wallflower.

Chabal, E. (2015) *A Divided Republic: Nation, State and Citizenship in Contemporary France*, Cambridge: Cambridge University Press.

Chute, H. (2008) 'The texture of retracing in Marjane Satrapi's Persepolis', *Women's Studies Quarterly*, 36(1/2): 92–110.

Dad Mohammadi, M. (2016) *Reading More than Marjane Satrapi's* Persepolis, PhD thesis, University of Chester.

Dave, P. (2006) *Visions of England: Class and Culture in Contemporary Cinema*, Oxford: Berg.

Ezra, E. and Rowden, T. (eds) (2006) *Transnational Cinema: The Film Reader*, London: Routledge.

Ezzatikarami, M. and Ameri, F. (2019) '*Persepolis* and human rights: unveiling Westernized globalization strategies in Marjane Satrapi's *Persepolis*', *International Journal of Applied Linguistics and English Literature*, 8(5): 122–30.

Gilmore, L. and Marshall, E. (2010) 'Girls in crisis: rescue and transnational feminist autobiographical resistance', *Feminist Studies*, 36(3): 667–90.

Gilroy, P. (1993) *The Black Atlantic: Modernity and Double Consciousness*, Cambridge, MA: Harvard University Press.

Golsorkhi, M. (2008) 'A partial history', *The Guardian*, 29 April. Available from: www.theguardian.com/commentisfree/2008/apr/29/apartialhistory (accessed 31 October 2023).

Hamid, R. (2007) 'Persepolis', *Cineaste*, 33(1): 61–3.

Hamidi, Y.N. (2022) 'Politics of location in *Persepolis*: the social and literary construction of the place, space, and belonging for Iranian women in *Persepolis* versus Iran', *Journal of Middle East Women's Studies*, 18(2): 238–59.

Higson, A. (2000) 'The limiting imagination of national cinema', in M. Hjort and S. MacKenzie (eds) *Cinema and Nation*, London: Routledge, pp 55–68.

Johnston, C. (2015) 'Tehran, Vienna, Paris: the cultural geographies of *Persepolis*', in P.I. Barta and P. Powrie (eds) *Bicultural Literature and Film in French and English*, New York: Routledge, pp 105–18.

Leservot, T. (2011) 'Occidentalism: rewriting the West in Marjane Satrapi's *Persepolis*', *French Forum*, 36(1): 115–30.

Maghbouleh, N. (2020) *The Limits of Whiteness: Iranian Americans and the Everyday Politics of Race*, Stanford, CA: Stanford University Press.

Malek, A. (2006) 'Memoir as Iranian exile cultural production: a case study of Marjane Satrapi's *Persepolis* series', *Iranian Studies*, 39(3): 353–80.

McClintock, A. (1995) *Imperial Leather: Race, Gender, and Sexuality in the Colonial Contest*, New York: Routledge.

Mottahedeh, N. (2004) 'Off the grid: reading Iranian memoirs in our time of total war', in *Middle East Research and Information Project*. Available from: https://bahai-library.com/mottahedeh_off_grid&chapter=all (accessed 31 October 2023).

Naficy, H. (2001) *An Accented Cinema: Exilic and Diasporic Filmmaking*, Princeton, NJ: Princeton University Press.

Naficy, H. (2008) 'Iranian emigrant cinema as a component of Iranian national cinema', in M. Semati (ed) *Media, Culture and Society in Iran: Living with Globalization and the Islamic State*, New York: Routledge, pp 167–92.

Naficy, H. (2012) *A Social History of Iranian Cinema. Volume 4: The Globalizing Era, 1984–2010*, Durham, NC: Duke University Press.

Naghibi, N. and O'Malley, A. (2005) 'Estranging the familiar: "East" and "West" in Satrapi's *Persepolis*', *English Studies in Canada*, 31(2): 223–47.

Nash, G. (2012) *Writing Muslim Identity*, London: Continuum.

Notting Hill (1999) Directed by Roger Michell [feature film], UK.

Palmer, L. (2011) 'Neither here nor there: the reproductive sphere in transnational feminist cinema', *Feminist Review*, 99(1): 113–30.

Persepolis (2007) Directed by Marjane Satrapi and Vincent Paronnaud [feature film], France.

Phillips, A. (2003) 'Hamid Naficy, an accented cinema: exilic and diasporic filmmaking', *Screen*, 44(3): 343–6.

Poya, M. (1999) *Women, Work and Islamism: Ideology and Resistance in Iran*, London: Zed Books.

Satrapi, M. (2000–03) Persepolis. Vols. I–IV, Paris: L' Association.

Satrapi, M. (2003–04) Persepolis I & II, London: Random House.

Satrapi, M. (2007) '*Persepolis* press kit interview', *Sony Classics*, March. Available from: www.sonyclassics.com/Persepolis/presskit/Persepolis.pdf (accessed 2 December 2020).

Satrapi, M. (2008) *Persepolis*, London: Vintage.

Warren, K. (2010) 'Animation, representation and the power of the personal story: *Persepolis*', *Screen Education*, 58: 117–23.

Whitlock, G. (2007) *Soft Weapons: Autobiography in Transit*, Chicago: University of Chicago Press.

Wolfreys, J. (2018) *Republic of Islamophobia: The Rise of Respectable Racism in France*, New York: Oxford University Press.

Zia-Ebrahimi, R. (2016) *The Emergence of Iranian Nationalism: Race and the Politics of Dislocation*, New York: Columbia University Press.

10

Sounds across Borders and the Ukraine War

Florian Scheding

Introduction

This chapter focuses on sonic responses to the Russia–Ukraine war during its first year, 2022. In many ways, it moves across lines familiar to migration studies, considering nationalism, politics and conflict. What I wish to add and emphasize in my contribution is fundamentally very simple. Through a close exploration and discussion of three musical case studies, I suggest that a focus on music as migratory has the potential to inform our thinking about migrant voices more broadly. Rather than accompanying geopolitical events from the sidelines, music and sound are crucial in narrating, influencing and shaping such real-world events and the lived experiences of those affected by them. In this chapter, I listen closely to three musical events that all sought to promote support for Ukraine and to protest, directly or indirectly, the Russian invasion: the Eurovision 2022 winning song 'Stefania' by Kalush Orchestra; the single 'Hey hey rise up' by Pink Floyd featuring Andriy Khlyvnyuk; and the Concert for Ukraine, organized by the British television broadcaster ITV. Rather than focusing primarily on the border crossing of people or goods themselves, my case studies emphasize the extent to which sound moves across borders and how it is bordered and either encouraged to, or prevented from, 'migrating'. I am interested in the extent to which migrant voices are envoiced or unvoiced, and the extent to which envoicement and silencing might occur simultaneously on different levels, thus directing our thinking towards questions of sonic access in the light of migratory experiences.

I use the term 'migration' broadly throughout the chapter to describe various facets of border crossing. There is much potential for conflict between concepts pertaining to globalization, transnationalism, interculturalism, cosmopolitanism, migration, emigration, displacement, mobility, diaspora, exile, immigration and several more. Terminology in music studies might seem messy. Use of the terms exile (Baily, 2015), displacement (Levi and Scheding, 2010), diaspora (Cohen, 2012), journey (Hinton, 2012), mobility (Gopinath and Stanyek, 2014), heterotopia (Bohlman, 2008a) and in-betweenness (Beckles Willson, 2007) or the avoidance of any one specific term (Feisst, 2011) suggest disagreement at first sight. And yet, the lack of a steadfast terminology in this field does not stand in the way of much common ground as far as the actual debate is concerned. It mirrors the long history of evolving terminologies of border crossing (see Brooke-Rose, 1998) as well as the diverse auto-descriptions of migrants themselves (see Scheding, 2010).

My three case studies all share seeming prestige settings and elite connotations. Richly funded, these musical performances reached millions of viewers and listeners. They remind us of music's potential to construct communalities and solidarities across borders. And yet each of these case studies also reinforces and bolsters nationalist ideologies in both methodological and practical terms. I therefore seek to open a discussion on the extent to which the three musical examples, while aiming to support refugee causes, aid the exceptionalization of migration and prop up narratives of marginalization and ideologies of nationalism, and do so in diverse and ever-changing ways. Unlike the visual, the sonic is inextricably linked to the temporal. Sound can only be experienced across a duration of time, and it eschews a sustained gaze in the way that an image, for example, allows (see Samuels et al, 2010, p 338). Despite the resulting ephemerality of the sonic, soundscapes are not placeless. They interplay strongly with the construction of the geographic and of social space. Sound is a crucial factor in creating (discourses of) citizenship, for example, but it is simultaneously complicit in restricting access to the discourses and practices of citizenship. My three examples all create sonic spaces that engage in a power dialectic. They are shaped by, and also shape, ideologies of political hierarchy and access.

'I ask all of you, please help Ukraine': Kalush Orchestra at the Eurovision Song Contest

On 14 May 2022, Ukrainian group Kalush Orchestra won the Eurovision Song Contest. The win was notable in several respects. Their song, 'Stefania', won the highest number of phone-in audience votes in the contest's 66-year history. While the final in Turin did not attract the largest television audience in Eurovision's history, by the end of 2022 'Stefania' had become the most-watched Eurovision song on the contest's YouTube channel. It is possible that 'Stefania' has reached a larger international audience than any other Ukrainian musical event in history. Notwithstanding the musical quality of 'Stefania', the huge audience vote suggests that the performance of the song was accompanied by an outpouring of solidarity with Ukraine, which had been invaded by Russia almost exactly three months earlier. Following their performance, Kalush Orchestra's Oleh Psiuk addressed the up to 161 million international television viewers, calling for help for the Ukrainian city of Mariupol, which was under siege by Russian forces and would be captured only days later. Referencing the steel plant that was the last Ukrainian-held position during the siege, he pleaded: 'I ask all of you, please help Ukraine, Mariupol. Help Azovstal, right now!' Eurovision contestants from Iceland and Germany, Systur and Malik Harris, also showed support for Ukraine, with Ukrainian flags on their instruments and calls for peace for the country at the end of their respective performances. It is difficult, then, to imagine an act of musical, indeed sonic, border crossing with an immediate wider global reach than on the night of 14 May 2022.

In this context, it seems perhaps surprising that the European Broadcasting Union (EBU), the organizer of the Eurovision Song Contest, insists on the contest being a non-political event. Its rules ban and prohibit political statements or messages. The EBU swiftly decided that no action would be taken against Kalush Orchestra, arguing that 'the comments of the Kalush Orchestra and other artists expressing support for the Ukrainian people [were] humanitarian rather than political in nature'. Indeed, the 2022 contest had been mired in what one might view as political, or at least politically motivated, incidents long before the night of the final. Following the call from broadcasters from ten participating countries (Denmark, Estonia, Finland, Iceland, Lithuania, the Netherlands, Norway, Poland, Sweden and Ukraine), the EBU had reneged on its initial decision to allow Russia to participate, excluding the country from the contest in the run-up to the Turin show.

There was controversy on the Ukrainian side too. In the national selection process, 'Stefania' had come second, beaten to top spot by singer Alina Pash and her song 'Тіні забутих предків' (Shadows of forgotten ancestors). Steeped in nationalism, the song's Ukrainian lyrics recount the country's long history of war and invasion until the Slavic gods Perun and Dazhboh hear the prayers of Ukraine's tribes and bring peace, calling for unity among the Ukrainian people. The song's title evidences a deep commitment to Ukrainian artistic and cultural history by continuing a cross-medial intertextual history. It references the 1965 Ukrainian film of the same name by Sergei Parajanov as well as the 1960 ballet by Vitaly Kyreiko, which are themselves based on the eponymous 1911 novel by Ukrainian author Mykhailo Kotsiubynsky. At the same time, the song faces west and positions Ukraine's cultural and, more specifically, artistic history as a part of the European cultural project more broadly. Pash likens Ukraine's longue *durée* of suffering to Dante's *Divine Comedy*, calls for Picasso's 'dove of peace', remembers a book of Shakespeare as her favourite toy and imagines the song as a continuation of the work of the Brothers Grimm.

Following her victory in the national selection process, it was, in fact, an act of border crossing that led to Pash's withdrawal from representing the country at the Eurovision Song Contest in Turin. After Russia's occupation of Crimea in 2014, the Public Broadcasting Company of Ukraine (UA:PBC), the organizer of the national selection for Eurovision, had decreed that artists who had performed in Russia or travelled from Russia to Crimea after 2014 were not eligible to represent Ukraine internationally. Following doubts over Alina Pash's border crossings, and suggestions that she had visited Crimea in 2015 via Russia, the singer's further participation in Eurovision was cancelled and the runner-up, Kalush Orchestra, was selected instead.

Why do these details matter? Against the background of daily news of bloodshed and battles between Ukrainian and Russian forces, the Eurovision Song Contest hardly seems to matter. Stephen Coleman (2008) has argued that Eurovision is seen as a ridiculous and embarrassing spectacle, and Graham Norton, who was a presenter at the 2023 Eurovision, held in Liverpool, and has hosted the British TV coverage on the BBC for several years, called Eurovision a 'silly song contest' on British broadcaster ITV's popular show *This Morning* on 26 September 2023. But, Norton continued, 'it does bring people together in a very serious way'. In fact, cultural studies scholars widely argue that Eurovision has the power to unite and forge communities along divergent lines of identity. George Cremona (2023) has invoked Eurovision as a vehicle to promote values propagated by the European Union, and Matt Weaver (2023) has called the contest the 'gay world cup', describing queer performers such as Austrian 2014 entry Conchita Wurst as invoking an alternative patriotism through a deliberate crossing and queering of national identities, a point also made by Catherine Baker (2015, 2019b). Performances of nationalism in Eurovision may be 'playful' (see Kyriakidou et al, 2018), but still provide 'a relatively long opportunity for small states to regularly promote themselves to a worldwide audience numbering in the hundreds of millions', as Dean Vuletic (2018, p 301) has highlighted.

Scholars widely debunk the EBU's claim of Eurovision as apolitical, so much so that Gad Yair and Chen Ozeri (2023) call the political nature of the contest an accepted truism. Ukraine's 2016 entry, '1944' by Jamala, sung in English with a chorus in Crimean Tatar dialect, won Eurovision with lyrics about the Soviet deportations of Tatars from Crimea, alluding to the Russian occupation of 2014. Displays of national mutual sympathies or antipathies reveal themselves in annual voting patterns, which frequently map onto geopolitical and migratory histories (see Yair, 2018). Ukraine, for example, has historically received high scores from other former Soviet bloc nations and from neighbouring Poland, while the Lithuanian diaspora in the UK (especially in Glasgow and London) and in Ireland frequently results in high scores for the Baltic country. The voting pattern between Russia and

Ukraine after the Russian occupation of Crimea likewise correlates with its geopolitical context. Since 2014, Russian and Ukrainian Eurovision juries have consistently refused to award points to each other's song entries. The televote paints a different picture, with Russian audiences awarding full points to Ukraine in the 2021 semi-final, less than one year before Russia's invasion in February 2022. The clash of diverse national performances on a stage of international broadcasting collaboration therefore simultaneously mirrors and reinforces varied forms of identities of national belonging within and against an international framework of border crossing and a history of mobility.

Andrea Bohlman and Alexander Rehding (2013) described Eurovision as 'soft politics' and suggested that music is ideally suited to reveal the complexities that define the interaction between the national and the transnational. Nations employ this soft power, according to Joseph Nye (2022), to garner transnational support. Indeed, Robert Seely (2016) has poignantly described Ukraine's win at Eurovision 2016 with Jamala's song '1944' as a Russian defeat. Eurovision, then, performs a politics of belonging and of difference, continuously negotiating between diverse identities and enabling nations to dance, as Bohlman and Rehding (2013) put it, to the varied tunes of the national and the transnational in the new Europe. Bohlman and Rehding's chapter forms part of a volume edited by Dafni Tragaki (2013), who chooses deliberately politicized language for the book and invokes Europe's long colonial history, entitling the collection *Empire of Song* (see also Meizel, 2015). The national, then, looms large in Eurovision, and it is in the interstitial space between national identity and transnational encounter that Eurovision can be situated.

Drawing on Eurovision in Kyiv in 2005, which played out against the backdrop of the pro-democratic Orange Revolution, Philip Bohlman (2011) has questioned the extent to which music, history and nationalism triangulate and either cohere or contradict one another. Bohlman pondered music's power to shape, reflect or give identity to the nation. We may love to hate music and nationalism, as Bohlman put it, reminding us that it is worth taking seriously the extent to which song not only sings the nation reflectively, but, in fact, sings it into being. Drawing on Johann Gottfried Herder's foundational theory of nationalism, Bohlman reminded us that it is the voicing of shared sound and communal sonic practice that are at the root of the nation. Who sings the nation state, Judith Butler and Gayatri Spivak (2010) asked provocatively, pointing to the access to voice as a constituent element of citizenship and the power of song to performatively construct, subvert and contradict the nation. Singing, and public singing in particular, are significant political acts and constitute claims to the rights of narrating the nation. Martin Stokes has argued that the access to and the practice of sound are crucial for a citizenship 'in conversational, multimodal, decolonizing, task-oriented terms' with a potential to 'shape collaborative democratic futures' (2023, p 6). With its huge international audience, Eurovision provides a stage, quite literally, for nations to perform their own 'historical fiction', as Catherine Baker (2019a) has called it. Further, in the moment of performing the nation through the transnational mobility of sound, song 'legitimises political structures', to use Ben Wellings and Julie Kalman's (2020, p 17) words.

The Eurovision Song Contest, then, simultaneously acts as a vehicle for transnational identity politics and relies on nationalist constructions of belonging. Marko Pavlyshyn has identified three factors in Ukrainian Eurovision entries: 'the potential and actual Russian reaction to the song; its meaning for Ukrainians in their domestic and international predicament; and potential and actual "Western" responses to it' (2020, p 131). This aspect is well illustrated by Kalush Orchestra's blend of global Western hip-hop with auto-orientalist tropes of folkishness. The Ukrainian song lyrics are directed towards a Ukrainian audience. While Kalush Orchestra suggested that 'Stefania' is about the mother of frontman Oleh Psiuk, the song likens the strong mother/child bond to that of the nation and the homeland, both heightened in times of hardship: 'She gave me a rhythm/ You can't take willpower from me, as I got it from her … I'll always come home, even on destroyed roads'. No sound is more closely associated with nationalism than folk song and folklore (Bohlman, 2008b, p 253) and the music of 'Stefania' signifies national identity, making use of the auto-orientalist strategies so common in Eurovision's narration of the nation on the international stage. Kalush Orchestra prominently pitch the telenka and sopilka, traditional Ukrainian flutes, against a more standard global pop music backing track. Members of Kalush Orchestra also wear traditional folkloric outfits on the Turin stage, with the keptar vest referencing the Hutsul ethnic group from western Ukraine.

At the same time, the sounds of 'Stefania' cross borders and seek to impact transnational discourses. While most non-Ukrainians will not understand the song's Ukrainian lyrics, the phonic message is nonetheless strong, suggesting a nation determined to sound and retain its voice on the international stage. Phonics matter. Ukraine's entry to the 2007 Eurovision, 'Денсінґ Лаша Тумбай' (Dancing Lasha Tumbai) by singer Verka Serduchka, appeared to sound like 'Russia goodbye' to several audiences and was described as offensive in Russian media (see Yekelchyk, 2010, p 229). (Since Russia's 2022 invasion of Ukraine, Serduchka has decided to sing 'Russia Goodbye' in concerts.) Phonics are thick with semantic meaning also with regards to the music. In addition to the nods to Ukrainian folklore, the perhaps overriding musical idiom of 'Stefania' is hip-hop and rap. The message is clear: on the 'arena for geopolitical debates', as Daniel Montoya (2017, p 8) has labelled Eurovision, Kalush Orchestra narrates the nation as fiercely protective of its identity and yet fully part of Western culture.

'Hey hey rise up': migratory aesthetics and transnational collaboration

On 27 February 2022, three days after the Russian invasion, Andriy Khlyvnyuk, singer of Ukrainian rock band BoomBox, posted a video on social media. The recording shows Khlyvnyuk in Sophia Square in Kyiv wearing a military uniform, sunglasses and a dark New York Yankees cap. Holding a rifle, he sings an unaccompanied version of 'Ой у лузі червона калина' (Oh, the red viburnum in the meadow). Khlyvnyuk had cut short a tour with BoomBox and returned from the US to join the armed forces of Ukraine. A month after posting his performance on social media, he was injured in battle. The song Khlyvnyuk chose, a patriotic march of Ukrainian resistance, is thick with meaning. Possibly based on folkloristic songs, it exists in numerous versions. It was first published in 1875 by Mykhailo Drahomanov and Volodymyr Antonovych, proponents of Ukrainian nationalism and Europeanization, and it soon became a well-known patriotic anthem, propagating independence. It has a specific history as a song of resistance against Russian rule, and during the Soviet era singing of the song was banned. This became punishable again in Crimea after Russia's occupation in 2014. Soon after posting, the video went viral and reached global audiences.

David Gilmour, singer and guitarist of Pink Floyd, was first shown Khlyvnyuk's recording by his daughter-in-law, Ukrainian artist Janina Pedan (see Grow, 2022). When Gilmour saw it, he asked Khlyvnyuk whether he could sample the song and issue it as a Pink Floyd charity single, with proceeds going to humanitarian aid for Ukraine. Gilmour had in fact performed with BoomBox at a benefit concert in 2015, although Khlyvnyuk was not present on that occasion. Pink Floyd had effectively disbanded in 2008, following the death of founding member and keyboard player Rick Wright, but on 30 March 2022, barely a month after Khlyvnyuk's post and with Khlyvnyuk's agreement, Gilmour, Pink Floyd drummer Nick Mason, bassist Guy Pratt and, on keyboards, producer Nitin Sawhney recorded 'Hey hey rise up'.

A promotional video followed soon afterwards. Directed by Mat Whitecross, it prefaces the song with sounds of war. We hear a Russian tank, identifiable by the 'Z' symbol used by Russian forces in Ukraine, presumably driving on a Ukrainian road, before we see and hear an explosion. The video cuts to Khlyvnyuk standing in military uniform in Kyiv while superimposed text informs audiences of Russia's invasion, Khlyvnyuk's artistic and armed resistance and Pink Floyd's support of the 'message of resistance'. From here, the video intercuts Khlyvnyuk's social media post and Pink Floyd's playing with images of war and refugees. Unexpectedly, the actual song does not begin with the voices of Pink Floyd or Khlyvnyuk, but with a brief excerpt of a traditional choral rendition of 'Oh, the red viburnum in the meadow' by the Veryovka Ukrainian Folk Choir. Led in by Mason's drums, Khlyvnyuk's sampled recording follows, harmonized and accompanied by Pink Floyd. After a full rendition of Khlyvnyuk's now accompanied version, Pink Floyd insert a middle section with different harmonic progression that consists of two guitar solos by Gilmour, intersected by Khlyvnyuk's 'Hey hey'. A second full accompanied version of Khlyvnyuk's sample completes the song. It is possible to argue that this is a sensitive sampling of Khlyvnyuk's original recording. Pink Floyd do not add vocals, thus platforming and emphasizing the Ukrainian original. During Khlyvnyuk's singing, the accompaniment is restrained. The final line, with the words, 'гей-гей, розвеселимо!' (Hey hey, we shall cheer!), is sung unaccompanied, Pink Floyd leaving the last word to Khlyvnyuk.

'Hey hey rise up' is a remarkable case of musical mobility and border crossing. It is remarkable precisely because it represents a case of ostensibly static performers collaborating across borders facilitated in part by Gilmour's connection through Pedan to a migratory history. While the musicians did not themselves cross borders for the recording – indeed, Khlyvnyuk had abandoned an international tour to return to his native Ukraine – they employ the technological potential of sound's mobility to narrate and cross aural borders. Technology is the vehicle of creative production, and it is also the vehicle, just as in the case of 'Stefania', to reach global audiences. The musical components, too, negotiate the dialectic of place and mobility. The rendition of 'Oh, the red viburnum in the meadow' by the Veryovka Ukrainian Folk Choir points towards the powers of folk song to signify nationalism. Khlyvnyuk's version, sung in the historic centre of metropolitan Kyiv, invokes the power of the local within a cosmopolitan space, while Pink Floyd's addition of global Western popular music adds transnational aspects.

That the song was issued as a Pink Floyd single 'featuring Andriy Khlyvnyuk of BoomBox' is instructive in this context. (One could perhaps equally imagine 'Hey hey rise up' as a song by Khlyvnyuk backed by Pink Floyd.) Pink Floyd's singer and guitarist David Gilmour made clear the rationale behind the decision to market the song as the first release in 28 years of new original music by one of the world's most famous musical groups:

> I've got a big platform. [Pink Floyd is] the biggest promotional vehicle … it's so vitally, vitally important that people understand what's going on there and do everything within their power to change that situation. And the thought, also, that mine and Pink Floyd's support of the Ukrainians could help boost morale in those areas: they need to know the whole world supports them. (Quoted in Petridis, 2022)

Song proceeds go to organizations for humanitarian aid in Ukraine. 'Hey hey rise up', then, employs the capitalist marketing pressures and strategies of the Western music industry to promote a transnational collaboration of a song that celebrates patriotism and agitates for support for Ukraine.

It is tempting to employ the theoretical framework of migratory hubs suggested by Nadia Kiwan and Ulrike Meinhof (2011) to disentangle this case of transnational musical collaboration. They posit that hubs are crucial for migrants, providing fixed points along the network of migrant flows and creating a nexus of transnational and transcultural mobilities. While Kiwan and Meinhof refer to migrant communities, their concept of human hubs through which migratory aesthetics travel maps onto the mobile collaboration of Pink Floyd and Khlyvnyuk. Further, acting as a strategic hub, the Pink Floyd brand is the entry point into the Western market and Western audiences. My suggestion to interpret 'Hey hey rise up' as migratory further chimes with the advocacy of Nina Glick Schiller and Meinhof (2011) to embrace music's potential to blur the migrant–native divide and enact a paradigm shift away from methodological nationalism towards transnational approaches.

In my reading, the aesthetics of 'Hey hey rise up' is markedly migratory, regardless of the fact that none of its performers are migrants. Migration is not a necessary, much less a sufficient, condition for migratory art. Mieke Bal (2007) introduced the notion of a migratory aesthetics that circumscribes possible relations with the migratory rather than pinpointing them, continuously escaping attempts to offer fixed definitions. For Jill Bennett (2011), migratory aesthetics may not be a unified or identifiable style, but rather a strategy that foregrounds transitional politics and interstitial spaces. She has suggested that a diverse migratory aesthetics is well suited as a subversive response to oppressive political systems. Bennett highlights the potential of migratory aesthetics to subvert fixed categories of identity, to invert tradition and question our understanding of it, and to form a transnational, mobile communality. 'Hey hey rise up' clearly invokes nationalism, but it also has the hallmarks of the migratory in that it was created in transnational collaboration and, in that sense, might be seen as 'exilic' art (Said, 2002), as the creation of an alternative space with the potential to subvert fixities and totalitarianisms.

In the West, reception following the release of 'Hey hey rise up' was almost exclusively affirmative, with several mainstream media in the UK praising and promoting the song (see, for example, Petridis, 2022, and Savage, 2022). At time of writing, the song's promotional YouTube video has been watched over 12 million times, and comments by viewers in English, French, German, Italian, Polish, Spanish and Ukrainian suggest that reactions across Europe are overwhelmingly positive. Critique emerged from a perhaps unexpected corner. Former bass player and founding member of Pink Floyd, Roger Waters, a controversial figure who left the band in 1985, referred to the song as 'lacking in humanity' and said that it 'encourages the continuation of the war', which he viewed as 'probably the most provoked invasion ever' (quoted in Willman, 2023; see also D'Souza, 2023).

Who sings for charity? ITV's Concert for Ukraine

On 16 March 2022, British broadcaster ITV announced a benefit concert to raise funds for Ukrainian victims of the Russian invasion. The concert took place less than two weeks later, on 29 March, in the Resorts World Arena in Birmingham. Following a well-established tradition of charitable concerts for humanitarian causes – perhaps the most famous being Live Aid, organized in 1985 by Bob Geldof and Midge Ure – the ITV Concert for Ukraine boasted a star-studded line-up, including performers such as Ed Sheeran, Snow Patrol, Billie Eilish, and the Manic Street Preachers. Ukrainian singer Jamala performed her song '1944', which won Eurovision in 2016. Several British actors and journalists, including newsreader Trevor McDonald, comedian Mel Giedroyc, actress Tamsin Greig and actor Eddie Marsan, read out tributes and reports from Ukrainian refugees. Broadcast in the UK, Ireland and Australia, the concert raised more than £13 million within 24 hours.

Despite the appearance of Jamala, the Concert for Ukraine was notable for its dearth of Ukrainian musicians. For example, Antytila's offer to appear was turned down. Formed in 2007, Antytila are a hugely successful group that, at the time of the Russian invasion, was releasing their seventh studio album. Their 2018 promotional video for the song 'Lego', which at the time of writing has been viewed more than six million times on YouTube, featured a cameo performance by future Ukrainian president Volodymyr Zelenskyy. Like Andriy Khlyvnyuk, Antytila's band members joined the Ukrainian armed forces following Russia's invasion. When Antytila heard of the planned concert, they contacted the organizers and posted a message on social media to headliner Ed Sheeran. The video shows Antytila in military uniform in front of a damaged apartment block in Kyiv. Singer Taras Topolia offered Antytila's participation in the concert, performing via video link from Kyiv:

> We are musicians of the Ukrainian band Antytila. ... In peacetime, our concerts gathered stadiums. ... The war has changed our lives and now we are fighting with weapons against the Russian occupiers. We thank you and all the British people for their support. Believe me, we are grateful, and we will always, always remember this. Today we learned about your charity concert for Ukraine, which will take place in Birmingham. And we offer to make a live broadcast between Kyiv and Birmingham with Antytila temporary [sic] joining the gig remotely. Our band will play our music in Kyiv, a city that has not

surrendered and will never surrender to the Russian occupiers. You will play in Birmingham. We are not afraid to play under the bombs. Through music, we want to show the world that Ukraine is strong and unconquered. We will fight and sing for victory in front of the whole world that supports us. So, on March 29, we are ready.

The concert organizers rejected Antytila's offer, arguing that 'for this specific concert, it would not be possible for us to feature them, as we are only able to focus on the humanitarian situation, not the politics or the military conflict' (quoted in Lavin, 2022). The parallels with Eurovision's claim to be non-political are apparent. And yet, while the EBU did not impose sanctions on Kalush Orchestra, the organizers of the ITV Concert for Ukraine decided to exclude Antytila.

The absence of performers representing the intended recipients of charitable events and benefit concerts is not unique to the Concert for Ukraine. Bob Geldof defended the decision not to include enough African performers in Live Aid by referring to their lack of popularity among Western audiences, arguing that the fame of participants directly correlates with the financial success of the event (see Davis, 2010). Moreover, the refusal to platform Antytila can be seen in the context of British Right-wing anti-migration politics, in which Ukrainian musicians were refused visas to perform on British soil. For example, members of the Khmelnitsky Orchestra were refused visas to perform in the UK in April 2023 (see Pidd, 2023). The performances were planned as part of a European tour of the orchestra, and in the autumn of 2022 the British government had, on its websites, trumpeted the concerts as a show of British solidarity with Ukraine (see British Embassy Brussels, 2022).

In the 1950s, Donald Horton and Richard Wohl coined the term parasocial interaction to describe the psychological phenomenon of audiences coming to think of on-screen celebrities as familiar or even as friends despite the fact that they have no personal interaction with them. This engenders a sense of ritualistic trust and identification, which, as Daniel Dayan and Elihu Katz (1992) have suggested, encourages audiences to back a cause, not because they believe in it, but because they believe that the cause is important to the performers on screen. In the political arena, imagined relationships with prominent media personas and the resulting parasocial interactions have huge potential for persuasion and real-world influence (Demetriades et al, 2023). It is in this context then that one may make sense of the organizers' seemingly peculiar strategy to ask well-known British actors and media personas to read out reports from Ukrainian refugees rather than invite refugees to speak (or sing) for themselves.

In fact, the absence of refugee voices is a common feature in debates about migration. While imagery is widely used to depict suffering, those persecuted are often portrayed as voiceless. The idea of voice or, rather, voicelessness, is a prominent trope in humanitarian campaigns and in the thinking about forced migration. It raises issues of agency and heterogeneity and invites us to examine humanitarian practices of using refugee voices and to listen to the tropes that emerge through them. Heath Cabot (2016) has pointed out how projects seeking to advocate for refugees in Greece follow the logic of using tragic tropes that fail to represent refugee voices and unwittingly silence them. Cabot argued that ethnographic and scholarly work is complicit in this silencing of oppressed voices, which, in turn, reinforces the power structures that led to the causes of oppression in the first place. Liisa Malkki (1997) has pointed out how narrative representations of charitable causes discursively infantilize and feminize refugees, while Nando Sigona has highlighted tensions 'between dominant representations of the refugee as an agency-less object of humanitarian intervention, and refugees' quest for recognition as political subjects' (2014, p 370).

In a fundamental sense, then, the ITV Concert for Ukraine constructed and reinforced what Josh Kun (2000) has termed aural borders. It is difficult to underestimate the sonic power of concerts reaching huge audiences, like the Concert for Ukraine, in these bordering processes. In fact, it seems to me that the aesthetics of bordering is as least as important as the lines on a map that separate nation states, if not more so. Borders 'are technologies of social circulation; and societies are the products of bordering, rather than the other way around' (Western 2018, p 481). Music may have the potential to engender transnational communality, then, but it also has the power to construct borders with rigid barriers between envoicement and unvoicement, between the access to being heard and silencing. Jopi Nyman and Johan Schimanski (2021) have suggested that artistic representations mediate borders and, as such, are integral parts of bordering processes. They posited that aesthetic forms 'are central to the political process' and remind us of Hannah Arendt's powerful advocacy for access for the voices of oppressed groups. Since ours is a 'world of appearance', visibility and being heard are necessary to achieving political participation and recognition (Arendt quoted in Nyman and Schimanski, 2021, p 3).

Conclusion

The three musical events I explored in this chapter have their own nuances, but they all engage with borders in sound, even in the moment of sonic border crossing. They create, narrate, transcend, reinforce and subvert aural borders. In highlighting the Russian invasion of Ukraine that began in February 2022 (and is ongoing as I write) and in drawing our attention to the human suffering it causes, they reinforce crisis narratives. They remind us of the idea of voice as a prominent trope in humanitarian campaigns, turning our attention to issues of agency and heterogeneity, and getting us to listen to the tropes that emerge through them. In so doing, one might argue that they further well-trodden paths of sonic essentialization in which representations of individual refugee stories often carry dehumanizing aspects. They tackle the issue of heterogeneity and the agency of individuals differently, but they all foreground the relationship between voice and silence, representation and exploitation.

Despite such reservations, songs like 'Stefania' and 'Hey hey rise up' do have the potential to engender trans-border communalities. If we highlight their migratory aesthetics, we may find an alternative focus on sound that has the potential to counter methodological nationalisms on which discourses of exceptionalization and lack of access to debates of citizenship rely. Rather than furthering narratives of urgency and crisis, I believe that a consideration of migration through the lens of sound and music can enrich wider understandings of migration and mobility. In a broader sense, my chapter seeks to remind readers that migration is sonic and that music and sound are not on the fringes, but at the centre of real-world politics and activisms. Amid the dominance of visually and textually based media and scholarship, this truism is sometimes drowned out from our engagement with human mobilities. The sometimes cacophonous public debates on migration leave little space for migrant voices, and migratory sounds themselves can seem unvoiced and unheard. The case studies in this chapter thus sit on a dialectic sliding scale between trans-border communality and bordering essentialization. In a disjunctural historical moment of border closures and talk of unprecedented numbers of refugees, of European war and of rising Right-wing extremism, discourses of crisis set by media and humanitarian narratives dominate and narrate movement as problematic. As Philip Bohlman (2012) has pointed out, music can sound the historiography of these disjunctures. Any song that has the potential to narrate, shape and counter them is worth listening to.

References

Baily, J. (2015) *War, Exile and the Music of Afghanistan: The Ethnographer's Tale*, Aldershot: Ashgate.

Baker, C. (2015) 'Gender and geopolitics in the Eurovision Song Contest', *Contemporary Southeastern Europe*, 2(1): 74–93.

Baker, C. (2019a) '"I am the voice of the past that will always be": the Eurovision Song Contest as historical fiction', *Journal of Historical Fictions*, 2(2): 102–25.

Baker, C. (2019b) '"If love was a crime, we would be criminals": the Eurovision Song Contest and the queer international politics of flags', in J. Kalman, B. Wellings and K. Jacotine (eds) *Eurovisions: Identity and the International Politics of the Eurovision Song Contest Since 1956*, Singapore: Palgrave Macmillan, pp 175–200.

Bal, M. (2007) 'Lost in space, lost in the library', in S. Durrant and C. Lord (ed) *Essays in Migratory Aesthetics: Cultural Practices between Migration and Art-Making*, Amsterdam: Rodopi, pp 23–35.

Beckles Willson, R. (2007) *Ligeti, Kurtág, and Hungarian Music during the Cold War*, Cambridge: Cambridge University Press.

Bennett, J. (2011) 'Migratory aesthetics: art and politics beyond identity', in M. Bal and M.Á. Hernández-Navarro (eds) *Art and Visibility in Migratory Culture: Conflict, Resistance, and Agency*, Amsterdam: Rodopi, pp 107–26.

Bohlman, A.F. and Rehding, A. (2013) 'Doing the European two-step', in D. Tragaki (ed) *Empire of Song: Europe and Nation in the Eurovision Song Contest*, Lanham, MD: Scarecrow Press, pp 281–97.

Bohlman, P.V. (2008a) *Jewish Music and Modernity*, New York: Oxford University Press.

Bohlman, P.V. (2008b) 'The nation in song', in S. Berger, L. Eriksonas and A. Mycokc (eds) *Narrating the Nation: Representations in History, Media and the Arts*, New York: Berghahn Books, pp 246–65.

Bohlman, P.V. (2011) *Focus: Music, Nationalism, and the Making of the New Europe* (2nd edn), New York: Routledge.

Bohlman, P.V. (2012) 'Historiographies of disjuncture, ethnographies of displacement', in M. Clayton, T. Herbert and R. Middleton (eds) *The Cultural Study of Music: A Critical Introduction*, London: Routledge, pp 28–39.

British Embassy Brussels (2022) 'The UK and Ukraine come together for the "Magical music of Harry Potter" in Belgium', *GOV.UK*, 24 November. Available from: www.gov.uk/government/news/the-uk-and-ukraine-come-together-for-the-magical-music-of-harry-potter-in-belgium (accessed 1 October 2023).

Brooke-Rose, C. (1998) 'Exsul', in S. Suleiman (ed) *Exile and Creativity: Signposts, Travellers, Outsiders, Backward Glances*, Durham, NC: Duke University Press, pp 9–24.

Butler, J. and Spivak, G.C. (2010) *Who Sings the Nation-State?* London: Seagull Books.

Cabot, H. (2016) '"Refugee voices": tragedy, ghosts, and the anthropology of not knowing', *Journal of Contemporary Ethnography*, 45(6): 645–72.

Cohen, B. (2012) *Stefan Wolpe and the Avant-Garde Diaspora*, Cambridge: Cambridge University Press.

Coleman, S. (2008) 'Why is the Eurovision Song Contest ridiculous? Exploring a spectacle of embarrassment, irony and identity', *The International Journal of Media and Culture*, 6(3): 127–40.

Cremona, G. (2023) 'A critical pedagogical Eurovision euphoria: the potential of the Eurovision Song Contest to promote values propagated by the European Union within formal learning contexts', in A. Dubin (ed) *The Eurovision Song Contest as a Cultural Phenomenon: From Concert Halls to the Halls of Academia*, Abingdon: Routledge, pp 111–28.

Davis, H.L. (2010) 'Feeding the world a line? Celebrity activism and ethical consumer practices from Live Aid to Product Red', *Nordic Journal of English Studies*, 9(3): 67–87.

Dayan, D. and Katz, E. (1992) *Media Events: The Live Broadcasting of History*, Cambridge, MA: Harvard University Press.

Demetriades, S.Z., Walter, N. and Cohen, J. (2023) 'Parasocial experiences in the political arena', in R. Tukachinsky (ed) *The Oxford Handbook of Parasocial Experiences*, Oxford: Oxford University Press, pp 335–53.

D'Souza, S. (2023) 'Pink Floyd lyricist calls Roger Waters an antisemite and "Putin apologist"', *The Guardian*, 7 February. Available from: www.theguardian.com/music/2023/feb/07/pink-floyd-lyricist-calls-roger-waters-an-antisemite-and-putin-apologist (accessed 1 October 2023).

Feisst, S. (2011) *Schoenberg's New World*, New York: Oxford University Press.

Glick Schiller, N. and Meinhof, U. (2011) 'Singing a new song? Transnational migration, methodological nationalism and cosmopolitan perspectives', *Music and Arts in Action*, 3(3): 22–39.

Gopinath, S. and Stanyek, J. (ed) (2014) *The Oxford Handbook of Mobile Music Studies*, 2 vols, Oxford: Oxford University Press.

Grow, K. (2022) 'David Gilmour: why I'm bringing back Pink Floyd after 28 years', *Rolling Stone*, 8 April. Available from: www.rollingstone.com/music/music-features/pink-floyd-david-gilmour-ukraine-interview-1334514/ (accessed 1 October 2023).

Hinton, S. (2012) *Weill's Musical Theatre: Stages of Reform*, Berkeley: University of California Press.

Kiwan, N. and Meinhof, U. (2011) 'Music and migration: a transnational approach', *Music and Arts in Action*, 3(3): 3–20.

Kun, J. (2000) 'The aural border', *Theatre Journal*, 52(1): 1–21.

Kyriakidou, M., Skey, M., Uldam, J. and McCurdy, P. (2018) 'Media events and cosmopolitan fandom: "playful nationalism" in the Eurovision Song Contest', *International Journal of Cultural Studies*, 21(6): 603–18.

Lavin, W. (2022) 'Antytila: Ed Sheeran-backed Ukrainian band told they cannot play fundraiser', *NME*, 26 March. Available from: www.nme.com/news/music/antytila-ed-sheeran-backed-ukrainian-band-told-they-cant-play-fundraiser-3190992 (accessed 1 October 2023).

Levi, E. and Scheding, F. (ed) (2010) *Music and Displacement: Diasporas, Mobilities and Dislocations in Europe and Beyond*, Lanham, MD: Scarecrow Press.

Malkki, L. (1997) 'Speechless emissaries: refugees, humanitarianism, and dehistoricization', in K. Fog Olwig and K. Hastrup (eds) *Siting Culture: The Shifting Anthropological Object*, London: Routledge, pp 223–54.

Meizel, K. (2015) 'Empire of song: Europe and nation in the Eurovision Song Contest [book review]', *Ethnomusicology Forum*, 24(1): 137–9.

Montoya, D. (2017) 'The Eurovision Contest: singing for the political upper hand', *Harvard International Review*, 38(4): 7–10.

Nye, J. (2022) 'Soft power after Ukraine', *Project Syndicate*, 3 May. Available from: www.project-syndicate.org/commentary/soft-power-after-russia-war-in-ukraine-by-joseph-s-nye-2022-05 (accessed 1 October 2023).

Nyman, J. and Schimanski, J. (2021) 'Introduction: images and narratives on the border', in J. Schimanski and J. Nyman (eds) *Border Images, Border Narratives: The Political Aesthetics of Boundaries and Crossings*, Manchester: Manchester University Press, pp 1–20.

Pavlyshyn, M. (2020) 'Ruslana, Serduchka, Jamala: national self-imaging in Ukraine's Eurovision entries', in J. Kalman, B. Wellings and K. Jacotine (eds) *Identity and the International Politics of the Eurovision Song Contest since 1956*, Singapore: Palgrave Macmillan, pp 129–50.

Petridis, A. (2022) 'This is a crazy, unjust attack: Pink Floyd reform to support Ukraine', *The Guardian*, 7 April. Available from: www.theguardian.com/music/2022/apr/07/pink-floyd-reform-to-support-ukraine (accessed 1 October 2023).

Pidd, H. (2023) 'Visa delay meant Ukrainian orchestra's key members missed UK concert', *The Guardian*, 13 April. Available from: www.theguardian.com/uk-news/2023/apr/13/ukrainian-orchestra-key-members-visa-delay-play-uk (accessed 1 October 2023).

Said, E.W. (2002) 'Reflections on exile', in *Reflections on Exile and Other Essays*, (3rd edn), Cambridge, MA: Harvard University Press, pp 173–86.

Samuels, D., Meintjes, L., Ochoa, A.M. and Porcello, T. (2010) 'Soundscapes: toward a sounded anthropology', *Annual Review of Anthropology*, 39: 329–45.

Savage, M. (2022) 'Pink Floyd reunite for Ukraine protest song', *BBC News*, 8 April. Available from: www.bbc.co.uk/news/entertainment-arts-61037080 (accessed 1 October 2023).

Scheding, F. (2010) '"The splinter in your eye": uncomfortable legacies and German exile studies', in E. Levi and F. Scheding (eds) *Music and Displacement: Diasporas, Mobilities and Dislocations in Europe and Beyond*, Lanham, MD: Scarecrow Press, pp 119–34.

Seely, R.W.H. (2016) 'Ukraine defeated Russia – at Eurovision. Here's why that matters', *The Washington Post*, 22 May. Available from: www.washingtonpost.com/news/monkey-cage/wp/2016/05/22/ukraine-defeated-russia-at-eurovision-heres-why-that-matters/ (accessed 1 October 2023).

Sigona, N. (2014) 'The politics of refugee voices: representations, narratives, and memories', in E. Fiddian-Qasmiyeh, G. Loescher, K. Long and N. Sigona (eds) *The Oxford Handbook of Refugee and Forced Migration Studies*, Oxford: Oxford University Press, pp 369–82.

Stokes, M. (2023) *Music and Citizenship*, Oxford: Oxford University Press.

Tragaki, D. (2013) *Empire of Song: Europe and Nation in the Eurovision Song Contest*, Lanham, MD: Scarecrow Press.

Vuletic, D. (2018) 'Public diplomacy and decision-making in the Eurovision Song Contest', in M. Dunkel and S.A. Nitzsche (eds) *Popular Music and Public Diplomacy: Transnational and Transdisciplinary Perspectives*, Bielefeld: Transcript, pp 301–13.

Weaver, M. (2023) 'The "gay world cup": why LGBTQ+ audiences love Eurovision', *The Conversation*, 16 May. Available from: https://theconversat ion.com/the-gay-world-cup-why-lgbtq-audiences-love-eurovision-205 524 (accessed 1 October 2023).

Wellings, B. and Kalman, J. (2020) 'Entangled histories: identity, Eurovision and European integration', in J. Kalman, B. Wellings and K. Jacotine (eds) *Eurovisions: Identity and the International Politics of the Eurovision Song Contest since 1956*, Singapore: Palgrave Macmillan, pp 1–20.

Western, T. (2018) 'Aural borders, aural bordering', in F. Scheding (ed) 'Forum: "Who is British music?" Placing migrants in national music history', *Twentieth Century Music*, 15(3): 439–92.

Willman, C. (2023) 'Roger Waters is "antisemitic to rotten core," says former Pink Floyd lyricist Polly Samson – and her husband, David Gilmour, emphatically agrees', *Variety*, 7 February. Available from: https:// variety.com/2023/music/news/roger-waters-antisemitic-says-polly-sam son-david-gilmour-agrees-pink-floyd-ukraine-1235515432/ (accessed 1 October 2023).

Yair, G. (2018) 'Douze point: Eurovisions and Euro-divisions in the Eurovision Song Contest – review of two decades of research', *European Journal of Cultural Studies*, 22(5–6): 1013–29.

Yair, G. and Ozeri, C. (2023) 'A march for power: the variety of political programmes on the Eurovision Song Contest stage', in A. Dubin (ed) *The Eurovision Song Contest as a Cultural Phenomenon: From Concert Halls to the Halls of Academia*, Abingdon: Routledge, pp 83–95.

Yekelchyk, S. (2010) 'What is Ukrainian about Ukraine's pop culture? The strange case of Verka Serduchka', *Canadian-American Slavic Studies*, 44(1–2): 217–32.

Beyond Migrants and Migration

Introduction

Natasha Carver, Brid Brennan and Holly Rooke

Anderson argues that we need 'to look *at and from* the border' (Anderson, this volume) and through doing so interrogate the vocabulary of bordering, including categories like 'citizen' and 'migrant'. How are these categories defined and represented, and by whom? And what impact do such articulations have? In Part 4 of the book, we attend to these challenges from different but complementary perspectives. In Chapter 11, Holly Rooke and Natasha Carver analyse the role played by the discourse of political elites (and the state) in the continual project of (re)producing national borders, through a critical discourse analysis of speeches on migration delivered by recent prime ministers and home secretaries in the UK. Brid Brennan's focus in Chapter 12 is on the work of the Transnational Migrant Platform – Europe and the Permanent Peoples' Tribunal. She explores the power of bottom-up, grassroots approaches in (re)claiming, contesting and going beyond the discourse on migration of governing elites. She considers how new narratives are articulated and co-generated within different collective framings which seek fundamental change through linking migrant and refugee people, social movements and engaged academe. These chapters amplify Anderson's argument that border crossing is never a singular, one-off event and that the border itself is far more than a geographical entity.

Contrary to what might be expected, neither ethno-national belonging nor the 'national order of things' (Malkki, 1995) are naturalized in either of these contexts. Politicians explicitly reassert the territorial sovereign nation state system as the only viable system – albeit whilst claiming it is currently unfit for purpose – and dismiss humanitarian challenges to their borderwork as the position of naive 'no borders' fantasists (for example, Johnson, 2022). Migrant and refugee campaign groups, on the other hand, argue that politicians are running roughshod over the flawed but essential architecture which underpins this nation state system: the national order of things is, after all, embedded within United Nations conventions, including the 1951 Refugee Convention and the 1990 Migrant Workers Convention. These instruments enshrine the power of nation states to label individuals, and thus call people into being in law as citizens/migrants/refugees as well as designate their belonging to a particular nation (Hacking, 1999; Carver, 2019). For many migrants, national identity only comes into significance as a category of belonging when the border is crossed. The extent to which migrants and allied citizens challenge this framing or reproduce it is raised in Brennan's interview. While politicians and many campaign groups present themselves as doing necessary and moral repair work to uphold the global nation state system on behalf of 'The People' they claim to represent, some abolitionist campaign groups attempt to resist and reject the system itself. This is a complex space of struggle and protagonism which migrant and refugee people inhabit together with other national and international social justice movements.

The nationalism produced in both contexts is often, seemingly, of the 'banal' (Billig, 1995) kind. Rooke and Carver highlight the use of references to 'national characteristics', like the British disposition for queuing, for example. Yet in the context of migration discourse, banal nationalism always has a sting in its tail in the work it does to naturalize the national order of things, whether utilized by elite politicians to justify divisive borderwork or by campaign groups to assert and claim rights. Ultimately, it is the system which produces 'migrants' and 'migration', not the movement of people. There is nothing intrinsic to the individual that makes them a migrant. Nor is there anything intrinsic to the movement of people that makes their journey a 'migration', inter-*nation*-al or otherwise. Migrants and citizens, 'illegal' and 'legal', refugees and workers, are all constructed externally with reference to national and often supranational legislation, which is itself underpinned by a global consensus and reliance on politically defined, territorially sovereign nation states (Carver, 2019).

'Who counts as a migrant?' is thus a never-answerable question, because 'migrant', like 'race' before it, is a floating signifier (Hall, 1996), which is not to say that the effects of migrancy are not real and often harmful, even deadly. The epistemology which held humans to be biologically distinguishable according to a hierarchical set of 'races' became mainstreamed through the slave trade and colonization. It is now widely understood that the notion of 'race' was a tool of exploitation, and thus a political rather than a biological construct (Quijano and Ennis, 2000). Nonetheless, the legal identities that colonial regimes generated on the basis of this epistemology – which designated the extent of one's social and physical (im)mobility – have proved long-lasting, not least because they continue to be politically useful for those in power. Following the disproving of scientific racism, in the West 'nationality' and/or 'ethnicity'/'ethnic minority' are now typically employed to do the heavy lifting required to legitimize and naturalize hierarchies of citizenship which render some people vulnerable to discrimination and exploitation. Adébísí argues that 'the increasing contemporary desire to replace "race" with "ethnicity" [or, in this case, national identity], attempts to disappear the unjust social production of racial categories, by among other things, diluting the reasons for studying race – injustice' (2023, p 70). The fact that the national order of things has become so established that it is taken for granted is testament to colonialism's longevity (Sharma, 2020).

While such identification is presented as being obvious, as with categorizations of 'race' in colonial contexts, it is never definitive. Racialized citizens continue to be at risk of misrecognition as migrants, sometimes with devastating consequences, as has been seen in the Windrush scandal (Bhattacharya et al, 2021). Meanwhile, migrants themselves continue to attempt to hide in plain sight, relying when they can on racist norms (Fox and Mogilnicka, 2019). The ambiguous position of former Prime Minister Rishi Sunak and former Home Secretary Suella Braverman as racialized/ post-racial citizens of the UK, Rooke and Carver argue, impacts their articulations on migration, including the delineation of 'migrant' into 'il/ legal migrant'. The hitherto classed and racialized subtext of *who we really mean* when we talk about 'who is a migrant' (Anderson, this volume) is, as a consequence, fast becoming explicitly labelled and categorized. Sharma (2020) is right to assert that defining citizens from migrants is work of existential significance to nation states: they *must* make 'migrants' if they are to be a nation state. They need not, however, make 'illegal migrants'.

What the complementary categories of migrant/citizen, il/legal migrant, refugee/worker serve to maintain is power relations within and between nation states: the national order of things. The global migration regime takes over from where colonialism left off (Sharma, 2020). But in producing and fetishizing these categories of 'citizens' and 'migrants', 'il/legal migrants', refugees and workers, the system also produces its own workload, for it now needs to know who belongs and who doesn't, and how they belong, in order to manage and control who is allowed to cross the border as well as the behaviour of 'migrants' within the territory. Such a workload is never-ending and insurmountable, and, measured against its own goals, resoundingly ineffective. Every year, more and more is spent on border surveillance and protection, passport control, extended monitoring of applicants both pre and post entry, and so on. This is also the model of 'Fortress Europe', imposed by the European Union on other states, including in the Maghreb, as described by Brennan in this volume. Huge spending on the most advanced technical security and military equipment is meant to ensure the implementation of both Europe's internal border policy and its externalization of borders to 'third' countries to prevent the entry of migrants and refugees (Akkerman et al, 2022; Council of the European Union, 2023). Yet with each added 'protection', the border's permeability and arbitrary sociopolitical construction becomes more apparent.

Reiman observed that 'criminology, alone among recognized social sciences, bears the burden of having the object of its study determined by the state' and has, therefore, a special responsibility to 'either declare its independence of the state or serve as an arm of the state' (2006, p 362). The shift within criminology to 'zemiology', or the study of social harm, was introduced to overcome this and thus allow for a more expansive academic critique of power, structure and definition (Canning and Tombs, 2021). As noted by Anderson in this volume, criminology is not actually alone in this; 'migration studies' has faced, and continues to face, a similar struggle, beholden to state definition and struggling to free itself from the methodological nationalism that has plagued analyses. As academics abandon the lens of the state and apply their critical gaze to denationalizing (El Miri, 2023) or 'demigrantizing' migration studies (Anderson, this volume), and instead analyse 'border harms' (Canning and Tombs, 2021), governments in the Global North increasingly entrench their policies in discourses of (il)legality, discourses which are gradually being realized in legislation and thereby creating new – criminal – legal identities (Rooke and Carver, this volume).

References

Adébísí, F. (2023) *Decolonisation and Legal Knowledge: Reflections of Power and Possibility*, Bristol: Bristol University Press.

Akkerman, M., Brunet, P., Feinstein, A., Fortin, T., Hegarty, A., Ní Bhriain, N. et al (2022) *Fanning the Flames: How the European Union is Fuelling a New Arms Race*, Amsterdam: Transnational Institute.

Bhattacharyya, G., Elliot-Cooper, A., Balini, S., Nişancloğlu, K., Koram, K., Gebrial, D. et al (2021) *Empire's Endgame: Racism and the British State*, London: Pluto Press.

Billig, M. (1995) *Banal Nationalism*, London: Sage Publications.

Canning, V. and Tombs, S. (2021) *From Social Harm to Zemiology: A Critical Introduction*, London: Routledge.

Carver, N. (2019) 'The silent backdrop: colonial anxiety at the border', *Journal of Historical Sociology*, 32(2): 154–72.

Council of the European Union (2023) 'Making the return systems more effective', *Statewatch*. Available from: www.statewatch.org/media/4107/eu-council-return-plans-return-decision-15277–23.pdf (accessed 28 May 2024).

El Miri, M. (2023) 'The weight of colonial cultural legacy in scholarly and political discourses on migration: for a denationalisation of the migration issue', in A. Miranda and A. Pérez-Caramés (eds) *Migration Patterns across the Mediterranean*, Cheltenham: Elgar Publishing, pp 67–82.

Fox, J. and Mogilnicka, M. (2019) 'Pathological integration, or, how East Europeans use racism to become British', *British Journal of Sociology*, 70(1): 5–23.

Hacking, I. (1999) *The Social Construction of What?* London: Harvard University Press.

Hall, S. (1996) 'Race: the floating signifier. Featuring Stuart Hall', Northampton, MA: Media Education Foundation. Available from: www.mediaed.org/transcripts/Stuart-Hall-Race-the-Floating-Signifier-Transcript.pdf (accessed 28 May 2024).

Hattam, V. (2022) 'Border economies/capitalist imaginaries: dispelling capitalism's system effects', *Borderlands Journal*, 21(1): 39–66.

Johnson, B. (2022) 'PM speech on action to tackle illegal migration: 14 April 2022', *GOV.UK*, 14 April. Available from: www.gov.uk/government/speeches/pm-speech-on-action-to-tackle-illegal-migration-14-april-2022 (accessed 27 November 2023).

Malkki, L. (1995) 'Refugees and exile: from "refugee studies" to the national order of things', *Annual Review of Anthropology*, 24(1): 495–523.

Quijano, A. and Ennis, M. (2000) 'Coloniality of power, Eurocentrism, and Latin America', *Nepantla: Views from South*, 1(3): 533–80.

Reiman, J. (2006) 'Review: *Beyond Criminology: Taking Harm Seriously*', *British Journal of Criminology*, 46(2): 362–4.

Sharma, N. (2020) *Home Rule: National Sovereignty and the Separation of Natives and Migrants*, Durham, NC: Duke University Press.

11

Constructing Illegality: Epistemic Borderwork in the Speeches of UK Political Elites

Holly Rooke and Natasha Carver[1]

Introduction

Migration has been a consistent topic of political debate in the UK since Margaret Thatcher set it on the agenda of the 1979 election (Francis, 2017). Successive governments of all political persuasions have introduced Bill after Bill restricting who can enter and under what conditions, resulting in an Act for every two years since 2004. Accompanying each Bill as it starts its passage through the Houses of Parliament are political speeches, typically given by the prime minister or home secretary, which introduce and justify the Bill and its (claimed) moral legitimacy to people and Parliament. While a hostile public and/or media is often cited as the justification for restrictive policies, this obscures the power of politicians to shape the terms of the debate (Goodfellow, 2020) and to convert rhetoric and discourse into legal fact. In this chapter, we focus on the 'epistemic borderwork' (Davies et al, 2023) in eight speeches on migration policy given by the most powerful politicians in the UK – two prime ministers (Boris Johnson, 2019–22, and Rishi Sunak, 2022–24), two home secretaries (Priti Patel, 2019–22, and Suella Braverman, 2022–23) and a secretary of state (Michael Gove, 2021–24) – between July 2021 and March 2023. This was a time of significant legislative and policy reform on immigration, including the introduction and enactment of the Nationality and Borders Act 2022 and the Illegal Migration Act 2023, as well as the Rwanda Partnership and the Homes for Ukraine policies.

Political discourse on migration is fundamentally nation-building: it separates 'us' from 'them', prescribes who belongs and who does not. In Westminster,[2] such discourse has frequently been explicitly racist and sexist.

However, in the age of postcolonial migration and associated neo- and post-racism (Sharma, 2020; Saini et al, 2023), the borderwork in political articulations can be surreptitious, coded and slippery. All the speeches analysed create a lexical connection in their representation (*Darstellung*) of 'the British People', 'the Nation' and government policies by describing them in the same value-laden terms. All also dehumanize migrant Others, constructing them as undeserving and exploitative. Three of the five speakers, however, are people of colour and thus subject to racialization and racism themselves. How they navigate and (re)articulate this racially coded discourse has not been subject to much scrutiny (Saini et al, 2023). We find that politicians are constrained by their own (perceived) positionality as insider/outsider in their ability to represent or speak as/for the people/ nation (*Vertretung*), which produces subtle but significant differences in their discursive constructions of migrant Others – constructions which are subsequently repeated and naturalized in media reporting, the popular imagination and the legislation itself. This borderwork, undertaken by the most powerful politicians, is not inconsequential rhetoric but epistemic violence (Spivak, 1988).

We start with a brief discussion of history, context and literature, then outline our methodology and develop our analysis. Taking up Bridget Anderson's call in the introduction to this volume for methodological denationalism, we make visible and analyse the relationship between the state-imposed category of 'illegal migrant' and the embodied – racialized – characteristics of political leaders.

Background and context

Politicians regularly refer to the UK's 'proud history' of welcoming refugees, obscuring a complex and far from generous reality bound up with race, class and colonialism (Mayblin, 2017; Carver, 2019; Sharma, 2020; Anderson, 2021). Systematic restrictions on immigration began with the Aliens Act 1905 (Dias-Abey, this volume), which stipulated that people classified as 'undesirable' could be denied entry (Kushner, 2003; Yeo, 2022). This classed, racialized and gendered classification has been repeatedly rearticulated and remains relevant today.

The United Nations 1951 Refugee Convention – to which the UK was a founding signatory – gave legal structure to the reception of people requesting asylum, placing an obligation on the government to assess protection claims from Europeans. Following the lifting of geographical limits in 1967, the rise in air travel and the end of the Cold War, increasing numbers of people from outside Europe began to seek asylum in the UK. By the 1990s, most applications came from people from the Global South (Mayblin, 2017). The prevailing representation of 'the refugee' changed from a 'white, male and anti-communist' individual (Chimni, 1998, p 351) to the non-White 'illiterate global poor' (Anderson, 2013, p 69), perceived as threatening both in their Otherness and their potentially unlimited numbers. Often fleeing persecution for non-Convention reasons and/or from non-state entities, many struggled to reconcile their histories within Convention constrictions and struggled therefore to be recognized as refugees in a system that constructed failure of recognition as evidence of falsehood and deception (Carver, 2019).

Systemic change occurred with New Labour's (1997–2010) reconceptualization of citizenship as membership of an imagined 'community of value'. While this was a major departure from the explicitly racialized construction of the nation state of the preceding decades (Maughan, 2010; Anderson, 2013), critical scholars argue that New Labour's approach re-entrenched racism in a dangerous and surreptitious form (Schuster and Solomos, 2004; Bhattacharyya et al, 2021). Entry was facilitated for European migrants and those considered 'the brightest and the best', yet restricted for asylum seekers and others from the Global South, including former colonies (Somerville, 2007). Asylum seekers were denied the right to work and their access to welfare was severely restricted. These punitive measures were bolstered under the Coalition and Conservative governments of David Cameron (2010–16), which also tightened the points-based system introduced by New Labour and further restricted family-based applications (Carver, 2016; Consterdine, 2020; Zotti, 2021). In 2012, then Home Secretary and later Prime Minister Theresa May (2016–19) introduced the hostile environment policy, which aimed to make life so difficult for 'irregular' migrants that they simply left the country (Zotti, 2021; Yeo, 2022). Without acknowledging the failure of this policy or recognizing its distressing effects, Prime Minister Boris Johnson ushered in the Nationality and Borders Act 2022, embedding hostility from the point of arrival by differentiating the asylum claims of those arriving 'irregularly' from those arriving under government-sponsored schemes or with visas. The Act curtailed the rights of the former to family reunion, further limited access to welfare, increased the scope for criminal prosecution for arriving undocumented, and enabled the warehousing of asylum seekers in quasi detention centres. The claimed intention was to deter people from risking their lives crossing the Channel, and in 2022 the legislation was enhanced through the announcement (by Johnson and Home Secretary Priti Patel) of a five-year partnership agreement to permanently relocate asylum seekers arriving in the UK to Rwanda.

At the same time, the war in Ukraine sparked cross party sympathy and solidarity, and in March 2022 Secretary of State Michael Gove announced the Homes for Ukraine scheme, offering any Ukrainian three years' residence with rights to work, healthcare, schools and most welfare benefits if they are sponsored by a UK resident who hosts them for six months. The scheme reinforced division between mode of arrival: Ukrainians who could wait for a visa were given a package enabling full integration, while those who made their own way struggled to gain entry or get support, and risked being treated like other asylum seekers (Easton, 2022; Syal and Taylor, 2022). The Illegal Migration Act 2023, introduced by then Prime Minister Rishi Sunak and then Home Secretary Suella Braverman, took this further, denying access to the asylum system altogether for those who arrive by their own efforts. It has been labelled an 'asylum ban' by UNHCR (2023) and effectively ends the UK asylum system as we know it.

A substantial body of research has examined how refugees, asylum seekers, immigrants and migrants are constructed in the media, but there has been little focus on political discourse, despite its significance (Taylor, 2020). While the relationship between politicians and media is symbiotic, those in office can construct, embrace, reject and shape discursive and legal constructions (van Dijk, 1997). Indeed, Crawley and Skleparis (2018) argue that the continual redefining of labels is so fundamental to each government's foray into legal exclusion that it amounts to 'categorical fetishism'.

Analysing Blair's parliamentary discourse on asylum, Maughan (2010, p 22) found that Blair constructed 'a new "us"' and 'a new "them"'. Blair associated 'asylum seekers rhetorically with the category of non-contributor' and then argued that the exclusion of non-contributors was ' "fair" as only those who contribute to society should be rewarded with citizenship rights' (Maughan, 2010, p 23). This conveniently overlooked the fact that it was New Labour who banned asylum seekers from working and contributing economically.[3] 'Asylum seeker' doubled up as a politically and socially pejorative term as well as a legal category (Schuster, 2003). Similarly, 'economic migrant' was employed simultaneously to recruit and celebrate Blair's economically and socially contributing migrant and as a disparaging term to signal the duplicity of 'bogus' asylum seekers (Maughan, 2010). Tracing the term 'economic migrant' from its first mention in Hansard (the official report of all parliamentary debates) in 1983, Goodfellow (2023) found that it is used to justify both inclusion and exclusion on classed and racialized terms.[4] Likewise, the (ab)use of the concept of fairness in political discourse on migration has a long history and is typically employed, as it was by Blair, as a means to deny or invisibilize racialization (van Dijk, 1997; Capdevila and Callaghan, 2008; Bates, 2022).

But how do the embodied racial characteristics of the speaker affect or change articulations on migration? Is there a relationship between the migrant heritage of the speakers and the policies they articulate? Priti Patel and Suella Braverman were the UK's second and third home secretaries of colour (the first was Sajid Javid in Theresa May's administration), while Rishi Sunak is the first prime minister of colour. All three were born in England to 'economic migrants' who had emigrated from India via East Africa (Kenya, Tanganyika,

Mauritius and Uganda) 'armed with hope for a better life' (Sunak in Palod, 2022). Post-Independence Africanization policies made life difficult for East African Indians; however, were a similar situation to arise today it would provide no basis for a UK asylum claim, not least because the Home Office would argue that claimants could or should relocate to India. At the time, however, all six future parents were, we presume, migrating as British passport holders/Citizens of the UK and Colonies within the British Empire, part of a group of people who have subsequently been termed 'the Windrush generation' (Taylor, 2020).[5] Like many White British people, Boris Johnson has migrant heritage in his family (albeit more distant than Patel, Braverman and Sunak). However, his appearance as a middle-aged, upper-class, White man obscures this, something also true for Michael Gove, despite his less auspicious start in life.[6]

In their analysis of campaign speeches by ethnic minority contenders in the 2022 Conservative leadership contest, Saini et al found that Sunak, Braverman and others undertook 'post-racial political gatekeeping', drawing implicitly or explicitly on their embodied racialization and migration histories to 'legitimise hard-right views on race, immigration and border politics' (2023, p 61). As members of a model minority (British Indians), Sunak, Braverman and Patel are well placed for this work and regularly 'co-opt mainstream nationalisms' and promote a 'hierarchy that "rewards" social conservatism and adherence to the White protestant work ethic', embedding themselves within the Conservative elite through 'shedding negative connotations of immigrant-hood that risk their becoming "othered"' (Saini et al, 2023, p 57). Here we consider *how* they tackle this discursive challenge and how that shapes their construction of migrant Others.

Materials and methods

We analysed eight purposively selected speeches on migration given by these five elite political figures (Table 11.1). Three relate to the introduction of legislation: the Nationality and Borders Act 2022 (Patel, 2021) and the Illegal Migration Act 2023 (Braverman, 2023; Sunak, 2023). Four relate to the introduction of migration policy: the Homes for Ukraine scheme (Gove, 2022), the Rwanda Partnership scheme (Johnson, 2022; Patel, 2022) and Sunak's (2022) statement to the House of Commons on illegal migration, specifically fast-tracking returns of Albanian nationals. The eighth was delivered by Braverman (2022) to Parliament following the Manston Asylum Centre scandal.[7] Excluding this last, these texts were meticulously crafted rhetorical acts. While we cannot establish the specific creation process for these particular speeches, government speech writer James Doughty (2017) explains that the procedure starts and ends with the minister: the speech writer has an initial meeting with the minister who outlines what they

Table 11.1: Speeches analysed

Date	Speaker	Office	Occasion
19 July 2021	Priti Patel	Home Secretary	Statement to Parliament introducing the Nationality and Borders Act 2022
15 March 2022	Michael Gove	Secretary of State for Levelling Up, Housing and Communities	Statement to Parliament on the Homes for Ukraine scheme
14 April 2022	Boris Johnson	Prime Minister	Speech to press from Downing Street on the Rwanda Partnership scheme
14 April 2022	Priti Patel	Home Secretary	Speech to press from Rwanda on the Rwanda Partnership scheme
31 October 2022	Suella Braverman	Home Secretary	Statement to Parliament on the Manston Asylum Centre
13 December 2022	Rishi Sunak	Prime Minister	Statement to Parliament on illegal migration
7 March 2023	Rishi Sunak	Prime Minister	Press statement outside Downing Street on the introduction of the Illegal Migration Bill
7 March 2023	Suella Braverman	Home Secretary	Statement to Parliament on the introduction of the Illegal Migration Bill

want to convey, followed by meetings with policy advisors, fact-checkers, other ministers, communications staff and so on, before the speech is finally returned to the minister, who will cut, add and recraft. None of the speeches are spontaneous, and the majority have been subject to careful creation by a team of writers over a period of time. Moreover, there are multiple intertextual references, so each speech builds on others, including those of previous prime ministers.

Our approach falls within the tradition of critical discourse analysis, which views discourse as a form of social practice that does not merely reflect but constructs and transforms the social world (van Dijk, 1997). Critical discourse analysis seeks to uncover the processes by which power relations are discursively constructed and the ideology at work when discourses are naturalized, becoming considered as common sense (Janks, 1997). Moving between the texts and context, we took a flexible and inductive approach to analysis, reading across the speeches to identify common themes, words and concepts while also taking each individually, tracking the development of discourses over time and exploring how speakers construct themselves, the nation and migrant Others. This uncovered the ways speakers used discourse and rhetoric to legitimize their ideological frameworks, exercising their political power to convert ideology into epistemology.

Representing the British people

> For centuries, our United Kingdom has had a proud history of welcoming people from overseas, including many fleeing persecution. My own great-grandfather came from Turkey in fear of his life, because our country offered sanctuary for his outspoken journalism. And when you look back over the centuries as people have come seeking refuge or simply in search of somewhere to build a better life, you see this is the very stuff our history is made of. From the French Huguenots, to the Jewish refugees from Tsarist Russia, to the docking of the Empire Windrush, to the South Asians fleeing East Africa, to the many, many others who have come from different countries at different times for different reasons, all have wanted to be here because our United Kingdom is a beacon of openness and generosity, and all in turn have contributed magnificently to the amazing story of the UK. (Johnson, 2022)

All five speakers reference *our* 'long' and 'proud history' of welcoming those in need with 'compassion' and 'generosity', discourse also found in the speeches of previous Conservative leaders including David Cameron, Theresa May and Michael Howard (Capdevila and Callaghan, 2008), as well as Labour leaders, particularly Tony Blair (Maughan, 2010). Through exophoric repetition of this claim across political parties and actors, and over time, the speakers construct a 'unitary and coherent version of the past' (Misztal, 2003, p 127) in which Britain unfailingly and without hesitation provided sanctuary to those in need and in which colonialism is notably absent. This is not a version of history supported by empirical evidence: on nearly every occasion Britain has been faced with a refugee situation, its government has sought to prevaricate, deny and make difficult any attempt at welcoming people. Consider the examples given by Johnson in the earlier excerpt: the Jewish people fleeing at the turn of the century were described in Parliament as engendering an 'evil of a very real and genuine kind' (HC Debate, 1902) and the government responded to their plight by introducing restrictions through the Aliens Act 1905; the racist reception of the Windrush generation is well documented, as is the continuing ungenerous, uncompassionate and alienating treatment of them and their descendants under the hostile environment policy (Taylor, 2020; Bhattacharyya et al, 2021); and the acceptance of East African Asians (the majority of whom held British passports) fleeing Idi Amin was undertaken extremely reluctantly and often with open hostility (Mamdani, 1973; Nasar, 2022).

These political articulations are 'heritage' rather than history, which is to say, 'the story we tell about ourselves in a way that gives meaning to our existence over time, explains the way we are now, and guides for the future' (Kirkwood, 2019, p 298). While the primary function is to instrumentalize 'the past […] to provide reassurance of moral rectitude in the present' (Kushner, 2003, p 273), through repeated articulation, it is a version of history that has taken on the illusion of truth and become widely accepted. The discursive purpose is not reflection and reparation but forging a positive national identity; it is a 'comforting mirage' (Yeo, 2022, p 28), which nonetheless does uncomfortable epistemic borderwork. What London (2000, p 17) calls the 'ritual invocation' of claiming nation and people to be welcoming, generous and compassionate is repeatedly wheeled out by government ministers as a prelude to introducing harsh restrictions.

A further necessary discursive step to justify each restrictive Act is the conflation of people/nation with government and government policy, accomplished through using the same terms to describe people and policy both within and across speeches. Consider how Patel deploys 'generosity', telling us: '*this country* is not mean-spirited nor ungenerous towards asylum seekers'; then: '*the system* is generous – costing the taxpayer over one billion pounds each year', and if other countries do not cooperate, 'their access to our generous, fast, and open visa *system* may be at risk'; and finally: '*The British people* are generous and compassionate. They simply want a system that is fair and firm. Fair to the British people, fair for those in genuine need, but firm against criminals and those who exploit our generosity by gaming the system' (2021, emphasis added). The lexical work done by 'generosity' links 'country' with 'system' and 'people', so the 'our' in the final assertion that 'our generosity' is being exploited, refers to all three as one.

Johnson (2022) and Gove (2022) do similar work with both 'generosity' and 'compassion', but although Sunak and Braverman rely on and reference the same discourse, their preference is to make 'fairness' the vehicle for connection. Patel's (2022) assertion that '[t]he British people are fair and generous' is amplified by Braverman's (2023) claim that 'the British people are famously a fair and patient people. But their sense of fair play has been tested beyond its limits. And they've seen the country taken for a ride and that patience has run out'. 'Fairness' allows Patel, Sunak and Braverman several additional dimensions: it provides for a claimed moral upper hand, portrays gentlemanly conduct, associates the speaker with dispensing justice and, importantly, provides a justification for being ungenerous and uncompassionate. Sunak (2022) simply states: 'the simplest moral framing for this issue … is fairness'. While Braverman (2023) invokes Shakespeare and cricket: 'The British people['s] […] sense of fair play has been tested beyond its limits'.[8] All three use the sporting idiom of *playing by the rules* – those who arrive in unregulated Channel crossings are 'gaming' (Patel, 2021,

2022), 'cheating' (Sunak, 2022) and 'abusing' (Patel, 2021; Braverman, 2022, 2023) 'the system', which is 'unfair' on both 'the British People' and other, rule-abiding migrants.

While the shift to fairness harks back to Blair and goes hand in hand with justifying increasingly harsh policies, this divergence between Johnson/ Gove's emphasis on generosity and compassion and Sunak/Braverman/ Patel's on fairness and playing by the rules (with Patel embracing both discourses equally) is also born of the fact that the latter are hesitant to speak *as the nation* or as *one of the people*, in contrast to Johnson and Gove. Although all five employ a royal 'we' to foster unity, Sunak, Braverman and Patel present 'the British People' – always adduced with the definite article to make them a singular cohesive group – as lexically separate to them. In Johnson's (2022) speech, he refers to 'our United Kingdom' twice, 'our country' and 'our history' just in the opening paragraph. The possessive pronoun functions to include the audience, but also places Johnson as *one of us*. Thus his opening does not simply invite 'identification and solidarity with the "we" group' (van Leeuwen and Wodak, 1999, p 93), but co-opts it for himself. In using the full 'United Kingdom', Johnson emphasizes the togetherness of (his) imagined community: this is not simply an 'arbitrary collection of people' but a 'community of value' (Anderson, 2013, p 2), a *kingdom* that is *united* by a shared history, values and beliefs, of which Johnson is part and parcel. He does not present himself as taking action on migration because he has the mandate of 'the British People', but because he *is* 'one of "us"' and therefore knows how *we* feel about *our United Kingdom*.[9] Gove (2022) too, albeit with less panache, confidently speaks simultaneously as and for the people, referring to 'our country' and 'our proud history'. Compare this to Patel, Sunak and Braverman, who instead present themselves as servants of the people, speaking for or on behalf of those people rather than as one of them.

> The British people have had enough of open borders and uncontrolled migration. [...] The British people have had enough of being told none of these issues matter – enough of being told it is racist to even think about addressing public concerns and seeking to fix this failed system. The British people have repeatedly voted to take back control of our borders. They finally have a government that is listening to them. Our priorities are the people's priorities. (Patel, 2021)

> Today we are introducing new legislation to keep my promise to you – to stop the boats. [...] So I say again: my policy is very simple, it is this country – and your government – who should decide who comes here, not criminal gangs. And I will do whatever is necessary to achieve that. (Sunak, 2023)

> Crucially, these are decisions supported by the British people precisely because they were decisions made by the British people, through their elected representatives – not by the people smugglers and other criminals breaking into Britain daily. […] This cannot and will not continue. Their government – this government – must act decisively. […] So, make no mistake. This government, this Prime Minister will act now to stop the boats. (Braverman, 2023)

There is a distance between these politicians and 'the British People' they repeatedly namecheck, implicitly marking that distance as something to be crossed. Their right to speak on behalf of the people must be justified: Patel's 'our' is the government rather than the public, and she expressly confirms the government's priorities are those of 'the people'; as the head of 'your' not *our* government, Sunak vows to keep his promise to 'you' rather than 'us'; while Braverman claims that 'this government', which is 'their government', will act decisively. At times this distance is so conspicuous that it jars (cf Braverman). This difference between Johnson/Gove and Patel/Sunak/Braverman, we suggest, is primarily due to their embodied characteristics as White vs People of Colour, in which Whiteness is assumed as a key marker of belonging. They (or their speech writers) are consciously or subconsciously positioning these speakers as not fully *one of us*, or assuming that 'the British People' are more comfortable thinking of them as *in the service of* the people rather than *one of us*.

This positioning produces subtly different accounts of *us* and *them*. Always at risk of being perceived as 'migrants', Patel/Sunak/Braverman cannot rely solely on the 'proud history' discourse of generous welcome. Instead, they use 'fairness' as the moral framework and *playing by the rules* as the arbitrator of good migrant from bad. This way, they too belong to Braverman's 'law-abiding patriotic majority'; implicitly, their parents *played by the rules* and are therefore legitimately here. This appeals to White Britons including ethnocentric voters who 'consistently favour stances which protect or enhance the position of their in-group' (Sobolewska and Ford, 2020, p 62) whose voices were amplified and legitimized through the Brexit campaign. It also gives permission to non-White Britons – who have been voting Conservative in increasing numbers and are therefore an important cohort for the Party (Saini et al, 2023) – to distinguish themselves from 'bad migrants' and support the Bill.

As White, middle-/upper-class men, Johnson and Gove have 'category entitlement' (Potter, 1996, p 121) to speak *as and for* 'the British People'. The other three only have entitlement to speak *for and on behalf* of 'the British People' due to their government positions. As the children of non-White migrants, however, Sunak, Braverman and Patel assume category entitlement to judge and distinguish migrants who 'play by the rules' from those who 'cheat'/'game'/'abuse' the system. Johnson, in contrast, has to assert his entitlement to do the same: 'My own great-grandfather came from Turkey'. Using his personal narrative to complement the national one, Johnson positions himself as the epitome of national belonging (emphasizing that '*our* country' gave his great-grandfather sanctuary, in case this heritage gives rise to doubts about his belonging), but also as having category entitlement – here moral entitlement – to determine who is un/deserving. Later in the speech he extends this category entitlement to 'colleagues of mine like Nadhim Zahawi who escaped with his family from Saddam Hussein's Iraq, Dominic Raab, whose Jewish father came to Britain from Czechoslovakia to escape Nazi Germany, and Priti Patel, whose family fled persecution in Uganda' (Johnson, 2022). The message is clear: this is a government composed of the descendants of refugees, who have moral legitimacy to judge contemporary asylum seekers. Importantly, all those mentioned fit the heritage discourse brief of the 'elite club of historically designated "genuine refugees"' (Kushner, 2003, p 267), having fled oppressive dictators *in the past* and gone on to success in their new country. Notably, Patel's refugee background is not drawn on by her in either of her speeches. A third-generation establishment White male, Johnson is in a stronger position to reference a migrant background – indeed he *must* reference it else the general public would not be aware of it – a strategy that is perhaps too risky for second-generation Patel, a woman of colour whose position within the imagined community of value is always precarious (Anderson, 2013). Braverman, also a second-generation woman of colour, does acknowledge her background, but underlines her own precarity vis-à-vis belonging in doing so: 'Indeed my own parents … decades ago found security and opportunity in this country, something for which my family is eternally grateful' (Braverman, 2023).

Thus, individual politicians are constrained by their own positionality and perceived racialized positionality as insider/outsider in their ability to represent or speak as/for the people/nation. This produces subtle but important differences in their discursive approaches, most notably relying more on 'fairness' to claim moral legitimacy. In the next section, we consider how these subtle differences in turn give rise to different articulations of migrancy.

Fetishizing categories

In 2023 the term 'illegal migrant' became established as the go-to term in political debates on migration, taking over from 'economic migrant'. This marks a watershed moment in migration discourse in two ways. First, for many, 'illegal migrant' is a dehumanizing oxymoron, as people cannot be 'illegal'.[10] While the tabloid press has previously used similar inherently contradictory labels, such as 'illegal asylum seeker' (Lynn and Lea, 2003;

Zaborowski, 2019), such terms have rarely been employed in political discourse, particularly by political elites in positions of responsibility. Second, while these discursive categories have a complex relationship with legal categories, leading to academic and policy confusion (Anderson and Blinder, 2019), the Illegal Migration Act 2023 gives this pejorative dehumanizing term legal footing.[11]

The term 'economic migrant' has seen frequent and regular use over the last 20 years in parliamentary debates, with a peak in the run-up to the Immigration Act 2016 (Goodfellow, 2023). 'Illegal migrant', on the other hand, is a relative newcomer, used rarely before 2015 but becoming more commonplace than 'economic migrant' in 2023.[12] This is reflected in the speeches, with Patel (2021, 2022) and Johnson (2022) both using 'economic migrant' to indicate illegitimacy and duplicity (for example, 'Enough of economic migrants pretending to be refugees'; Patel, 2021), whereas Sunak and Braverman talk instead of 'illegal migrant',[13] primarily in relation to numbers and cost: 'It's completely unfair on the British people who have opened their homes to genuine refugees but are now having to spend nearly £6 million a day to put up illegal migrants in hotels' (Sunak, 2023). While there is no definition of 'migrant' in international law, policy definitions (for example, see European Commission, nd; International Organization for Migration, nd) align with dictionary definitions, conceptualizing 'migrant' as an umbrella term for all people who have left their country of origin.[14] In this case, the 'illegal migrants' being 'put up ... in hotels' are asylum seekers: those who arrive irregularly and do not claim asylum are sent to a detention centre to await removal, as Braverman (2023) acknowledges. However, the Illegal Migration Act 2023 essentially eliminates the status of 'asylum seeker' by restricting refugee entries to those few preselected by the government, meaning it is no longer necessary to even attempt to determine whether a person is, to use Sunak's tautology, a *genuine* refugee.

This shift in discourse from 'economic' to 'illegal' stems at least in part from the migration backgrounds of these speakers and lawmakers: Sunak's, Braverman's and Patel's parents fled from the upheavals of East Africa seeking economic security and opportunity. Politically, it would be difficult if not impossible for these politicians to use 'economic migrant' in the same way as Johnson and others before him, without at the very least being accused of throwing stones while living in a glasshouse. But while they could readily be accused of being the descendants of recent 'economic migrants' (and, implicitly, not 'genuine' refugees), they cannot be accused of 'not playing by the rules'. Sunak and Braverman thus assert that it is those who arrive without government permission who are, by definition, insufficiently deserving or bogus, but at the same time they allow that *some* unregulated arrivals *may* be genuine, so the only 'fair' system is to stop all of them and rely on resettlement policies, which allow the government to select. According to Braverman (2023), 'by some counts there are 100 million people around the world who could qualify for protection under our current laws. And let's be clear: They are coming here'. According to Sunak (2023), this is 'unfair' on 'the British people', 'taxpayers' and 'those who most need our help but can't get it as our asylum system is being overwhelmed by those travelling illegally'. Unregulated arrivals are 'skipping' (Sunak, 2023), 'bypassing' or 'jumping the queue' (Braverman, 2022).

This image of a queue, where the neediest are being pushed from their rightful place at the front, is a development of the 'fair play' and 'playing by the rules' metaphors used by Patel, Sunak and Braverman. As Martin (2021) highlights in an Australian context, the queue-jumping metaphor presents the receiving nation as civilized, orderly and paternalistic, rescuing those in *real*/more need. Braverman (2023) states that stopping the boats and capping the annual number of refugees will 'ensure an orderly system'. The metaphor has additional significance in these speeches given the mythology of Britain as a nation of queuers (see Newburn, 2022), meaning those arriving irregularly are not only harming the 'genuine' (feminized, helpless) refugees waiting in camps, but disrespecting a British value, thereby reinforcing their Otherness and undeservingness. Queue-jumping is all the more inexcusable in the context of the often-repeated claim that there are 'safe and legal' routes. This claim is demonstrably false: only a tiny proportion of people access protection through government schemes (Lenegan, 2023). In 2022, for example, 10 Iranians were resettled via formal schemes, but 5,642 crossed the Channel 'irregularly' (Refugee Council, 2023). Grant rates for Iranians were 80 per cent in the UK at initial decision in the same period, indicating that the majority are determined by the UK Home Office to be refugees.

As well as constructing the British government as responsible, just and fair, the queue-jumping metaphor also channels broader problematic humanitarian discourses of un/deserving and the 'ideal refugee' (Fiddian-Qasmiyeh, 2010; see also Ticktin, 2016). Throughout the speeches, deservingness is instantiated through vulnerability or proximity to 'innocence', which is in turn constructed through nationality, gender, disability and age. For example, the groups most consistently humanized across the speeches are the totally helpless dead, always referred to as 'people' or the even more humanizing 'men, women and children'. Consider also the case of nationality. Ukrainians are typically talked about in the most humanizing way as 'the people of Ukraine', as in 'everyone in the United Kingdom, continues to be in awe of the bravery of the people of Ukraine' (Gove, 2022). Afghans are assigned the epithet 'brave' by Patel (2021) along with the more humanizing 'nationals', as in 'brave Afghan nationals'. Similarly, Sunak (2022) tells us that 'we have opened our hearts and homes to people from Hong Kong, Afghanistan and Ukraine'.[15] All these constructions present the specific national groups as deserving of sanctuary. Albanians, in contrast, are dehumanized and constructed as undeserving, with Albanian used as an adjectival attribute of 'arrivals' (Braverman, 2022; Sunak, 2022), 'cases' (Braverman, 2022), 'asylum seekers' and 'illegal migrants' (Sunak, 2022), and never paired with 'people' in any construction. Similar work is done by gender and age, whereby those who Patel (2021) tautologically terms 'grown adults – mostly men' are undeserving, while women and children are deserving: 'It's a striking fact that around seven out of ten of those arriving in small boats last year were men under 40, paying people smugglers to queue jump and taking up our capacity to help genuine women and child refugees' (Johnson, 2022). This is a trope that has sustained currency in the UK from the Kindertransport of World War II to the Dubs amendment to the Immigration Act 2016 (McLaughlin, 2018) and was also prominent in the press reporting on the Mediterranean Crisis in 2015 (Strasser, 2022). The explicit humanizing term 'human beings' is only used once across all the speeches – 'We have a moral obligation to stop this vile trade. Because human beings are not cargo' (Patel, 2021) – to implicitly reference the slave trade (which Patel does explicitly later in the speech in a passive construction), positioning the government as modern-day abolitionists fighting a just cause against modern-day slave traders or people smugglers.[16]

Use of 'people smugglers' has increased in parallel with that of 'illegal migrants'. It was used sparingly until 2015 but extensively in the Houses of Parliament in 2022 and 2023[17] and occurs frequently in the speeches analysed, with Sunak and Braverman building on the constructions set up by Patel. The term is used interchangeably with 'criminal gangs' by all speakers except Gove, and is typically coupled with 'ruthless' and/or 'organized'. These collocates emphasize agency and sophistication, as does the repeated use of the phrase 'business model', as in 'we will break the business model of these people smugglers' (Sunak, 2023). In this construction the agentic 'vile' and 'evil' 'people smugglers' are placed in opposition to the passive, helpless people being smuggled. However, these two are also frequently conflated with each other through criminalization (both are 'illegal') and through characterization as abusers and exploiters of 'the British People'/ nation/system, constructed as a holy trinity through generosity/compassion/ fairness. 'People smugglers', 'criminal gangs' and 'illegal migrants' are all 'abusing our human rights laws and other protections' (Braverman, 2022), thus depriving those 'in genuine need of protection' (Patel, 2022) and indeed undermining 'the very principle of seeking refuge' (Patel, 2021), all of them guilty of 'breaking into Britain daily' (Braverman, 2023).

Braverman's metaphorical allusion to the nation as a family home – which is also evoked by Patel (2021), who wants 'to slam the door on foreign criminals' – positions the government as a paternalistic and protective father figure, a metaphor with a long history in conservatism (Lakoff, 1995) and migration discourse (Walters, 2004; Taylor, 2020). It is also prominent in the metaphorically titled Homes for Ukraine policy, which invites *us* to offer *Ukraine* (the title suggests we will house a nation rather than individual families) 'a home' (Gove, 2022). This contrasts with the much-debated large-scale accommodation for asylum seekers: 'sites such as disused holiday parks, former student halls, and surplus military sites […] locations that could accommodate 10,000 people' (Sunak, 2022). Patel, Johnson, Braverman and Sunak all repeatedly express outrage (on behalf of 'the British people' and 'taxpayers') that unregulated arrivals are being accommodated in hotels, as if this was due to migrants' choice rather than government policy. The metaphor positions migrants as un/wanted guests or unwelcome 'invaders'.[18] While we are urged to make Ukrainians 'feel at home' (Gove, 2022), asylum seekers are conflated with 'failed citizens' (Anderson, 2013) and as 'people of no fixed abode' and 'in our care', who, like criminals, should not be 'free to wander' (Braverman, 2023).

Conclusion

Anderson argues that '[t]o label a person as a "migrant" is to label them out of place, and this labelling itself can be a means of displacement' (2021, p 300). Here we have demonstrated how the label has been further fetishized along an axis of il/legality (Crawley and Skleparis, 2018). There is continuity with the prevailing discourse on migration going back to Blair's tenure, with harsher measures being justified through harsher discourse. Dehumanizing discourse has been written into legislation, creating new pre-denigrated legal identities. The Illegal Migration Act 2023 marks a major shift in the UK's approach to sanctuary, and we suggest that the notable acceleration in this nationalist and superficially post-racial trajectory is in part facilitated by the embodied racialized characteristics of the elite politicians responsible for migration policy. We have demonstrated that Patel, Sunak and Braverman position themselves as *serving* 'the British People' rather than speaking as or for them. Their migrant heritage and racialized status push them to put more discursive emphasis on concepts such as 'fairness' and 'playing by the rules' for determining entry criteria rather than the (supposedly national) characteristics of generosity and compassion. This, in turn, lends itself to the construction and division of 'migrants' as il/legal. Their presentation of themselves, their life trajectories and their powerful government roles further signal post-racialism, which overrides and obscures the racial colonial logic inherent in their discourse and policies on migration.

Notes

[1] We would like to thank Bridget Anderson, Dan Godshaw and Amanda Schmid-Scott for their helpful comments.

[2] UK immigration policy is controlled by central government rather than the devolved authorities in Northern Ireland, Scotland and Wales. The rhetoric that accompanies such policy typically ignores this complex landscape and assumes a singular nation state, conflating England with Britain (Sobolewska and Ford, 2020; Honeyman, 2023).

[3] Until 2002, asylum seekers could apply to work if they had been waiting more than six months for an initial decision.

[4] Others have found similar political constructions in Europe (see, for example, Szmagalska-Follis, 2011, and Paynter, 2022).

[5] Both Sunak and Braverman had a parent recruited to work in the NHS (Palod, 2022; Braverman, nd).

[6] Gove started life in care and was adopted into a working-class family in Aberdeen. Alexander Boris de Pfeffel Johnson has Turkish, Swiss, Bavarian and Saxon heritage and was born in the US. Sunak and Johnson attended elite education establishments, followed by the University of Oxford where they were joined by Gove. Braverman was an undergraduate at Cambridge and Patel at Keele.

[7] In October 2022, it emerged that an estimated 4,000 people – including children – were being held for long periods at the Manston Centre in Kent, a processing facility intended for 1,000–1,600 people. The extreme overcrowding led to a diphtheria outbreak (BBC, 2022).

[8] See Duke-Evans (2022) for the etymology of the term and its association with being British.

[9] Johnson, renowned for his discursive competence and flair, is a long-standing admirer of Winston Churchill and frequently styles his rhetoric on that of the wartime leader (Abramicheva, 2022; Honeyman, 2023).

[10] Cf Migrants' Rights Network (nd) and Brennan, this volume.

[11] The Illegal Migration Act 2023 amends the Immigration Act 1971 (s 33(1)), which previously referred to 'illegal entrants', defined as those '(a) unlawfully entering or seeking to enter in breach of a deportation order or of the immigration laws, or (b) entering or seeking to enter by means which include deception by another person'.

[12] This is based on a Hansard search, via https://hansard.parliament.uk/ search, undertaken on 1 August 2023.

[13] Although neither prime minister makes extensive use of either term in Hansard, both home secretaries use both terms frequently, Patel favouring 'economic' and Braverman 'illegal'.

[14] This is still problematic, as Anderson and Blinder (2019) point out, since many are born outside their supposed or claimed country of origin and many are also stateless and therefore have no country of origin.

[15] The resettlement policies for those from Afghanistan and Hong Kong are limited to specific groups, but this is not made clear in these speeches.

[16] In his analysis of UK parliamentary discourse on the European asylum crisis in 2015, Kirkwood (2017) found that most uses of 'human beings' were by those on the political Left.

[17] This is based on a Hansard search, via https://hansard.parliament.uk/search, undertaken on 1 August 2023.

[18] Braverman was strongly criticized for her use of the term 'invasion' in the parliamentary debate following the 2023 speech analysed here, but has refused to apologise (The Guardian, 2023). While the other speakers have not gone so far as to call unregulated arrivals 'invaders', war metaphors permeate the speeches of Sunak (2022) in particular, who talks about 'boots on the ground patrolling ... beaches', 'officers ... embedded in respective operations' and '[h]ostile states ... using migration as a weapon'.

References

Abramicheva, O. (2022) 'Johnsonism as a linguistic phenomenon: professional discursive personality of Boris Johnson', *Scientific Bulletin of the International Humanitarian University*, 53(1): 4–10.

Anderson, B. (2013) *Us and Them? The Dangerous Politics of Immigration Control*, Oxford: Oxford University Press.

Anderson, B. (2021) 'Methodological de-nationalism: de-exceptionalizing displacement, re-exceptionalizing citizenship', *Humanity*, 12(3): 300–11.

Anderson, B. and Blinder, S. (2019) 'Who counts as a migrant? Definitions and their consequences', *The Migration Observatory*. Available from: https://migrationobservatory.ox.ac.uk/resources/briefings/who-counts-as-a-migrant-definitions-and-their-consequences/ (accessed 5 August 2023).

Bates, D. (2022) '"The jobs all go to foreigners": a critical discourse analysis of the Labour Party's "left-wing" case for immigration controls', *Critical Discourse Studies*, 20(2): 183–99.

BBC (2022) 'Manston migrant centre: what were the problems?', 21 December. Available from: www.bbc.co.uk/news/explainers-63456015 (accessed 5 August 2023).

Bhattacharyya, G., Elliott-Cooper, A., Balani, S., Nişancıoğlu, S., Koram, K., Gebrial, D., et al (2021) *Empire's Endgame: Racism and the British State*, London: Pluto Press.

Braverman, S. (2022) 'Western jet foil and Manston Asylum Processing Centres', Hansard: House of Commons Debates, vol 721, cols 637–65, 31 October. Available from: https://hansard.parliament.uk/commons/2022-10-31/debates/ea4c1c3a-4ad5-4b5e-bf9e-411e7f47cd79/Commons Chamber (accessed 1 September 2024).

Braverman, S. (2023) 'Home Secretary statement on the illegal immigration Bill', *GOV.UK*, 7 March. Available from: www.gov.uk/government/speeches/home-secretary-statement-on-the-illegal-immigration-bill (accessed 1 September 2024).

Braverman, S. (nd) 'About Suella'. Available from: www.suellabraverman.co.uk/about-suella (accessed 5 August 2023).

Capdevila, R. and Callaghan, J. (2008) '"It's not racist. It's common sense." A critical analysis of political discourse around asylum and immigration in the UK', *Journal of Community and Applied Social Psychology*, 18(1): 1–16.

Carver, N. (2016) '"For her protection and benefit": the regulation of marriage-related migration to the UK', *Ethnic and Racial Studies*, 39(15): 2758–76.

Carver, N. (2019) 'The silent backdrop: colonial anxiety at the border', *Journal of Historical Sociology*, 32(2): 154–72.

Chimni, B.S. (1998) 'The geopolitics of refugee studies: a view from the south', *Journal of Refugee Studies*, 11(4): 350–74.

Consterdine, E. (2020) 'Parties matter but institutions live on: Labour's legacy on Conservative immigration policy and the neoliberal consensus', *British Journal of Politics and International Relations*, 22(2): 182–201.

Crawley, H. and Skleparis, D. (2018) 'Refugees, migrants, neither, both: categorical fetishism and the politics of bounding in Europe's "migration crisis"', *Journal of Ethnic and Migration Studies*, 44(1): 48–64.

Davies, T., Isakjee, A. and Obradovic-Wochnik, J. (2023) 'Epistemic borderwork: Violent pushbacks, refugees, and the politics of knowledge at the EU border', *Annals of the American Association of Geographers*, 113(1): 169–88.

Doughty, J. (2017) 'What's it really like being a government speechwriter?', *Civil Service World*. Available from: https://www.civilserviceworld.com/in-depth/article/whats-it-really-like-being-a-government-speechwriter (accessed September 2024).

Duke-Evans, J. (2022) *An English Tradition? The History and Significance of Fair Play*, Oxford: Oxford University Press.

Easton, M. (2022) 'Ukraine: refugees to UK turned back at Calais over paperwork', *BBC News*, 8 March. Available from: www.bbc.co.uk/news/uk-60659786 (accessed 1 July 2023).

European Commission (nd) 'Migrant'. Available from: https://home-affairs.ec.europa.eu/networks/european-migration-network-emn/emn-asylum-and-migration-glossary/glossary/migrant_en (accessed 5 August 2023).

Fiddian-Qasmiyeh, E. (2010) '"Ideal" refugee women and gender equality mainstreaming in the Sahrawi refugee camps: "good practice" for whom?', *Refugee Survey Quarterly*, 29(2): 64–84.

Francis, M. (2017) 'Mrs Thatcher's peacock blue sari: ethnic minorities, electoral politics and the Conservative Party, c. 1974–86', *Contemporary British History*, 31(2): 274–93.

Goodfellow, M. (2020) *Hostile Environment: How Immigrants Became Scapegoats* (2nd edn), London: Verso.

Goodfellow, M. (2023) 'Interrogating the "economic migrant" in British political discourse: race, class, the economy and the human', *Ethnic and Racial Studies*, 46(8): 1553–75.

Gove, M. (2022) 'DLUHC Secretary of State's update on Ukrainian Sponsorship scheme', *GOV.UK*, 15 March. Available from: www.gov.uk/government/speeches/dluhc-secretary-of-states-update-on-ukrainian-sponsorship-scheme (accessed 1 September 2024).

HC Debate (1902) 'Immigration of destitute aliens', vol 101, cols 1269–91, 29 January.

Honeyman, V. (2023) 'The Johnson factor: British national identity and Boris Johnson', *British Politics*, 18: 40–59.

International Organization for Migration (nd) 'Who is a migrant?'. Available from: www.iom.int/who-migrant-0 (accessed 5 August 2023).

Janks, H. (1997) 'Critical discourse analysis as a research tool', *Discourse: Studies in the Cultural Politics of Education*, 18(3): 329–42.

Johnson, B. (2022) 'PM speech on action to tackle illegal migration: 14 April 2022', *GOV.UK*, 14 April. Available from: www.gov.uk/government/speeches/pm-speech-on-action-to-tackle-illegal-migration-14-april-2022 (accessed 27 November 2023).

Kirkwood, S. (2017) 'The humanisation of refugees: a discourse analysis of UK parliamentary debates on the European refugee "crisis"', *Journal of Community & Applied Social Psychology*, 27(2): 115–25.

Kirkwood, S. (2019) 'History in the service of politics: constructing narratives of history during the European refugee "crisis"', *Political Psychology*, 40(2): 297–313.

Kushner, T. (2003) 'Meaning nothing but good: ethics, history and asylum-seeker phobia in Britain', *Patterns of Prejudice*, 37(3): 257–76.

Lakoff, G. (1995) 'Metaphor, morality, and politics, or, why conservatives have left liberals in the dust', *Social Research*, 62(2): 1–22.

Lenegan, S. (2023) 'What safe and legal routes are available for refugees to come to the United Kingdom?', *Free Movement*, 12 July. Available from: https://freemovement.org.uk/what-safe-and-legal-routes-are-availa ble-for-refugees-to-come-to-the-united-kingdom/?mc_cid=3263c35 821&mc_eid=06b6848db6 (accessed 1 August2023).

London, L. (2000) 'Whitehall and the refugees: the 1930s and the 1990s', *Patterns of Prejudice*, 34(3): 17–26.

Lynn, N. and Lea, S. (2003) '"A phantom menace and the new apartheid": the social construction of asylum seekers in the United Kingdom', *Discourse & Society*, 14(4): 425–52.

Mamdani, M. (1973) *From Citizens to Refugees*, London: Peter Lane.

Martin, C.A. (2021) 'Jumping the queue? The queue-jumping metaphor in Australian press discourse on asylum seekers', *Journal of Sociology*, 57(2): 343–61.

Maughan, B. (2010) *Tony Blair's Asylum Policies: The Narratives and Conceptualisations at the Heart of New Labour's Restrictionism*, Working Paper Series no 69, Oxford: Oxford Refugee Studies Centre.

Mayblin, L. (2017) *Asylum after Empire: Colonial Legacies in the Politics of Asylum Seeking*, London: Rowman & Littlefield.

McLaughlin, C. (2018) '"They don't look like children": child asylum-seekers, the Dubs amendment and the politics of childhood', *Journal of Ethnic and Migration Studies*, 44(11): 1757–73.

Migrants' Rights Network (nd) 'Words matter: "illegal migration". How many "illegal immigrants" are in the UK?'. Available from: https://mig rantsrights.org.uk/projects/wordsmatter/illegal-immigration/ (accessed 1 July 2023).

Misztal, B. (2003) Theories of Social Remembering, Berkshire: McGraw-Hill Education.

Nasar, S. (2022) 'When Uganda expelled its Asian population in 1972, Britain tried to exclude them', *New Lines Magazine*, 12 August. Available from: https://newlinesmag.com/essays/when-uganda-expelled-its-asian-population-in-1972-britain-tried-to-exclude-them/ (accessed 1 July 2023).

Newburn, T. (2022) 'First come, first served: why Britain leads the world in queueing', *The Express*, 3 August. Available from: www.express.co.uk/entertainment/books/1650014/dover-travel-chaos-airports-britain-queuing (accessed 1 July 2023).

Palod, A. (2022) 'Punjab to London via Africa: all you need to know about Rishi Sunak's family', *The Quint*, 24 October. Available from: www.thequint.com/news/world/all-you-need-to-know-about-rishi-sunaks-family-history#read-more (accessed 5 August 2023).

Patel, P. (2021) 'Home Secretary opening speech for Nationality and Borders Bill', *GOV.UK*, 19 July. Available from: www.gov.uk/government/speeches/home-secretary-opening-speech-for-nationality-borders-bill (accessed 1 September 2024).

Patel, P. (2022) 'UK and Rwanda migration and economic development partnership', *GOV.UK*, 14 April. Available from: www.gov.uk/government/speeches/home-secretarys-speech-on-uk-and-rwanda-migration-and-economic-development-partnership (accessed 1 September 2024).

Paynter, E. (2022) 'Border crises and migrant deservingness: how the refugee/economic migrant binary racializes asylum and affects migrants' navigation of reception', *Journal of Immigrant & Refugee Studies*, 20(2): 293–306.

Potter, J. (1996) Representing Reality: Discourse, Rhetoric and Social Construction, London: SAGE Publications.

Refugee Council (2023) *The Truth about Channel Crossings – March 2023*, Briefing Paper. Available from: www.refugeecouncil.org.uk/wp-content/uploads/2023/01/Refugee-Council-Channel-Crossings-briefing-March-2023.pdf (accessed 1 July 2023).

Saini, R., Bankole, M. and Begum, N. (2023) 'The 2022 Conservative leadership campaign and post-racial gatekeeping', *Race and Class*, 65(2): 55–74.

Schuster, L. (2003) 'Common sense or racism? The treatment of asylum-seekers in Europe', *Patterns of Prejudice*, 37(3): 233–56.

Schuster, L. and Solomos, J. (2004) 'Race, immigration and asylum: New Labour's agenda and its consequences', *Ethnicities*, 4(2): 267–300.

Sharma, N. (2020) *Home Rule: National Sovereignty and the Separation of Natives and Migrants*, Durham, NC: Duke University Press.

Sobolewska, M. and Ford, R. (2020) *Brexitland*, London: Cambridge University Press.

Somerville, W. (2007) *Immigration under New Labour*, Bristol: Bristol University Press.

Spivak, G. (1988) 'Can the subaltern speak?', in C. Nelson and L. Grossberg (eds) Marxism and the Interpretation of Culture, Basingstoke: *Macmillan Education*, 271–313.

Strasser, S. (2022) 'Ambivalences of (un)deservingness: tracing vulnerability in the EU border regime', in J. Tošić and A. Streinzer (eds) *Ethnographies of Deservingness*, New York: Berghahn Books, pp 251–77.

Sunak, R. (2022) 'PM statement on illegal migration: 13 December 2022', *GOV.UK*, 13 December. Available from: www.gov.uk/government/speec hes/pm-statement-on-illegal-migration-13-december-2022 (accessed 1 September 2024).

Sunak, R. (2023) 'PM statement on the Stop the Boats Bill: 7 March 2023', *GOV.UK*, 7 March. Available from: www.gov.uk/government/speec hes/pm-statement-on-the-stop-the-boats-bill-7-march-2023 (accessed 1 September 2024).

Syal, R. and Taylor, D. (2022) 'Ukrainians who come to UK illegally could be sent to Rwanda, Johnson says', *The Guardian*, 23 June. Available from: www.theguardian.com/uk-news/2022/jun/23/ukrainians-who-come-to-uk-illegally-could-be-sent-to-rwanda-johnson-says (accessed 1 July 2023).

Szmagalska-Follis, K. (2011) 'What is an economic migrant? Europe's new borders and politics of classification', in R.M. Smith (ed) *Citizenship, Borders and Human Needs*, Philadelphia: University of Pennsylvania Press, pp 115–32.

Taylor, C. (2020) 'Representing the Windrush generation: metaphor in discourses then and now', *Critical Discourse Studies*, 17(1): 1–21.

The Guardian (2023) 'Suella Braverman tells Holocaust survivor she will not apologise for "invasion" rhetoric', 14 January. Available from: www. theguardian.com/world/2023/jan/14/suella-braverman-wont-apolog ise-to-holocaust-survivor-for-calling-migrants-invasion (accessed 5 August 2023).

Ticktin, M. (2016) 'Thinking beyond humanitarian borders', *Social Research*, 83(2): 255–71.

UNHCR (2023) 'Why the UK Illegal Migration Bill is an asylum ban'. Available from: www.unhcr.org/uk/media/65150 (accessed 1 July 2023).

van Dijk, T. (1997) 'Political discourse and racism: describing others in Western parliaments', in S. Riggins (ed) *The Language and Politics of Exclusion: Others in Discourse*, Thousand Oaks, CA: Sage, pp 31–65.

Van Leeuwen, T. and Wodak, R. (1999) 'Legitimizing immigration control: A discourse-historical analysis', *Discourse Studies*, 1(1), 83–118.

Walters, W. (2004) 'Secure borders, safe haven, domopolitics', *Citizenship Studies*, 8(3): 237–60.

Yeo, C. (2022) *Welcome to Britain: Fixing Our Broken Immigration System*, London: Biteback Publishing.

Zaborowski, R. (2019) 'Between the vulnerable and the dangerous: representations of refugees in the British press', in T. Thomas, M.M. Kruse and M. Stehling (eds) *Media and Participation in Post-Migrant Societies*, London: Rowman & Littlefield International, pp 49–60.

Zotti, A. (2021) 'The immigration policy of the United Kingdom: British exceptionalism and the renewed quest for control', in M. Ceccorulli, E. Fassi and S. Lucarelli (eds) *The EU Migration System of Governance: Justice on the Move*, Cham: Palgrave Macmillan, pp 57–88.

12

Communities of Resistance: Migrant Organizing and Transnational Campaigning Past and Future

Brid Brennan, interviewed by Bridget Anderson

Introduction

This volume discusses how the 'migrant' identity is unstable and ill-defined. And yet often, together with its companion terms 'refugee' and 'asylum seeker', it becomes a focus for organizing. In this context, the fuzziness of the term 'migrant' can be in productive tension with ideas of 'national communities', as it establishes connections between people who experience immigration controls and who come from different countries. Moreover, migrants embody and facilitate connections between multiple issues, from extraction to dictatorship, that stretch across borders. What this means in practice is explored in this interview with Brid Brennan, who coordinates the Corporate Power project at the Transnational Institute, Amsterdam. She has a long history of organizing with migrant workers across Europe and participates in the Facilitation Work Group of the Transnational Migrant Platform – Europe (TMP-E). Bridget Anderson held this interview with Brid in November 2023.

Q: Brida, you've been an active campaigner for the rights of migrants and refugees in Europe for more than 40 years. Can you start by telling us how you came into this field, and what the context was?
I entered this field through engagement with the Commission for Filipino Migrant Workers (CFMW), established as an international foundation in the Netherlands in 1979. It was a response to Filipino migration to Europe,

that had really picked up in the 1970s. This was the time of the Marcos dictatorship or, as it was then called in the Philippines' liberation movement, 'the US–Marcos dictatorship'. Marcos developed the export of labour as a major pillar of the Philippine economy – which it continues to be to this day. This meant Filipino migrant workers, like seafarers, construction workers, medical staff and domestic workers, became major actors in the restructuring of the global labour supply, especially in Europe, the US and the Middle East.

At the same time, Europe became home to Filipino political refugees fleeing persecution. Many of these were organizers, and they became involved in establishing the international solidarity networks of Philippines support groups alongside volunteers and missionaries who had returned from the Philippines after being active in civil society organizations there. Together, they started supporting the organizing of migrant communities. This began with pilot programmes in Rome and London, which fought for resident rights and against deportation and the compulsory remittances demanded by President Marcos' Executive Order 508. These campaigns then linked up with grassroots initiatives and migrant groups in other European countries. In 1985 the International Office of the CFMW was established in Amsterdam.

It's worth saying that the Philippines is a highly diverse country with more than 120 languages, so even though I talk about the *Filipino community*, I don't want to suggest it is a homogenous group. Indeed, it was in the Netherlands in the context of the seafarers' migration that Filipinos from Luzon and Visayas met and collaborated with Filipinos from the Muslim Bangsamoro region in Mindanao, where for many years there had been struggles for independence and autonomy.

The CFMW wanted to facilitate the organizing and networking of Filipinos especially, but not only, in London, Rome, Barcelona and Athens, where there were many Filipino migrant workers. We collaborated with the Philippine Seafarers Assistance Programme to support Filipino seafarers often working on the huge ships docking at Rotterdam, Hamburg and Piraeus. That was my introduction to the migrant scene, starting in the 1980s when I was a member of CFMW's Women's Committee and supported the publication of the monthly *Kababayan* newsletter.

This combination of international solidarity work and migrant organizing was not without its tensions. Migrant workers sometimes felt that their struggles as workers or their role as political activists were not sufficiently acknowledged, and refugees could be impatient that migrant self-organizations prioritized organizing and campaigning around their rights in Europe above campaigning for solidarity with the Philippines' democratic struggle. Conversely, some migrant organizations, while drawing on the Philippines' rich organizing tradition, shied away from being extensions of Philippine political movements and parties. But overall, both strands of work were complementary and drew on a strong tradition of Filipino community and political organizing, remaining deeply connected in their different ways with the political situation in the Philippines.

And this connection with politics in what we now call the Global South was not confined to the Philippines. I realized this when I worked for a time in the CFMW London office. In the UK in particular, activists and community organizers from the 1950s onwards had taken colonialism's legacy as central to their work. They were highly attuned to the connections between empire and the politics of race and migration. 'We are here because you were there', as Ambalavaner Sivanandan used to say. For migrants and those working in solidarity with them, the connection between immigration law and racism was direct – immigration law was racist and there was a continuity between colonialism and immigration controls.

Q: So how did the migrant organizing develop after the establishment of CFMW? And can you tell me some of the achievements?
The CFMW had a clear class focus, but the specifics of organizing varied depending on the challenges faced by migrants in different countries. In the UK, for instance, the issue of migrant domestic workers was very much to the fore – in fact that was, as I recall, how you and I first met! Domestic workers were not given visas independent of their employers, and if they left their employers, even in cases of severe exploitation and abuse, they were forced into *illegality*. So there was a self-organized group of domestic workers, and a support group set up to campaign for a change in immigration law and policy. We had strong allies in the trades union movement, especially TGWU,[1] today's Unite. This campaign was a good example of how Filipinos started to organize with other migrant and refugee communities, as this was a campaign for the rights of all migrant domestic workers, not only Filipinas.

The 1980s was a formative decade in that respect. The experience of the workplace was a transnationalized space where workers from all continents worked and lived the same exploitation and precarity of migration status, so migrant workers discovered the importance of organizing and acting together. Filipino migrant organizations were well linked with other migrant and refugee communities. So, in the Netherlands there was a lot of collaboration with Moroccan and Turkish migrant workers – in Italy, with Eritrean migrants and refugees, and in the UK we worked with groups like the African Refugee Housing Action Group and the Refugee Forum.

A very vibrant and active migrant community – what I would call a *protagonist* community – developed, which was alive to the importance of cross-community initiatives. One event I particularly remember was the Communities of Resistance Conference in London on 11 November 1989, co-convened by the Institute of Race Relations with other migrant, refugee and anti-racist organizations. The CFMW participated alongside groups based in the Netherlands, France, Germany, Denmark and other countries, and we launched a Communities of Resistance campaign across Europe to contest the establishment of *Fortress Europe* and to demand equal rights and have this community recognized as a star on the EU flag.

In the 1980s, there was a lot of finding of common ground across different nationalities around struggles such as anti-deportation, anti-racism and for regularization, but by the late 1980s and early 1990s we were seeing the emergence of Fortress Europe and a new common language of racism and borders, and it was clear we needed cross-community organizing across Europe and not only at a country level. By the 1990s, Filipino migrant organizing had three components – organizing and campaigning around conditions of work, immigration status, and security and conditions of stay; campaigning for freedom and democracy in the Philippines; and building *communities of resistance* with other migrant communities. We'd also chalked up some victories, both individual anti-deportation campaigns and structural changes – like the UK migrant domestic worker campaign, which was won in 1997.

In November 1997, a Europe-wide conference was convened by the CFMW in Athens which launched the integrated Filipino Migrant Agenda for Europe and the Philippines, calling for equal rights in Europe and participative democracy and development in the Philippines. The conference established the Platform of Filipino Migrant Organizations in Europe, which had representation from Filipino migrant self-organizations across 14 countries on its council and the CFMW as its facilitating secretariat. One particularly important initiative was Panahon Na! meaning 'The Time Has Come!', the global campaign for the right to overseas voting and dual citizenship. Panahon Na! formed the International Coalition for Overseas Filipinos' Voting Rights, which sent three international delegations – from Europe, the US and the Middle East – to lobby the Senate and House of Representatives in the Philippines. The campaign was the first time the collective, cross-continental voice of overseas Filipinos reverberated in the country's political arena, and in the Philippines it gave high visibility to migrants as significant actors. It also got attention from other migrant communities who built on it and launched similar campaigns towards their own governments. The campaign was won and the law was enacted in 2003.

What I am highlighting here is that the development of Filipino migrant organizing was a process that had roots in particular political contexts – in the Philippines, in specific so-called host countries and in the EU – but that crucially Filipino migrants were active protagonists. They were engaging with other migrant communities and with citizens' organizations, and through this transnational activism, they were enriching Filipino political culture and demands.

Q: What you say about the global networking is really interesting. Has this global organizing continued? What are its aims and who does it direct its demands to?
We need to set migrant global networking in the context of global networking and movement building more generally. I'm thinking particularly of the World Social Forum (WSF) and its affirmation 'Another world is possible – let's build it!' Participation in the WSF and its regional gatherings exposed migrant and refugee organizations to new political horizons and a wide range of political traditions and struggles. One of the key developments arising from these experiences was the co-convening of the TMP-E in 2008. This was set up to bring together diverse migrant communities and build transnational alliances. As we've already seen with the Filipino community, when migrant and refugee people move, they bring their political, cultural and religious roots with them and plant them in new ground. They also connect different kinds of struggles – against dictatorship, extractivism, climate change, conflict and war. So the TMP-E draws on knowledge, experiences and capacities – being a migrant/refugee, taking on the struggles for resident rights, labour rights, against racism; relations with family and community and through this a direct, lived connection to political developments in their country of origin; and the capacity to forge transnational community relations with other nationalities, including with citizens in the country of residence.

In 2016, the TMP-E called a Europe-wide conference in Amsterdam with representatives from migrant and refugee networks in the African and Latin American communities, the Europe Platform of the Moroccan Organizations, and the network of the CFMW and Platform of Filipino Migrant Organizations in Europe. Also involved were trade unions – the Belgian Christian Trade Union, ACV/CSC; and SOC-SAT,[2] Spain – and La Via Campesina (LVC), a global movement of peasant and rural workers struggles. The LVC became involved through their organizing of migrant rural workers, such as the Moroccan women in vegetable production in southern Spain, those at the US–Mexico border and internal migrants in the rural economies of Bangladesh and India. This is proving a very positive collaboration. There has been a lot of learning and sharing of organizing strategies. The LVC takes an anti-imperialist and anti-capitalist approach to its analysis and organizing, including articulating very specific strategies on corporate issues and the development of alternatives on the ground. Working with a global movement active in both the Global South and North is very generative for migrant workers' struggles, at the same time as working with migrants is generative for LVC. The partnership is an example of *demigrantizing* and finding common ground with engaged citizens, including around the current economic model and corporate domination.

The Amsterdam meeting was called to develop a strategy addressing the EU's immigration policy, captured in Sarkozy's statements on zero tolerance for illegal immigrants,[3] and to challenge the European response to the forced displacement following the Syrian war. We also wanted to strategize about the international direction of the United Nations Global Compact for Safe, Orderly and Regular Migration and Global Compact for Refugees, which were then in development. The key international body leading these global compact initiatives was the Global Forum on Migration and Development (GFMD). While some migrant organizations had participated at the beginning of the GFMD process, there were growing concerns about its nature. It is led by states but has non-transparent partnerships with corporations and the private sector and although it operates under the umbrella of the United Nations, it has no clear lines of accountability. Moreover, we saw this as encapsulating a shift from internationally binding human rights instruments to non-binding global compacts.

After two days of lively debate, the Amsterdam conference concluded with two resolutions – to initiate a process with the Permanent Peoples' Tribunal and to challenge the proposed global compacts on migration and refugees.

Q: Can you tell me a bit more about the Permanent Peoples' Tribunal (PPT) and what it meant for migrant organizing?
The PPT's founding document is the Universal Declaration of the Rights of Peoples, adopted in Algiers in 1976, which demands the freedom of all peoples in the face of new forms of imperialism and domination. It was a response to the threats to the achievements of decolonization processes and the efforts to establish the New International Economic Order. The PPT was founded in 1979 at the last session of the Second Russell Tribunal on dictatorships in Latin America, convened by the Italian senator Lelio Basso, who had also been a key player in the development of the Algiers Declaration. It is a permanent institution that listens to peoples who are forced to deal with the absence of law and the impunity of the powerful. It highlights state and corporate violations in economic, ecological and systemic crimes by organizing sessions, or hearings, where an international panel of experts listens to witnesses. It isn't only – or even mainly – about the hearings though. What is key is that it brings people together around particular issues and introduces groups to new networks and struggles. It creates a meeting space for practitioners, people's organizations, lawyers and activist scholars to engage in new analysis and strategizing. It is a kind of organizing and mobilizing tool that builds new relationships. Leah Bassel has written very interestingly about this in her article on the London PPT hearing.[4]

The PPT was known to some of the migrant and refugee organizations and movements convening the Amsterdam conference, as it had a history of engagement with peoples of the Global South. From the perspective of the TMP-E and the participant organizations and networks, the PPT was an opportunity to project a public voice that could contest the dominant policy discourse and challenge the role of law in legitimizing the violence of the migration and refugee policy regime of the EU and member states. The 45th Session of the PPT on The Violations with Impunity of the Human Rights of Migrant and Refugee Peoples, held from 2017 to 2020, was migrant and refugee led and undertaken with engaged citizen solidarity organizations and networks. Several of the organizations who participated in the Amsterdam 2016 conference agreed to be co-convenors. This meant developing an overarching framework and an indictment as well as a strategy of mobilization and outreach communication, but also organizing the hearings, finding resources, and coordination. Communities were encouraged to come forward and request a hearing, and in the end seven hearings were held, two in Barcelona, and one each in Palermo, Paris, London, Brussels and Berlin. Some 500 organizations, networks and movements participated, with organizing committees at city and national level undertaking the preparation of specific hearings, and a PPT Working Group, anchored by the TMP-E, that facilitated preparation, communication and follow-up. One of the overarching aims was movement building, so it was important that the individual hearings were not separate events but part of an organic process that built on what had gone before. That meant connecting different hearings, but also respecting the specificity of each hearing and using this to strengthen the capacity of organizations in the different cities and countries and to support the development of alliances across issues and across borders.

The hearings confirmed the systematic and widespread violations of human and people's rights and identified system crimes in the implementation of the EU immigration, securitization, externalization and militarization of borders policy.[5] The PPT process helped expose the systemic nature of the oppression of migrants, but it also highlighted the protagonism of migrant resistance and facilitated the building of migrant transnational communities together in collaboration with engaged citizens. It was very enriching for strategizing and developing a strong sense of migrant and refugee organizations as human rights bearers and defenders. Indeed, one of the most significant outcomes was an understanding and a recognition by the PPT that migrants and refugees are a *people* – a people imagining a more just world, taking an active role and seeking partners to begin to build it and move from inequality to equality and from injustice to justice, not only for migrants and refugees but for all peoples.

Q: What is the PPT countering? What is it responding to in terms of debate?
We can read the movement of people, whether as *migrant* or *refugee*, as a great global protest against the unsustainability of the current neoliberal capitalist world order. It is also a stark reminder of how deeply unfinished the decolonization process is and how this has been prolonged by the false solutions of trickle-down development. The movement and presence of

migrant and refugee people create a significant learning opportunity and a chance to forge new relations, knowledge and strategies. Migrant and refugee people individually and collectively are a reservoir of rich politico-social experiences that demonstrate not only resistance and resilience, but also the creativity and transformation capacity so urgently needed to reinvigorate the movements in the Global North.

But in the face of this opportunity, we are confronted with a loud babble that places migrant and refugee people *outside* even when they are *inside* European society. By babble, I mean conflicting voices all speaking at the same time. You have the official speak that says migrant and refugee and Black and Brown people are not fully persons and not deserving of social support or legal assistance. They are represented as criminals or terrorists or people smugglers, and a threat to the security of Europe's citizens. Exceptions can be made for Ukrainian refugees or for highly skilled – for which read, middle-class – people, but even people in these categories shouldn't assume that they will be secure in the welcome extended. Then there's the media speak – headlines and interviews about disaster and death, frequently without context and implying people are irresponsible when they bring their children on precarious journeys or are the victims of exploitation. And there's the everyday forked tongue speak – 'We need you to do the dirty work, but you have to work for a pittance, or without a contract. And please no cooking of your own food in our neighbourhoods – it smells ghastly!' Of course, there is also the voice of solidarity and welcome, and those speakers can risk criminalization themselves when they rescue or provide sanctuary.

However, the voice we heard in the PPT process was of organizations refusing to be bound by the representations of migrant/refugee as problem, as criminal, as terrorist. It asserted instead, as Gianni Tognoni, Secretary General of the PPT, put it, 'migrant/refugee as human person, as human rights bearer, as defender of democracy'. I was struck by one of the witnesses who spoke at the London hearing. She was called Clara, and was an activist with the RMT[6] trade union. She explained how Shell operations in Nigeria were implicated in impoverishment and displacement, leading people, including her, to seek work abroad. Describing her struggles as an undocumented woman, and the racism and abuse she experienced both from individuals and systemically, she denounced: 'You can't be a robber and call me a thief!' At the launch of the PPT in Barcelona in July 2017, another witness represented the Senegalese street vendors of Barcelona, constantly pursued by police clearing the streets of illegalised vendors. They formed an association, trade union and livelihood cooperative, and successfully transformed their *street-sheet* into a label asserting that 'No one is illegal' – it promised those who bought from them that they would be doing so in solidarity with undocumented workers and those displaced by global capital. One of their leaders insisted that 'We are all migrants and refugees – it is not a crime to migrate or seek refuge'. I was reminded of him when I read your introduction to this volume, as we can see this as exemplifying demigrantizing and claiming the right to be a worker in a worker-run cooperative.

Q: So where now for migrants in Europe?
I previously mentioned the GFMD. Midway through the PPT hearings, the GFMD presented two non-binding global compacts at its Marrakesh Summit – a Compact for Management of Migration (GCM) and a Compact for Refugees (GCR). This was a rubicon moment for migrant and refugee people's organizations. As I said, some had originally engaged with the GFMD process, but became convinced that the GCM/GCR were just more of the same. Quite a number of civil society organizations welcomed and continue to engage with the global compacts, but those of us involved in the PPT process saw them as a legitimation of those same killing fields that were documented and identified as system crimes in the PPT hearings.

The LVC convened a People's Summit at the Marrakesh Summit with participation from the TMP-E and migrant organizations, particularly from the Maghreb region and dealing with the Europe–Mediterranean borders. The People's Summit made a strong statement that rejected these initiatives and proposed an alternative, a Global Pact of Solidarity for the Rights of Migrants and Refugees, premised on rights not profits or state and corporate interests. As well as a rejection of the state–private sector partnership to control migration envisaged by the global compacts, the Global Pact of Solidarity recognized the importance of popularizing a new narrative of migration, one that rejected criminalization and victimhood. We rejected the idea that migration is a problem and that migrants need to be helped by NGOs, and migrants insisted that they are protagonists who bring political opportunities and networks and new narratives to the places they move to. One of the ways we think about it is the demand and rallying cry to 'Look *with* us not *at* us! Stand in our shoes and see our viewpoint to build a better world'.[7]

The Global Pact of Solidarity is a call to action that stretches into a future that migrant people will build together with citizens. It has become a popular organizing framework across borders and movements, particularly by helping link migrant and refugee struggles with efforts to fundamentally transform our social and economic relations across the planet. It's also a living text, to be further developed in the light of new events and struggles. So, for instance, it was rewritten and commitments were reinvigorated with the introduction of the EU Pact on Migration and Asylum, 2020 – a European version of the global compacts. This specifically Fortress European version of the Global Compacts – EU legislation since June 2024 – is a priority campaign for the TMP-E related networks. With a horrible irony, this pact was announced at the very moment of the devasting fire at the Moria Camp in Lesbos, a catastrophe that underlined the normalization of the violations of the rights of migrants and refugees confined in sites without rights.[8] At the time of this conversation, the EU pact is in the phase of finalization for full implementation, but there is considerable alarm on the ground that the model of Fortress Europe is being imposed now on Tunisia with disastrous consequences for the people of Tunisia and their relations with the peoples of sub-Saharan Africa and the Maghreb.

All of which is to say that the Global Pact of Solidarity that was reiterated at the final hearing of the 45th Session of the PPT in Berlin in December 2020 is now taken as the focus of organizing across the network. It is an instrument for reaching out beyond Europe and for connecting with other global struggles for justice and has been the reference point for many summits and convergences. So in answer to your question, where now, I think the Global Pact of Solidarity has started to integrate migrant and refugee people and their organizations into new coalitions for global social justice, connecting migration with many other struggles. The next step is building on this.

Q: Can you be a bit more specific? What are the campaign priorities initiated by the pact, for instance?
We want to globalize the Pact of Solidarity in an action plan that links borders and regions. This was initiated at the Caravana March Summit Brussels (30 September to 1 October 2022[9]) when we decided to hold two Europe-wide campaigns.

First is the campaign on regularization, which coordinates the now multiple struggles on regularization at national level. Its goals include the popularization of the new narrative drawn from the process of the PPT, and the contestation of the categories of 'regular' and 'irregular'. This is important, as a key problem with most regularization campaigns is that they remake the legal/illegal binary by their very success. Yes, they widen who is included in the 'legal' category, but they typically don't challenge the binary itself and the border regimes that exclude and illegalize people. An alternative approach is to simply demand 'work, housing, papers and rights', as articulated by the Unione Sindacale di Base (an Italian trade union) – a demand that could equally be made by impoverished citizens across Europe, especially given austerity and the cost-of-living crisis of the past decade. The campaign led by migrants therefore reaches out to trade unions, cost-of-living crisis networks and climate movements.

The second campaign focuses its efforts against the militarization and externalization of borders. These can join up different anti-border and no borders campaigns in three regions – Europe, Africa and the Middle East; the US and Mexico; and South-East Asia and South Asia. For example, there were important commemorations organized for the first anniversary of the massacre of at least 37 migrants and the deliberate injury of more than a hundred others on 24 June 2022 at the Nador–Melilla[10] border, including at Nador and in Melilla. Organizations from across the region participated, including a big mobilization of the Association of the Relatives of the Dead and Disappeared, which is becoming a significant organizing and mobilizing space. Commemorative sites of *killing fields* and *sites without rights* – places of mass deaths at sea, land or desert, and massacres of migrant and refugee people on the move, such as Nador–Melilla and Cutro – are also becoming sites of transnationalized protest and struggle.

We see campaigns as spaces to deepen our analysis as well as invigorate our action, and as ways of helping to develop new networks and solidarities. Part of the new narrative we promote is to recognize the connective capacities of migrants. This is particularly important in a context of fragmentation across progressive social and political movements, some of which have become issue based or identitarian. Migrant organizing pushes against identitarianism, by its very nature – who counts as a migrant is, as you say in your introduction, not sharply defined and it is most definitely transnational. It also offers possibilities for developing joint strategies and convergence across the borders of states, interests and communities.

Q: What are your thoughts on migrant and scholarly collaboration?
The PPT was a great example of how the expertise of lived experience can be enriched and analysis deepened by perspectives of engaged academics. We learned more about the international economic and development model, the global restructuring of labour, gender, racism, international law and the law of the sea. Academics also served on the multidisciplinary bench of jurors. Through dialogue with scholars and experts, we generated new ways of framing migrant issues that came from grassroots experiences. For instance, we started thinking about how migrants can be confined in *sites without rights*, and that these are not only camps and detention centres but also workplaces, such as the domestic hells of live-in workers and the agricultural glasshouses for growing Europe's fruit and vegetables.

The challenge for academics, especially those engaged in migration studies, and those still designated in our societies as *migrants* and *refugees* is to collaborate not only in contesting categorizations and the processes and relations that construct them – racism, nationalism, colonialism and imperialism – but in co-generating new strategies to win a more just and equal world. I appreciate that many migrants are academics and many academics are activists, but very often the questions posed to migrants and refugees are still designed principally to provide evidence-based arguments on the *wrongs* and *impacts* of migration policy. We can do better than that by drawing on migrants' own understandings and analyses of their experiences of exploitation, barbarism and necropolitics. Perhaps we can blur the borders between academia/public scholarship and solidarity/activism[11] so that the conceptual work done by migrants and refugees is recognized and the politics of the academic/public scholar is acknowledged.

Final note from Brid

This interview owes much of its insights to the collective knowledge, activism and art-ivism of colleagues and comrades, practitioners, experts and activist scholars in academe over decades of migrant organizing in social and political struggles. These initiatives and campaigns have been mainly, but not exclusively, in Europe and organically connected with struggles in different regions of the Global South.

Notes

[1] Transport and General Workers' Union.
[2] Sindicato de Obreros del Campo –Sindicato Andaluz de Trabajadores.
[3] See A. Sage (2014) 'Back on centre-stage with a flourish, France's Sarkozy still divides', *Reuters*, 19 September. Available from: www.reuters.com/article/uk-france-sarkozy-idAFKBN0HE21820140919 (accessed 4 December 2023).
[4] See L. Bassel (2022) 'A promise of listening: migrant justice and the London Permanent Peoples' Tribunal', *Race and Class*, 63(4): 35–55.
[5] The overall judgement and specific hearings of the 45th Session can be viewed on the PPT website at: https://permanentpeoplestribunal.org/45-session-on-the-violat ion-of-human-rights-of-migrants-and-refugee-people-2017-2020/?lang=en (accessed 5 December 2023).
[6] National Union of Rail, Maritime and Transport Workers.
[7] 'Look *with* us not *at* us' is a call first made by a worker active in the migrant domestic workers' group Waling Waling and since popularized in several migrant communities and adopted by the TMP-E.
[8] PPT Steering Group (2019) 'How the hostile environment creates sites without rights: evidence presented to the London Hearing of the Permanent Peoples' Tribunal on the violations with impunity on the rights of migrants and refugees'. PPT. Available from: https://www.statewatch.org/media/documents/news/2019/nov/ppt-evidence-hostile-environment-sites-without-rights-11-19.pdf (accessed 5 December 2023).
[9] The Caravana took place 30 September to 1 October 2022.
[10] Nador is in Morocco, Melilla is a Spanish enclave surrounded by Moroccan territory. You can read more about the massacre here at https://www.borderforensics.org/investi gations/nadormelilla/
[11] See S.M. Borras and J.C. Franco (2023) *Scholar-Activism and Land Struggles*, Rugby: Practical Action Publishing.

Index

References to figures appear in *italic* type; those in **bold** type refer to tables. References to endnotes show both the page number and the note number (231n3).

Printed and bound by CPI Group (UK) Ltd, Croydon, CR0 4YY

07/07/2026

14916220-0004